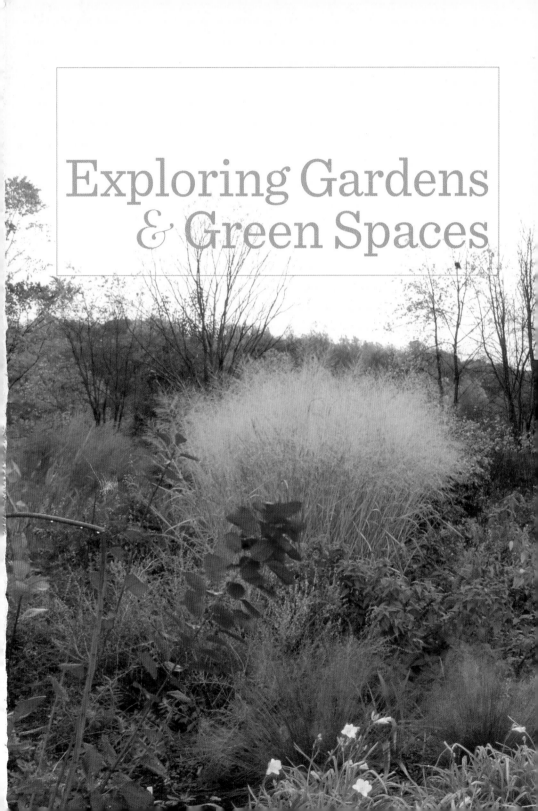

Exploring Gardens & Green Spaces

Exploring Gardens & Green Spaces

From Connecticut to the Delaware Valley

Magda Salvesen

W. W. Norton & Company
NEW YORK · LONDON

For information about permission to reproduce selections
from this book, write to Permissions, W. W. Norton &
Company, Inc., 500 Fifth Avenue, New York, NY 10110

For information about special discounts for bulk purchases,
please contact W. W. Norton Special Sales at
specials@ ww.norton.com or 800-233-4830.

Book design by Guenet Abraham
Manufacturing by KHL Printing Co. Pte Ltd
Production Manager: Leeann Graham
Electronic Production: Joe Lops

Library of Congress Cataloging-in-Publication Data

Salvesen, Magda.
Exploring gardens and green spaces from Connecticut to
the Delaware Valley / Magda Salvesen. – 1st ed.
     p. cm.
Includes index.
ISBN 978-0-393-70626-0 (pbk.)
1. Gardens—Northeastern States. I. Title.

SB466.U6N67 2011
712.0974—dc22

                              2010045641

ISBN 13: 978-0-393-70626-0 (pbk.)

W. W. Norton & Company, Inc., 500 Fifth Avenue,
New York, N.Y. 10110
www.wwnorton.com
W. W. Norton & Company Ltd., Castle House, 75/76 Wells
St., London W1T 3QT
9 8 7 6 5 4 3 2 1 0

"A Garden really lives only insofar as it is an expression of faith, the embodiment of a hope, and a song of praise."
—Russell Page, *The Education of a Gardener* (1962)

To Diane Cousineau,
whose keen intelligence guided this writing project
from beginning to end.

Storm King Art Center, Mountainville, NY

CONTENTS

Exploring Gardens & Green Spaces

Longwood Gardens, Kennett Square, PA

INTRODUCTION

To a large extent, I wrote this book for myself. I needed to know more about gardens within reach of New York City and their geographic relation to one another. For years, in conjunction with my work as an art historian, I was immersed in the thrill of eighteenth-century houses in Britain and their landscapes and gardens, with my interest expanding to include the ambitious high-Victorian horticultural developments and the smaller, delightful Arts and Crafts style. I also gravitated towards the Italian and French gardens of Europe, and followed their variations in other countries, including Germany, Portugal, and Sweden. Each summer brought a particular focus, and I gradually filled in some gaps.

Teaching garden history at the New York Botanical Garden and elsewhere since 1990 encouraged this European bias, but also challenged me to expand upon it. Three weeks in Kyoto deepened my knowledge of the Japanese aesthetic, while at home I began exploring American gardens under the wing of Priscilla Dunhill. A well-published writer and coauthor of *Glorious Gardens to Visit* (1989), a guidebook to the Northeast and Mid-Atlantic states, she whisked me off in her little car to the Mohonk Mountain House, LongHouse Reserve, Untermyer Park, and many other gardens and designed landscapes in the tri-state area. As the years passed, I urged her to update the book and to add maps and additional practical information, such as public transportation. I offered to help, but to no avail, as she was always too busy with new projects.

When Andrea Costella at W. W. Norton asked me, after my lecture on Regency gardens at the Horticultural Society of New York, if I had a garden book up my sleeve, out came the proposal that had been incubating for some time: *Exploring Gardens & Green Spaces from Connecticut to the Delaware Valley*. Taking on the geographical parameters of Priscilla's book—gardens within approximately three hours of New York City—I revisited familiar sites with a fresh eye, made long lists of new ones, and sought out innovations and environmentally-sensitive transformations in public spaces. I enlisted the help of patient directors, head horticulturalists, and steadfast Friends of the gardens.

Temporarily putting my work as curator of the Jon Schueler estate on the back burner, I spent most of the growing season of 2009 and part of 2010 immersed in this pursuit, corralling fellow garden historian, Patricia Taylor, my eldest sister, an inveterate gardener, and various friends for a week or a day's outing. More often, though, because of the length of time I liked to spend at each place and the challenges of the photography, I whizzed out of New York by myself at the crack of dawn, amazed at my ability (with my trusty GPS) to manage the New Jersey motorways or the criss-crossing parkways northeast of the city.

Enthralled by what I found—and being an inveterate proselytizer—I wanted to spread the word to garden lovers, urban friends, and landscape design students and professionals, and to make it easier for them to both revisit and take in new gardens on their travels or weekend outings. The variety of offerings is indeed stunning.

Gardens that specialize in daffodils, spring ephemerals, azaleas, irises, peonies, roses, summer perennial borders or mature trees invite us through the changing seasons. Elsewhere, Japanese gardens draw us into a broader investigation of Asian culture. Exciting restorations, given impetus by a growing awareness of garden and estate history, acquaint us with the formal gardens designed by Beatrix Farrand and other landscape design greats, and are, at times, complemented by ambitious long-term plans for the surrounding parks. The sculpture gardens included in the book bring the museum outside and mingle art with horticulture and the physical delight of moving through designed spaces with their myriad vantage points.

Visitors will discover that some historic cemeteries are reestablishing their identities as arboretums, and colleges are proudly connecting students to new environmental practices and luring alumni back to leafy campuses and gardens.

On other occasions they will be surprised by the extraordinary survival of a conservatory, which opens up the history of plants and the advances of technology.

Some of these gardens are horticulturally superb, others used to be but are maintained on a shoestring; still others have periodic injections of public money and then years of drift. Initiatives often depend on supporting foundations—or Friends—who fundraise, agitate, and volunteer as gardeners. The facts given on the total number of professionals and helpers caring for the properties reveal just how challenging their task often is.

While a few gardens included here may seem modest—especially compared to many of the superbly designed and well-kept private gardens open to the public once a year through the Garden Conservancy—they provide an important element in the narrative and social history of each house.

Cultural habits remain engrained—my British background inevitably leads me to associate garden visiting with a pause for lunch or the necessary cup of tea. Frequently surprised by the unavailability of cafés at the gardens or parks, or by the unpredictability and shortness of their hours, I felt that including information on picnicking facilities and "eateries" was vital. Equally perplexed by how few people seem to explore the (carriage) trails in the parks of some of the larger properties, I have also drawn attention to such opportunities. This allows visitors to experience the house and garden in their relationship to the formerly managed estate, essential to a historical understanding of, for instance, the Roosevelt, Vanderbilt, and Frederic Edwin Church properties.

The references to nearby places of interest stem from my love of extended walks and my curiosity about the pleasures that unknown surroundings might yield. If the garden is quite small or doesn't encourage picnics, if a visitor suddenly desires a change of pace, or if the weather becomes inclement, information on nearby attractive villages and towns or art museums might be invaluable.

Although I have looked after my own little gardens in various places from the age of eight up until a few years ago, I remain in awe of those who are the true horticulturalists, and especially those whose vocation is in the public sphere. This book is a tribute to them. I also extend my sincere thanks to W. W. Norton for bringing it to fruition with such flair.

New York, 2010

CONNECTICUT

1. Bartlett Arboretum & Gardens, Stamford
2. Bellamy-Ferriday House & Garden, Bethlehem
3. Boothe Memorial Park & The Boothe Park Rose & Wedding Garden, Stratford
4. Bush-Holley Historic Site, Cos Cob
5. Bushnell Park, Hartford
6. Butler-McCook House & Garden, Hartford
7. Cedar Hill Cemetery, Hartford
8. Amy Cogswell Garden at the Webb-Deane-Stevens Museum, Wethersfield
9. Connecticut College Arboretum & The Caroline Black Garden, New London
10. Cricket Hill Garden, Thomaston
11. Edgerton Park, New Haven
12. Elizabeth Park, Hartford
13. Beatrix Farrand Garden at Three Rivers Farm, Bridgewater
14. Garden of Ideas, Ridgefield
15. The Glass House, New Canaan
16. Glebe House Museum & The Gertrude Jekyll Garden, Woodbury
17. Goodbody Garden at Fort Stamford, Stamford
18. Florence Griswold Museum, Old Lyme
19. Harkness Memorial State Park, Waterford
20. Hill-Stead Museum & Garden, Farmington
21. Hollister House Garden, Washington
22. Laurel Ridge Foundation, Litchfield
23. George & Olive Lee Memorial Garden, New Canaan
24. The Mystic Seaport Gardens, Mystic
25. Osborne Homestead Museum, Derby
26. Pardee Rose Garden in East Rock Park, Hamden
27. Riverfront & Lincoln Financial Sculpture Walk, Hartford
28. Roseland Cottage, Woodstock
29. Shoyoan Teien: The Freeman Family Japanese Garden, Middletown
30. Harriet Beecher Stowe Center, Hartford
31. Walnut Hill Park, New Britain
32. Weir Farm National Historic Site, Wilton
33. Wheeler Farm Gardens, Portland
34. Whitney Water Treatment Plant & Park, Hamden
35. Wickham Park, Manchester
36. Yale University Campus, New Haven
39. Caramoor Center for Music & the Arts, Katonah, NY
46. Hammond Museum & Japanese Stroll Garden, North Salem, NY
48. Innisfree Garden, Millbrook, NY
49. John Jay Homestead State Historic Site, Katonah, NY
52. Lasdon Park, Arboretum & Veterans Memorial, Katonah, NY
71. Wethersfield Garden, Amenia, NY

See Connecticut's Historic Gardens: *www.cthistoricgardens.org*

16

CONNECTICUT

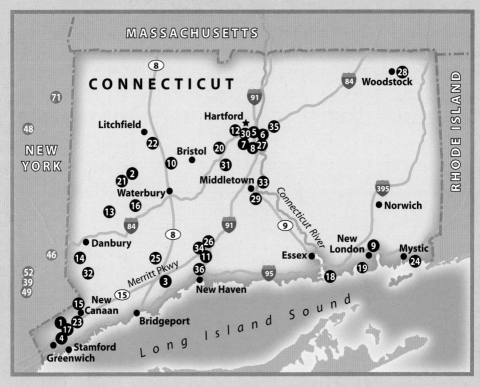

MASSACHUSETTS

CONNECTICUT

8

84 Woodstock

28

71

48

Litchfield

Hartford

84

91

12 30 5 6 35
7 8 27

Bristol

22

20

NEW
YORK

10

31

2
21

Middletown

33

Waterbury

16

29

Connecticut River

395

Norwich

13

84

91

9

Danbury

8

46

26
34
11

New
London

Essex

9

Mystic

14

25

Merritt Pkwy

36

24

32

52
39
49

3

New Haven

18

19

15

15 New
Canaan

Bridgeport

95

1
17
4

23

Greenwich

Stamford

Long Island Sound

RHODE ISLAND

STAMFORD/NEW CANAAN AREA

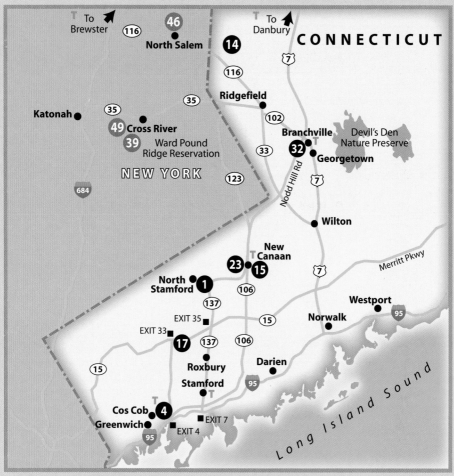

1. Bartlett Arboretum & Gardens, Stamford, CT
4. Bush-Holley Historic Site, Cos Cob, CT
14. Garden of Ideas, Ridgefield, CT
15. The Glass House, New Canaan, CT
17. Goodbody Garden at Fort Stamford, Stamford, CT
23. George & Olive Lee Memorial Garden, New Canaan, CT
32. Weir Farm National Historic Site, Wilton, CT

39. Caramoor Center for Music & the Arts, Katonah, NY
46. Hammond Museum & Japanese Stroll Garden, North Salem, NY
49. John Jay Homestead State Historic Site, Katonah, NY

LITCHFIELD AREA

2 Bellamy-Ferriday House & Garden, Bethlehem, CT

10 Cricket Hill Garden, Thomaston, CT

13 Beatrix Farrand Garden at Three Rivers Farm, Bridgewater, CT

16 Glebe House Museum & The Gertrude Jekyll Garden, Woodbury, CT

21 Hollister House Garden, Washington, CT

22 Laurel Ridge Foundation, Litchfield, CT

NEW HAVEN AREA

3 Boothe Memorial Park & The Boothe Park Rose & Wedding Garden, Stratford, CT

11 Edgerton Park, New Haven, CT

25 Osborne Homestead Museum, Derby, CT

26 Pardee Rose Garden in East Rock Park, Hamden, CT

34 Whitney Water Treatment Plant & Park, Hamden, CT

36 Yale University Campus, New Haven, CT

NEW LONDON AREA

9 Connecticut College Arboretum & The Caroline Black Garden, New London, CT

18 Florence Griswold Museum, Old Lyme, CT

19 Harkness Memorial State Park, Waterford, CT

24 The Mystic Seaport Gardens, Mystic, CT

ARROW TO:

28 Roseland Cottage, Woodstock, CT

5 Bushnell Park, Hartford, CT

6 Butler-McCook House & Garden, Hartford, CT

7 Cedar Hill Cemetery, Hartford, CT

8 Amy Cogswell Garden at the Webb-Deane-Stevens Museum, Wethersfield, CT

12 Elizabeth Park, Hartford, CT

20 Hill-Stead Museum & Garden, Farmington, CT

27 Riverfront & Lincoln Financial Sculpture Walk, Hartford, CT

29 Shoyoan Teien, Middletown, CT

30 Harriet Beecher Stowe Center, Hartford, CT

31 Walnut Hill Park, New Britain, CT

33 Wheeler Farm Gardens, Portland, CT

35 Wickham Park, Manchester, CT

CENTRAL HARTFORD

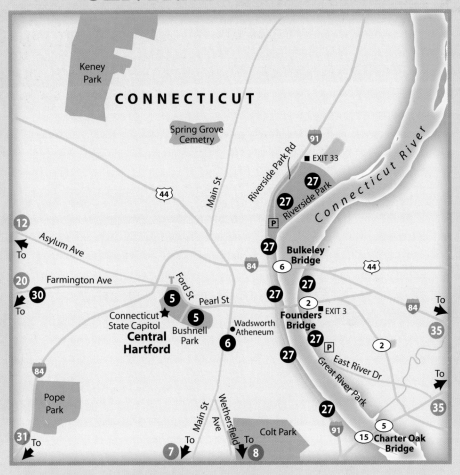

- **5** Bushnell Park, Hartford, CT
- **6** Butler-McCook House & Garden, Hartford, CT
- **27** Riverfront & Lincoln Financial Sculpture Walk, Hartford, CT
- **30** Harriet Beecher Stowe Center, Hartford, CT

ARROWS TO:

- **7** Cedar Hill Cemetery, Hartford, CT
- **8** Amy Cogswell Garden at the Webb-Deane-Stevens Museum, Wethersfield, CT
- **12** Elizabeth Park, Hartford, CT
- **20** Hill-Stead Museum & Garden, Farmington, CT
- **31** Walnut Hill Park, New Britain, CT
- **35** Wickham Park, Manchester, CT

1 BARTLETT ARBORETUM & GARDENS

151 Brookdale Road, Stamford, CT 06903
TEL: (203) 322-6971
WEBSITE: *www.bartlettarboretum.org*
SEE MAPS: pp. 17 & 18

Grounds open: 9am–sunset; visitor center Monday–Friday 9am–4:30pm, closed national holidays. Admission fee (sometimes)

Location: 43 miles from New York City

Public transportation: Metro-North or Amtrak to Stamford, taxi 7-1/2 miles

Facilities: Maps from the shelter in the car park, and also from the visitor center in the main house, where there are restrooms, a gallery, and a horticultural resource library; no refreshments; picnicking; not wheelchair accessible; dogs on leash

Programming: Educational courses, classes for adults and for children; summer concerts; ongoing plant clinics

Nearby eateries: South on High Ridge Road (approx. 2 miles), many diners, etc.; downtown Stamford, 7-1/2 miles

Also of interest: Stamford Museum & Nature Center, 39 Scofieldtown Road, 1-1/4 miles, 118-acre former estate of Henri Bendel

A checkered history of care and neglect and changing botanical research interests has left the Bartlett Arboretum with the challenge of reinvigorating the property and forging new directions.

The former home, from 1913, of Dr. Francis A. Bartlett (1882–1963), the founder in 1907 of the F. A. Bartlett Tree Expert Company, it was also the site of his training school and research laboratory. He collected and planted a large number of plant specimens, and when the research laboratories moved to North Carolina in 1965 the state of Connecticut purchased the arboretum. Transferred to the neighboring University of Connecticut in 1993, it lost its significance once the campus moved to downtown Stamford

in 1998. Finally, in 2001 the land was transferred to the city of Stamford, and the nonprofit Bartlett Arboretum Association assumed operational responsibility.

The association took over some seventy-five acres of woodlands and wetlands—depleted by disease, deer, and invasives—and the remnants of the collections, which occupy sixteen acres near the house. Many of the rhododendron cultivars planted and bred by Professor Gustav Mehlquist (1906–1999) had disappeared. The renowned conifer collection, across the road, was overgrown and had lost its natural water supply. Few people visited. Since then the management, replanting, and interpretation of native

species in the woodlands, wetlands, and meadows have become a high priority, and trails allow access to these areas. Educational programs for schoolchildren have also been developed.

Closer to the house, the Mehlquist area has been cleared and replanted, magnolia and viburnum collections have been initiated, and new acquisitions in the tea family (*Stewartia, Franklinia*, and *Camellia*) have been made. The botanical research of staff members has taken two of them to the Amazon rainforests and the Caribbean, and in winter the greenhouse holds an array of unusual tropicals, which in summer are planted in display islands with useful labels. A clicking system is used as a deterrent for deer.

Other small gardens, borders, and curiosities reflect various interests, new and old, and some notable champion trees survive. Lacking a strong sense of design, the importance of this

area is mainly as an educational resource. Additions are being made once again to the herbarium. A new greenhouse for propagation and a conservatory for enlarged displays, are long-term goals of the small group of staff members: five full-time and five seasonal gardeners assisted by master gardeners and volunteers. The conifer area, still closed to visitors (about 25,000 annually), may be replanted. In the meantime, the trails through the woodlands are a bonus.

② BELLAMY-FERRIDAY HOUSE & GARDEN

Main Street North, Bethlehem, CT 06751
TEL: (203) 266-7596
WEBSITE: *www.ctlandmarks.org*
SEE MAPS: pp. 17 & 19

Hours: House and garden open May–August, Wednesday, Friday, Saturday, and Sunday 11am–4pm; September–Columbus Day weekend, Friday, Saturday, Sunday 11am–4pm. Also Memorial Day, Labor Day, Columbus Day, same hours. Admission fee

Location: 95 miles from New York City

Public transportation: None

Facilities: Visitor center; good brochure and map; gift shop with books on related history and exhibit space; no refreshments but list of local restaurants available; restrooms; picnic tables; not wheelchair accessible; dogs on leash; SCVNGR texting hunt for families

Programming: Exhibitions, workshops, talks

Garden tours: About five per season, and by appointment

Nearby eateries: Bethlehem; Woodbury (9 miles south); Litchfield (8-1/2 miles north)

As the name suggests, the lives of two families intertwine here, the last owners, Eliza Ferriday and her daughter, Caroline Ferriday (1902–1990), especially nurturing the ten-acre garden and grounds. Generous lawns around the circular drive dissolve into grassy areas on the south, with large, mature specimen trees and white-flowering shrubs (both native and introduced) visible against a backdrop of dark eastern hemlocks. A stone terrace behind the house gives access to the formal parterre garden (1915–1918). Its strong design—low clipped hedges and upright cones of yew (*Taxus cuspidata*) around a putto in a little pool—appears to advantage from Caroline Ferriday's bedroom on the second floor where irrigation pipes for the roses and perennials are less noticeable. Below the parterre garden and down a gentle slope, one can see more perennials and the special collections of peonies, roses on a tunnel arbor, and then early, middle, and late flowering lilacs and magnolias. A semicircular, clipped yew hedge at the bottom defines the layout, and another planting of eastern hemlocks produces a sense of enclosure on the north.

Although no longer productive, the adjoining orchard is a reminder of its importance for generations of the Bellamy family (1740–1868). The

Reverend Joseph Bellamy (1719–1790), who became a well-known Puritan preacher, author, and educator, acquired a hundred acres of land when he became Bethlehem's minister in 1740. The clapboard house was built for him in 1754 and enlarged in 1767 to accommodate his large family and resident theological students. Pastures for cows and sheep, a large kitchen garden, and the orchard extended out from the house, with the woods supplying fuel. His descendents added the entrance piers and gates, as well as the stone walls on the eastern and western borders. The existing outbuildings are mainly nineteenth-century replacements of the originals.

Henry and Eliza Ferriday bought what they called "The Hay" in 1912 as a summer country estate, adding on the northern wing. After Mr. Ferriday died in 1914, his wife and daughter continued to visit from New York every year and focused on the development of the garden. Caroline Ferriday's interest in the Reverend Bellamy and his period led her to remove the nineteenth-century additions and restore the home and its interiors to their possible eighteenth-century appearance, in harmony with her imagined recreation, in Colonial Revival style, of the parterre.

When Caroline Ferriday (a staunch supporter of the French Resistance during World War II, civil rights activist, and philanthropist) died in 1990, the outer eighty-nine acres were donated to the Bethlehem Land Trust (trail map from the visitor center), and ten acres, including the house and garden, to the Antiquarian & Landmarks Society, now Connecticut Landmarks. The grounds, visited by some 2,000 people a year, are taken care of by two part-time gardeners. Future plans include refurbishing the apple orchard and replanting grape vines on the tunnel arbor.

3 BOOTHE MEMORIAL PARK & THE BOOTHE PARK ROSE & WEDDING GARDEN

5744 Main Street Putney, Stratford, CT 06614
TEL: (203) 381-2046
WEBSITE: *www.boothememorialpark.org*
SEE MAPS: pp. 17 & 20

Hours: Garden and grounds open year-round. Museum tours available June 1 through November 1, Tuesdays and Fridays 11am–1pm; Saturdays and Sundays 1pm–4pm. Admission free to grounds, charge to museum

Location: 68 miles from New York City

Public transportation: Metro-North to Stratford, CT; taxi 4-1/4 miles

Facilities: Restrooms; picnic tables in the Park; wheelchair accessible; dogs on leash

Nearby eateries: Stratford and Milford (4-1/2 miles)

Also of interest: Beardsley Park, 1875 Noble Ave, Bridgeport, 7 miles—a 100-acre Frederick Law Olmsted city park, rather run-down now; Beardsley Zoo in the park, 1920; Merritt Parkway, from NY/CT border to north of Milford, CT, landscaping originally by Weld T. Chase

The brothers David and Stephen Boothe donated thirty-two acres in 1949 to the town of Stratford. Included was their home of around 1840, remodeled in 1914, their grounds, and a collection, also begun in 1914, of odd and unique buildings and their contents that formed the museum. These are clustered near the main entrance to the park and include a windmill (1844), a barn (c. 1880) topped by a 1913 clock tower, a faceted blacksmith shop (c. 1935), and the Putney Chapel (1844). Perhaps the most fascinating is the Technocratic Cathedral (c. 1932) built of striations of redwood in undulations, with glass-block windows stacked like the bottom two stories of a modernist pagoda.

Since the initial gift, other structures have arrived in the park, catering to the interests of a new set of aficionados.

A local astronomical society has a working planetarium (1957), the Stratford Amateur Radio Club (1951) and the Boothe Memorial Railway Society (2002) have centers, while an attraction for the general visitor is the toll booth from the Merritt Parkway that sits in the park as a separate showpiece. Designed in 1940 by George Dunkelberger (who was also responsible for the sixty-eight bridges along the $37\frac{1}{2}$ miles), to fit in with the intended parklike setting of the road, it resembles a shingle-roofed, open wooden cabin, with divisions for three streams of cars. In 1988, when tolls were ended, it was rescued and joined the museum.

The park itself, beyond the nondescript car park, has appealing sweeps of grass, nicely graded, sloping toward the Housatonic River (cut off by River Road) with clumps of trees and wooded sections providing shade and picnic areas along with a children's playground. No playing fields have to be accommodated in this hilly terrain, but a circuit path that would allow walkers, strollers, and joggers to fully enjoy its extent is absent. The grounds are minimally maintained and the pond has lost its former aesthetic appeal.

Within this park, with all its special-interest claims, an unexpected feature appears: the Rose and Wedding Garden, designed and planted in 1990 at a cost of $36,000, and donated by the Friends of Boothe Park, formed in 1984. It is surrounded by a wooden fence, with climbing roses adorning its entrance and exit archways. A central brick pathway defines the axis, with two Victorian ornaments (a cast-iron fountain and a cast-iron vase) at the center of two compartments of shaped beds. Except for the hostas around the fountain, every bed is filled with roses, a lovely display in season, which draws wedding and prom groups for

photographs. The Friends valiantly raise money for the expenses, and six volunteers look after this well-loved garden, annually attracting, it is estimated, some 89,000 visitors.

Adjacent to the rose garden lies the Stratford Sister Cities Friendship Garden. The symbolic importance of this simple rectangular bed of flowers belies its modest proportions. In a display of cultural and horticultural cooperation, Stratford, CT and its five sister cities in Britain, Australia, Canada (two), and New Zealand (all with Shakespeare theaters) create a new design each year, selecting plants (mostly annuals) that will thrive in all five countries.

In a town that had two locations so contaminated that they were designated as Superfund sites, with an estimated clean-up cost of $200 million, the Boothe Memorial Park, is certainly underfunded. Thus, the well-tended little rose garden is a special bonus, not to be taken for granted.

4 BUSH-HOLLEY HISTORIC SITE

39 Strickland Road, Cos Cob, CT 06807
TEL: (203) 869-6899
WEBSITE: *www.hstg.org*
SEE MAPS: pp. 17 & 18

Hours: House (by tour) and grounds open March through December, Wednesday–Sunday noon–4pm; January and February, Friday–Sunday noon–4pm. Closed major holidays. Admission free to grounds, fee for house tour
Location: 35 miles from New York City
Parking: Under I-95 overpass
Public transportation: Metro-North to Cos Cob, walk 2 blocks
Facilities: Visitor center, museum, shop, restrooms in former post office (c. 1805) on property; no refreshments; picnicking; limited wheelchair accessibility; Green Market on Tuesday 9am–3pm and Friday noon–6pm, in season; dogs on leash
Nearby eateries: Cos Cob, within walking distance; Greenwich, 2-1/4 miles
Also of interest: Audubon Center, 613 Riversville Road, Greenwich (285 acres), 8 miles; Bruce Museum, 1 Museum Drive, Greenwich, 2-1/4 miles; in Bruce Park (opposite the museum) an innovative children's playground (2009) integrates plantings and nature with the "Boundless" theory of play

The Bush-Holley House mirrors some of the economic and social changes that have taken place in Cos Cob. Built in the 1730s, with comfortable additions appended from 1755 to 1771, it was the home of David Bush (1733–1797), a wealthy merchant with ten children, who owned land and a gristmill and negotiated his business connections with New York through the busy port of Cos Cob. The Greenwich Historical Society bought the property in 1957 for its colonial and early nineteenth-century history, and furnished it accordingly. It focused on the time frame of 1820–1825, when the family slaves were being emancipated and the Bush finances were less stable.

But since 1997, the growing interest in the Cos Cob colony of American Impressionists has brought about a second interpretation.

Between 1892 and 1920, Cos Cob became (like Old Lyme a little later) a favorite summer gathering place for artists. Josephine and Edward P. Holley (1848–1916 and 1837–1913), with limited resources and living in a village that had become a quiet, rather dilapidated and picturesque backwater (yet within easy reach of New York by train), had started taking in boarders. The ambiance of their house attracted John Henry Twachman (1835–1902), J. Alden Weir (1852–1919; see p. 88), Childe Hassam (1859–1935), and many others over the years. Elmer MacRae (1875–1953) even married the Holley daughter, Emma Constant (1871–1965), and one of the rooms upstairs is set up as his studio. The artists posed their models inside the "Old House" or moved outside, painting the exterior with its good-looking porches, as well as the garden, the boats in the harbor, and the surrounding countryside. Examples of their work, seen on the guided tour, vividly bring into focus this period of American art and also reflect the influence of Japanese woodblock prints in its development.

The modest bits of garden—interpreted to the time of the artists and the household around 1900—have been recreated from their paintings, photographs of the time, and written material. They add a nice touch, creating visual links and extending the narrative from indoors to outdoors. A few lilacs at the front of the house, a grape arbor, and some fruit trees recalling the orchard are supplemented by a well-maintained mixed flower and vegetable patch. Nasturtiums, tobacco plants, cabbage, zucchini, poppies, squash, cornflowers, tomatoes, chards, beets, and lettuce are all intermingled and are edged by marigolds, bringing to mind the produce once used for the evening meal when family and boarders gathered in the dining room and fresh flowers were arranged in the many vases.

The Greenwich Historical Society owns three other building on the property, using them for visitor, educational, and archival centers. Six master gardener volunteers care for the garden.

5 BUSHNELL PARK

Ford, Jewell, and Elm Streets
surround the park, Hartford, CT 16103
TEL: (860) 232-6710 (BUSHNELL PARK FOUNDATION)
WEBSITE: *www.bushnellpark.org*
SEE MAPS: pp. 17 & 23

Hours: Park open dawn to dusk. Admission free

Location: 117 miles from New York City

Parking: On streets at weekends, or parking garages

Public transportation: Amtrak to Hartford, and walk south one block to park

Facilities: No refreshments; portable toilets; picnic tables; wheelchair accessible; dogs on leash

Programming: Summer concerts and some seasonal events

Nearby eateries: Adjacent downtown Hartford

Nearby plazas and parks: Constitution Plaza (1964, Charles Dubose and landscape architects Sasaki Associates), bordered by Market, Talcott, and State Streets and Columbus Boulevard; Burr Mall (1969, landscape architect Dan Kiley), Main and Prospects Streets; Pope Park, Pope Park Drive (1-1/4 miles), with schematic drawings by Jacob Weidenmann (1893) and, after his death, the Olmsted firm, 1898

Also of interest: Wadsworth Athenaeum, 600 Main Street

The creation of City Park, renamed Bushnell Park after the articulate promoter, the Reverend Horace Bushnell (1802–1876), reflects strong optimism and democratic intent. The plan was that a new park—located on forty acres just beyond the railroad station—would get rid of an unsightly array of ramshackle houses and factories, clean up the polluted Hog River, and bring together citizens from all walks of life to enjoy nature. The beautiful landscaped park would be a cause for civic pride and bring admiring visitors, thereby attracting more business to the city. In 1854 the electorate of Hartford voted overwhelming to authorize the expenditure of $105,000, and thus City Park, over the next sixteen years, became the first U.S. public park built entirely with taxpayers' money.

The landscape designer and engineer Jacob Weidenmann (1829–1893) entered the scene in 1860, after the 1858 competition produced unsatisfactory results. The Hartford-born Frederick Law Olmsted (1822–1903) may have been considered, but he was busy with New York's Central Park. Weidenmann, who was born in Switzerland, educated in Germany, and arrived in the United States in 1856, had all the professional credentials. He supervised the surveying, draining, grading, and fountain work, selected the planting, and laid out the carriage drives and pathways to connect the two parts of the park divided by Trinity Street. His plan, in a restrained modern and picturesque landscape style, informed by European models, made a feature out of the river. Five bridges connected the park to downtown Hartford, and a terrace at the top of the hill created a viewing point. Weidenmann selected 1,100 trees from 157 varieties.

Changes have taken places over the years: the Victorian-Gothic Connecticut State Capitol, designed in 1871 by Richard M. Upjohn (1828–1903), with its oddly proportioned tall tower and gold cupola (replacing Trinity College) looms over the park from the top of the hill; the river, after disastrous flooding in 1936 and 1938, was moved underground by the Army Corp of Engineers. Weidenmann's central fountain has been replaced on the north side by the 1898 Corning Fountain (installed in 1899) with a stag, or hart (connecting it with "Hartford"), and a group of Saukiog Indians, by John Massey Rhind (1860–1936). The flower bedding reflects that Victorian period. Memorial monuments too find a place: the 1886 Soldiers and Sailors Memorial Arch over Trinity Street by George Keller (1842–1935) commemorates Civil War participants with innovative friezes and sculptures.

The west side of Bushnell Park is now more open, with swathes of lawn and a new performance pavilion (1995), by Buttrick White & Burtis, for concerts and festivals. The east side has a greater variety of trees (cucumber magnolia, Turkey oak, black tupelo, catalpa, bald cypress, locust, pagoda

tree, maple, cherry) and also features a children's playground and a pool with two spraying fountains and a Charles Perry sculpture, installed in 1990. The much-loved wooden carousel from 1914, by Stein & Goldstein, was placed in the park in 1974, and operates from May through mid-October.

Since its formation in 1981, the Bushnell Park Foundation has been cooperating with the city in efforts to renovate the park. The tree count, down to a mere 339 in the late 1980s, is now up to 750. Four state champions survive, along with a scion of the famous Charter Oak which hid Connecticut's charter of independence from 1687 to 1689. Difficulties remain: portable toilets are useful but unsightly, and the Bushnell Park Café and Gallery in the 1947 domestic-Gothic pump house at 60 Elm Street was closed in 2009. The foundation estimates that about a million people use the park each year, reason enough for the city to invest in this important public space.

6 BUTLER-McCOOK HOUSE & GARDEN

396 Main Street, Hartford, CT 06103
TEL: (860) 522-1806
WEBSITE: *www.ctlandmarks.org*
SEE MAPS: pp. 17 & 23

Hours: Garden always open. House open for tours: April, Saturday and Sunday 11am–4pm; May through October, Thursday–Sunday 11am–4pm; November and December, Saturday and Sunday 11am–4pm. Admission fee to house
Location: 116 miles from New York City
Parking: In rear from South Prospect Street
Public transportation: Amtrak to Hartford, walk 3/4 mile or taxi
Facilities: Visitor center; gift shop; no refreshments; restrooms; picnic table; first floor and garden wheelchair accessible; dogs on leash
Programming: Several exhibitions, concerts
Garden tours: Included in house tour in season and by appointment
Nearby eateries: Adjacent, in downtown Hartford
Also of interest: Wadsworth Athenaeum, 600 Main Street (3/4 mile)

One of only five eighteenth-century houses left in Hartford, the clapboard 1782 Butler-McCook home, with its Victorian additions, was lived in until 1974. Painted a mustard color with blue window sashes and shutters— its front area adorned with lilacs, a great plane tree, and a green picket fence—it sits proudly on Main Street, formerly a residential neighborhood. Inside is a veritable treasure trove of social history relating to the four generations of occupants, read through the furnishings, paintings, travel mementoes, photographs, and archival material. An excellent exhibition contextualizes their involvement with medicine, religion, Hartford industries, and social reform,

as well as the neighbors and family activities.

The garden, which stretches in a rectangle behind the house, is of similar historical interest. It was designed in 1865 by Jacob Weidenmann (of Bushnell Park and Cedar Hill Cemetery fame). The original plan hangs in the house and is his only known design of such a small town garden (one acre). It shows a compromise between the strictly utilitarian (retaining the traditional kitchen garden and its central access path) and design ideas of the period. The latter are seen (to the southwest) in the serpentine, a short, roughly oval-shaped path around a lawn with clusters of shrubs, backed by more shrubs and trees, leading to a pool with bases for four cast-iron urns; a formal parterre of small beds symmetrically laid out within two circles below the back of the house; and at the far end, beyond the kitchen garden, another area in the natural style, of lawn, looping path, shrubs, trees, and a garden pavilion. The still-existing pit house and cold frames are seen tucked against the north wall in the plan.

In 1885 the kitchen garden was replaced by a tennis court, and that space remains as an open lawn. The whole of the far (eastern) end of the garden has given way to an informal car park, and another eighteenth-century house (1788) was moved there in 2008. Despite such changes, the 1865 design remains visible: the attractive parterre garden with its little box hedges containing roses, perennials, and annuals, a form of the original pool, and some of the trees from that period (Carolina silver bell, dawn redwood). There is also a Lady Banks rose, a descendant of the one planted in 1853. These, and others known from journals, attest to the great interest in mixing regional with ornamental plantings.

The house and all its contents were deeded to the Antiquarian and Landmarks Society (now Connecticut Landmarks) in 1974, when Frances Cook died, to be "a sort of oasis in the hustle and bustle of a World's Main Street." The garden is looked after by twenty-five volunteers from the West Hartford Garden Club, with

Connecticut Landmarks budgeting for lawn mowing and tree/leaf removal. Some 3,000 people visit the house and garden annually. A return to the complete planting and layout of the Weidenmann 1865 design would be a most valuable contribution to garden history.

7 CEDAR HILL CEMETERY

453 Fairfield Avenue, Hartford, CT 06114
TEL: (860) 956-3311
WEBSITE: *www.cedarhillcemetery.org*
SEE MAPS: pp. 17, 22 & 23

Hours: Grounds open daily 7am–dusk; admission free

Location: 112 miles from New York City

Public transportation: Amtrak to Hartford, walk 1/2 mile to Main & Pearl, CT Transit bus #61 to Maple Avenue stop

Facilities: Office (Monday–Friday 8am–4pm) in Northam Memorial Chapel; *Guide by Cell* leaflet on notable residents, and restrooms. Also information box inside entry gates; no refreshments; no picnicking; no dogs; wheelchair accessible

Programming: Tours and events May through October, organized by the Cedar Hill Cemetery Foundation

Nearby eateries: Scattered; downtown Hartford

Hartford, with the creation in 1859 of City Park (Bushnell Park), was in the forefront of the urban park movement (see p. 32), but lacked a cemetery in the modern rural style. This was remedied in 1865 by a group of prominent citizens, who purchased parcels of land for a 268-acre tract (some three miles from the city center), which answered the requirements for views, water, a diversified terrain, good trees, and woods. Cedars grew on the ridges—hence the name. They invited Jacob Weidenmann (1829–1893), superintendent of City Park (which he had designed), to lay out this new nonsectarian park for the living as well as for the dead. For some reason the entrance gate and house he designed were not built, and the ones we see today are by his colleague,

George Keller (1842–1935): the superintendent's house, on the right, built in 1880; Northam Memorial Chapel, on the left, in 1882; and the handsome gate, in 1889.

Cedar Hill Cemetery was to flow over hill and dale, with no curbs, fences, hedges, or barriers. Weidenmann planned large family plots with only one central monument surrounded by gravestones flush with the ground, or single, upright columns, obelisks, or memorials, standing in the grass, never in lines, and scattered among the trees and shrubs. Drives and paths for carriages or strolling pedestrians wound their way between the various areas. The approach to the heart of the cemetery from the entrance gates was totally distinctive, making a beautiful landscape statement out of a problem.

The water table in this swampy area (some sixty acres) being too high for graves, Weidenmann created a series of five interconnected, artificial lakes (one was eight acres in extent) set within the grassland. The drive passed by the dam and its cascade, with serene views of water and plantings beyond. Today there are just three lakes, and the land around is only minimally managed, but the effective alliance between nature and art is still evident.

The concept of an "open lawn system" was not consistently followed, and today there are many upright memorials, and the views are less open. But the proportion of 40 percent trees, plantings, and meadow to 60 percent for burial sites presents a most attractive landscape for contemporary pursuits such as birdwatching, walking, jogging, and tree admiring. Pick up *A Guide to the Notable Trees of Cedar Hill Cemetery* at the entrance gate office and follow the route to find twenty-three labeled, special specimens, or join the infrequent tree tours with Ed Richardson. West coast conifers, regional natives, and European and Japanese imports are featured, many being over one hundred years old.

The mission of the Cedar Hill Cemetery Foundation, established in 1999, is to work with the board of Cedar Hill Cemetery to preserve and protect the art, history, and natural resources of this historic cemetery. Besides nurturing the trees and the designed landscape, the foundation organizes thematic tours on, for example, funerary iconography or

the lives of prominent figures from the arts (Jacob Weidenmann, William Glackens, Katherine Hepburn) and big business (J. P Morgan, Samuel Colt). It also reaches out to new audiences with such events as scavenger hunts and lantern tours at night. The grounds are managed by three full-time and eleven seasonal gardeners. Some 5,000 people visit annually.

8 AMY COGSWELL GARDEN AT THE WEBB-DEANE-STEVENS MUSEUM

211 Main Street, Wethersfield, CT 06109
TEL: (860) 529-0612
WEBSITE: *www.webb-deane-stevens.org/garden_and_grounds.html*
SEE MAPS: pp. 17, 22 & 23

Hours: House (by tour) and garden open May 1 through October 31, daily (except Tuesdays) 10am–4pm; Sundays 1pm–4pm. Closed Memorial Day, July 4, and Labor Day. Garden free; house fee

Location: 112 miles from New York City

Parking: On street or in town parking lot

Public transportation: Amtrak to Hartford, CT Transit bus #53W or 55 to Wethersfield, or taxi 5-1/2 miles

Facilities: Visitor center in the museum for garden plan and various brochures, gift shop, restrooms; no refreshments; picnic tables; garden and first floor of house wheelchair accessible; dogs on leash

Programming: For the three historical museums

Garden tours: By appointment

Nearby eateries: Cafés and restaurants within walking distance

Also of interest: The town of Wethersfield has the largest historic district in Connecticut, with 150 pre–Civil War houses and 150 built shortly thereafter

Three superb clapboard and brick eighteenth-century houses adjacent to each other make up the Webb-Deane-Stevens Museum. One finds the charming Colonial Revival garden at the back of Joseph Webb's 1752 merchant house. Colonial Revival, the early twentieth-century interpretation of what an American eighteenth-century garden might have looked like, includes ingredients such as an enclosed, rectangular space, crossed by paths (usually of brick) at right angles; beds filled with "old-fashioned" flowers (rather than semitropicals or bedding-out in blocks of color); arbors and

arches for an abundance of climbing roses, clematis, and honeysuckles; and a sundial.

The Webb House garden draws upon these components. In fact, it is a revival of a revival, since the 1921 garden designed for the Colonial Dames by Amy Cogswell (1867–1958) fell into disrepair, and then was much changed. But the rediscovery of Cogswell's design and planting arrangements in 1996 gave impetus to the reconstruction of 1999, which is what we see today. Broad borders lining the main and transverse paths are filled with roses and hardy perennials reflecting, whenever possible, the list of ninety-nine plants specified by Cogswell—some indeed colonial, others favorites of the time. White heirloom trellised wooden arches carry additional roses. Although Joseph Webb originally had a pleasure garden, no descriptions remain.

The view past the sundial on the main axis takes in the large trees and

volunteer Ann Foley, in the next few years.

The Webb House has been owned by the National Society of the Colonial Dames of America in the State of Connecticut since 1919. The house tour presents the history of its previous owners and functions, including the fact that it served as George Washington's headquarters in 1781.

a small meadow outside the hedged garden, along with the period-style barn on the right, now used for receptions. Plans to reinterpret this outer area, the larger section of the eight-acre grounds, and to plant native trees and shrubs there are under way. The resulting nature walks will then be used as an educational tool for children. Charles Lyle, the director, underscores the commitment to Cogswell—"this elusive garden designer of the Golden Age of Women Landscape Architects"—and hopes to publish a pamphlet on her, based on the illuminating research of garden

The Colonial Revival garden and the little herb garden and plantings around the other two houses are cared for by one part-time buildings and grounds professional, and some twenty-five to thirty volunteer Garden Angels, who meet once a month under the direction of a part-time master gardener, and a part-time coordinator of volunteers. Some 400–500 visitors discover the garden annually. Currently there is no plant or tree labeling.

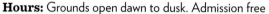

⑨ CONNECTICUT COLLEGE ARBORETUM & THE CAROLINE BLACK GARDEN

270 Mohegan Avenue, New London, CT 06320 (MAIN CAMPUS)
(SEE PARKING INFO FOR CORRECT DETAILS)
TEL: (860) 439-5020
WEBSITE: *http://arboretum.conncoll.edu*
SEE MAPS: pp. 17 & 21

Hours: Grounds open dawn to dusk. Admission free
Location: 125 miles from New York City
Parking: On Williams Street for Native Plant Collection; for the Caroline Black Garden, take entrance to the Connecticut College Athletic Center, on the east side of Route 32 (Mohegan Avenue), and park behind Vinal Cottage
Public transportation: Amtrak or Shore Line to New London, then taxi 2-1/2 miles
Facilities: Trail maps at the entrances to the Native Plant Arboretum and the Caroline Black Garden, and in the Olin Science Center, Room 103 (arboretum headquarters); restrooms in the Olin building or the Harkness Chapel; Oasis snack shop in the Crozier-Williams College Center; picnicking; wheelchair accessibility in central campus area; dogs on leash
Programming: Lectures and workshops for adults and children
Arboretum tours: Usually May through October, Sunday at 2pm. Also by appointment
Nearby eateries: New London
Also of interest: Lyman Allyn Art Museum, 625 Williams Street, 1/2 mile

The whole 750 acres of Connecticut College was designated an arboretum in the mid-1990s, and, indeed, wonderful trees grow in the core area of the campus. A brochure and map, *Trees of the Connecticut College Campus*, picks out sixty of them for a self-guided walk, giving a short description, including country of origin, and their location. When the college was founded on the broad plateau of a hill in 1911, the area was treeless and used for pasture, so these specimens stem from that period onward.

In addition, two specific arboretum destinations beckon. Directly opposite the Williams Entrance (to the west) is the Native Plant Collection, established in 1931 and then expanded to 450 acres in the early 1990s. The view is immediately dramatic: a formal avenue of round-topped *Kalmia* (a blaze of pinks in early June) leading to the lake, where large quantities of water lilies reside. The self-guided tour maps out a route stopping at nine "stations," with some detours to the fenced-in special collections of wildflowers, viburnums, and azaleas. The walk takes one through natural habitats based on varying ground, water, and light conditions, with managed areas for other collections, such as the magnolias or the satisfying display of conifers, including dwarf and cultivated varieties of natives. Key woody plants are labeled.

The Caroline Black Garden, on the opposite side of campus, offers very different plantings, and is a much smaller (five acres) and more tightly designed garden space. Despite the ongoing noise from the road, it has a surprisingly intimate feel, with open areas of graded and well-shaped

such as botany, environmental studies, and conservation biology, draw upon it on a regular basis. Although visitors are welcome, the mission is to prepare "the next generation of citizen-leaders, whose diverse responsibilities will include crafting a sustainable relationship with the natural world."

College grounds staff maintain the central campus, while three full-time arboretum staff members manage the Caroline Black Garden, the Native Plant Collections, and the natural areas. Students join them on

lawn enclosed or punctuated by superb (mostly) nonnative conifers, an enormous European beech, rhododendrons, viburnums, spireas, hydrangeas, Japanese maples, cherries, and other Asian exotics. Its circumference is defined by woodland planting, encompassing also a native holly collection. This garden was established in 1928 by Professor Caroline Black, and her legacy is reflected in the college's continued commitment to using all parts of the arboretum as a living laboratory. Currently some twenty-five courses,

a regular basis. Currently Japanese garden designer Stephen Morrell is redesigning the water feature area in the Black Garden, and additional stone installations and planting are expected. A new public entrance to the Native Plant Collection is also planned.

10 CRICKET HILL GARDEN

670 Walnut Hill Road, Thomaston, CT 06787

TEL: (860) 283-1042

WEBSITE: *www.treepeony.com*

SEE MAPS: pp. 17 & 19

Hours: Nursery open during the Peony Festival, six weeks in May and June, Tuesday–Sunday 10am–4pm, and Memorial Day Monday. Also open preseason and postseason (see website). Admission free

Location: 104 miles from New York City

Public transportation: Metro-North to Waterbury, taxi 11-1/2 miles; Peter Pan bus to Waterbury, taxi

Facilities: Peony sales; brochure; gift shop and books on peonies and Chinese gardens; no refreshments; restrooms; picnicking; not wheelchair accessible, but view from drive; dogs on leash

Nearby eateries: Thomaston, 2 miles; Litchfield, 7 miles; list available

Also of interest: White Memorial Conservation Center, 80 Whitehall Road, Litchfield (4,000 acres), 9-1/2 miles; Topsmeade State Forest (see p. 68), 7-1/2 miles; Guy Wolff Pottery, 1249 Bantam Road, Bantam, 11-3/4 miles; Cornwall Bridge Pottery, 415 Sharon Goshen Turnpike (Route 1280), West Cornwall (in the village) 23 miles

Spread over seven acres, under a light canopy of deciduous trees, the peonies in this nursery are planted along fluidly formed terraces on what was once a stony hillside. The first dry roots arrived in 1988 from China, and since then the growing of tree (and herbaceous) peonies has become a focused passion (and a second career) for David Furman and his wife, Kasha, and now their two sons. Visits to suppliers in China and Japan ensure the quality of this collection of some 400 labeled varieties. The peonies bloom at different times throughout a six-week period: the Chinese tree peonies first, followed by Japanese tree peonies, and then the American varieties. Twenty-one more acres of woodland are ideal for bird watching, and a little walk around a pond provides a seat and an extended view. A teahouse will be constructed over the next few years and, when complete, regular musical performances during bloom time are planned.

11 EDGERTON PARK

75 Cliff Street, New Haven, CT 06511
TEL: (203) 624-9377 (ON SUNDAYS 1–4 PM
AND FOR MESSAGES)
WEBSITE: *www.edgertonpark.org*
SEE MAPS: pp. 17 & 20

Hours: Grounds open daily, dawn to dusk; conservatory daily, 10am–4pm, except
for major holidays; horticultural library and historical exhibits in the Carriage House,
Sunday 1pm–4pm. Admission free

Location: 81 miles from New York City

Parking: On Cliff Street

Public transportation: Metro-North or Amtrak to New Haven, taxi 3-1/2 miles
or bus, CT Transit J line, from downtown to Cliff Street on Whitney Avenue

Facilities: *Discover Edgerton Park* brochure (including guide to ten trees) from
notice board at Cliff Street entrance; restrooms in greenhouse complex; plant sales;
no refreshments; picnicking; conservatory and grounds wheelchair accessible;
dogs on leash

Conservatory tours: Call (203) 624-8941

Nearby eateries: Five at corner of Putnam and Whitney Avenues, Hamden,
1-1/4 miles

The remnants of a country house estate endure here: the stone wall that surrounds the twenty-two-acre property, the gatehouse, great mature trees, open lawns, and a carriage house. A pleasant view over a grassy dell opens up from the terrace with its balustrade and fountain (replaced in 1991 with a modern design). But the conservatory, greenhouses, and kitchen garden are perhaps the most important legacy of Frederick F. Brewster (a New Haven industrialist), who willed Edgerton to the city of New Haven in 1957 on condition that the main house be demolished after his wife's death (1963). He had bought the property in 1906 from Caroline Whitney, a niece of the renowned Eli Whitney, building a new house designed by Robert Storer Stephenson, who also laid out the grounds in the eighteenth-century English landscape tradition. Photos show the residence filled with enormous displays of potted flowers and cut flowers—another of their great interests.

Currently (although funding is threatened) sixteen people with disabilities work in the conservatory—with its rainforest, tropical, and dry landscape displays—and in one of the greenhouses, funded through the Greenbriar program of the

Easter Seals Rehabilitation Center. Their horticultural skills have led to the development of an educational program to bring in New Haven schoolchildren from third through sixth grade for science and environmental classes. Since 1981, other greenhouse spaces have been rented out to community members, extending the gardening season throughout the winter.

The large, enclosed former kitchen garden and shrub nursery have now become the Community Gardens, divided up into wood or tile-edged

plots, and filled with flowers and vegetables in the summer. An area surrounded by a hedge is set aside for sitting or eating. Local residents can be seen walking their dogs or jogging in the grounds—which are cared for by just one gardener. The city provides for lawn mowing and fallen tree removal. The greenhouse initiative—a hive of activity—and other projects have been supported by the all-volunteer Edgerton Park Conservancy, formed in 1982, whose goal is to raise $125,000 annually. It plans for the eventual preservation and restoration of the park in tandem with the city.

12 ELIZABETH PARK

Prospect and Asylum Avenues, on border of
Hartford and West Hartford, West Hartford, CT 06119
TEL: (860) 231-9443
WEBSITE: *www.elizabethpark.org* (FRIENDS OF ELIZABETH PARK)
SEE MAPS: pp. 17, 22 & 23

Hours: Park open daily, dawn to dusk. Admission free
Location: 120 miles from New York City
Public transportation: Amtrak to Hartford, bus #72 from Union Station
(no buses on weekends) or taxi 2-1/2 miles
Facilities: Information office by greenhouses; restaurant, outdoor café, and
restrooms at the Pond House; picnic tables; wheelchair accessible. *Elizabeth Park:
A Century of Beauty* by Alicia Cornelio with photographs by William Shepard (2003,
not available on site); dogs on leash
Programming: Ongoing garden tours in season; concerts
Nearby eateries: Hartford or West Hartford
Also of interest: Spring Grove Cemetery, 2035 Main Street, Hartford, 3-1/2 miles;
Noah Webster House, 227 South Main Street, West Hartford, 3-1/2 miles

The star attraction in June at Elizabeth Park is the two-and-a-half acre rose garden. Designed and planted by Theodore Wirth (1863–1949) in 1904, it is the oldest public rose garden in the United States. Creating a glorious profusion of color, roses are planted in a pattern of 476 beds (each usually displaying one variety) within a square, with semicircles at each end added in 1912 and 1936. Roses also grow over the seventy-eight high arches placed along the eight pathways, converging at the delightful gazebo on a mound, canopied by Virginia creeper. Around the garden, fences provide further opportunities for climbers. In all, some 650 varieties stem from 15,000 plants.

The flamboyant Charles M. Pond (1837–1894) left the land for Elizabeth Park—to be named for his wife—to the city of Hartford with an endowment of $160,000. The gift was challenged by his brother and sister, and the ninety-six-acre estate of flower gardens, good ornamental trees and shrubs, farmland and house (razed in 1956) was transferred only after a sensational two-year court case. Swiss-born Theodore Wirth was hired in 1896 to superintend the transformation, and he in turn worked with John Charles Olmsted (1852–1920) to design the new layout of carriage drives, paths, an attractive man-made lake, and bridges across the stream. The display gardens at the bottom of the slope occupy the site of the former race track.

Opposite the rose garden, the large square perennial garden, redesigned in 1987 around a hexagonal central pavilion, is bedecked with clematis and offers beds of cool, pastel shades along with those of warmer colors. Adjacent, recalling the park's historic beginnings, is the annual garden—a display of tulips in spring followed by a blaze of traditional bedding-out plants in summer, grown in the neighboring Lord & Burnham greenhouses (1898). Passing through a pendent Atlas cedar archway, one comes to a rock garden, redesigned in 1981 as a shade garden with an emphasis on hostas and groundcovers among the stones.

Clustered at the other side of the greenhouses are more displays, each one reflecting a particular horticultural

expertise. Two berms recall the Victorian delight in carpet-beds: in 2009 the United States flag and the name "Elizabeth Park" were planted out. The Connecticut Dahlia Society and the Connecticut Iris Society are represented along with the Herb Society of America, whose attractive garden is arranged around a circle of creeping thyme. Planters and lush

tropicals ornament the area round the Pond Café, which overlooks the lake with its two spraying fountains. Quiet walks through the woods lead past playgrounds, ball fields, and tennis courts—carefully sited away from the main vistas—to additional land across Prospect Avenue with views extending to downtown Hartford.

The Friends of Elizabeth Park, formed in 1977 when the rose garden and the park were in dire straits, raise money, agitate to keep up horticultural standards on the 102 acres, organize events, and cooperate with the city of Hartford. Every rose bed is labeled as well as some of the special trees. Some 300,000 visitors use the park annually. In addition to the city's three maintenance staff and a supervisor, the Friends supply two seasonal gardeners, two garden consultants, one part-time administrator, and a part-time office clerk in summer. They plan to increase the gardening volunteers to 100 by 2015, replace the outdoor stage with a permanent stone one, and continue rehabilitating the separate Heritage Rose Garden.

13 BEATRIX FARRAND GARDEN AT THREE RIVERS FARM

694 Skyline Ridge Road, Bridgewater, CT 06752

TEL: (860) 350-8226

WEBSITE: *www.promisek.org*

SEE MAPS: pp. 17 & 19

Hours: For garden hours see website; usually several days only in summer, or by appointment. Admission: suggested donation

Location: 82 miles from New York City

Public transportation: None; nearest Metro-North station Danbury, 13 miles

Facilities: Pamphlets and a trail map available on the porch; also photocopy of 1922 Farrand planting plan; no refreshments; restroom in house; picnic tables; not wheelchair accessible, though could view from terrace; no dogs

Nearby eateries: Bank Street in New Milford, 9-1/2 miles; list available

Also of interest: A walk leads down to the right of the bamboo grove to the lake and on toward the end of the promontory (pick up a trail map at entrance to garden)

In this small, enclosed garden facing south, the hand-picked quality of the irregular stones on the walls, terraces, paths, edging, and steps play as important a part as the planting. Wisteria grows on the main terrace, whose steps lead down to an intermediate level and then to an attractive pattern of rectangular and L-shaped beds arranged around a little central pool. The abundance of planting softens the geometry: sedum, alyssum, and thyme spreading into paths, and peonies, roses, irises, hydrangeas, foxgloves, astilbes, lilies, artemisia, ladies' mantle, and many others reflecting a palette of softer shades of yellow, white, cream, and pink.

New York neurologist Dr. Frederick Peterson (1859–1938) and his wife,

Antoinette Ronan, bought the three hundred acre property in 1916 and named the new house Three Rivers Farm, drawing attention to its site. In 1921 Beatrix Farrand (1872–1959) was commissioned to design the garden; however, there is no proof that the actual planting plan within the constructed hardscape was ever followed, as the earliest photos of the garden show the rectangular space divided into simple quadrants, and an article in *Country Life in America* (March 1931), is effusive about the Asian plants that Dr. Peterson had imported or acquired from the Arnold Arboretum and other sources. The three stunning summer-blooming Japanese lilac trees (*Syringa reticulata)*, in the formal garden are thought to stem from this horticultural interest, which complemented his collection of Chinese paintings.

Years later, in 1978, after the house, outbuildings, greenhouse, and teahouses had long lain empty and decaying, and the garden and Farrand planting scheme lodged in her archives at the University of California at Berkeley. In spite of certain adaptations, the spirit and intention of the garden emerge. A deer fence is a necessary but unfortunate intrusion.

surrounding area were completely overgrown, eight Connecticut neighbors saved the property from intensive residential development by purchasing it, forming Promisek, Inc., a Catholic educational and environmental association dedicated to facilitating the emergence of a lay spirituality. Slowly they cleared areas around the house, revealing the walls and paths of the garden, and realized that the main axis continued through two sets of piers, and then to a deep teardrop-shaped pool and curved, stone-built sitting area. When local landscape designer Pamela Edwards discovered in 1992 that it was Farrand who had designed the enclosed garden, Promisek bravely decided to restore that garden and to follow not Dr. Peterson's arrangements but the

The Farrand garden is maintained entirely by six to nine volunteers. The surrounding area is kept cleared from the encroaching woods, although the views to the rivers (dammed as lakes in the 1950s) are obscured in summer by tree foliage. Promisek, Inc., has made its own additions, including a grove for remembrance. Whether the abandoned pool and seating in the woods were designed by Farrand is uncertain. No sign of the special collection of Asian trees and shrubs beyond the sunken garden is visible except for a bamboo grove and a cork tree. Three magnificent native sugar maples stand to the east of the house. There are plans to label the main specimen trees for the 300–500 annual garden visitors.

14 GARDEN OF IDEAS

647 North Salem Road, Ridgefield, CT 06877
TEL: (203) 431-9914
WEBSITE: *www.gardenofideas.com*
SEE MAPS: pp. 17 & 18

Hours: Garden and farm stand open May 15 through October 30, daily 10am–6pm. Admission: suggested contribution

Location: 70 miles from New York City

Public transportation: Metro-North to Brewster, NY, and taxi 8 miles

Facilities: Visitor center; brochures at entrance to garden; plants and produce shop; no refreshments; restrooms; picnic tables; dogs on leash

Group garden tours: By appointment

Nearby eateries: Ridgefield, 3-1/2 miles

Also of interest: Ballard Park, Main Street and Barry Avenue, Ridgefield; Ward Pound Ridge Reservation, Routes 35 and 121, Cross River, NY, 9 miles (4,315 acres); Aldrich Contemporary Art Museum, 258 Main Street, Ridgefield

The Garden of Ideas combines whimsy and serious horticulture, marshland and intensive organic vegetable farming. Poems and sayings on placards delight or annoy, and handcrafted benches and seats appear at just the right points. One senses that the owners, Joseph Keller and Ilsa Svendsen, who also do landscape contracting, are responding to the challenge of being commercially viable and, at the same time,

developing their eight acres in ways
that are aesthetically satisfying.
A walk around the lake toward their
house passes—by means of
a boardwalk—over the wetlands, where
wild rice thrives, to new plantings of
Metasequoia, Cryptomeria, native azaleas,
and perennials. A stroll in the opposite
direction arrives at the mature garden
of Joseph Keller's parents' house,
which looks down on big islands of
evergreens (many variegated or golden)
and tall perennials, strong yuccas,
and waving grasses, with a view over
the greenhouse to the marshland and
woods beyond. Trumpet vine grows
lushly over an arch, some of the
viburnum and dogwood collections are
in evidence, and emerging from the
vegetation here and throughout the
rest of the property are figurative and
sometimes abstract sculptures by Steve
Cote—fabricated from new or found
steel, and full of humor.

The farm stand has many repeat
visitors, and perhaps 1,000–2,000
people visit the ornamental areas,
which were started in 1985 and
expanded with many revisions.
Currently plants are not labeled. Ilsa
Svendsen writes, "It is our goal to
create a perfect cohesion of wildlife
habitat, stunning horticultural/
sculpture displays, and working farm."
They do all the work themselves with
occasional help from their landscape
contracting crew.

15 THE GLASS HOUSE

199 Elm Street, New Canaan,
CT 06840 (VISITOR CENTER)
TEL: (866) 811-4111 (TICKETS)
VISITOR CENTER: (203) 594-9884 x0
WEBSITE: *www.philipjohnsonglasshouse.org*
SEE MAPS: pp. 17 & 18

Hours: Open by reservation only for tours of different lengths, May 1 through November 30, daily except Tuesday. Only several of the interiors are visited, but most of the buildings can be viewed in the landscape. Admission fee

Location: 46 miles from New York City

Parking: For guests with special needs only. Municipal parking lots one block away

Public transportation: Metro-North to New Canaan, cross the road to the visitor center

Facilities: Visitor center with media presentations on the life and work of Philip Johnson, book and gift store, restrooms, no refreshments; tour wheelchair accessible with prior arrangements; no dogs

Nearby eateries: New Canaan; list from website

The Glass House (1945–1949) and its pavilions, set in forty-seven acres of the Connecticut countryside, must be the most intriguing twentieth-century riposte to the eighteenth-century landscape tradition of follies: temples, towers, sculptural forms, grottoes, and other constructs used as eye-catchers, destination points, or places of entertainment. Just as his British and continental antecedents reveled in architectural and literary allusions, Philip Johnson (1906–2005), an informed and playful architect, created conversations with other architects, historical periods, and contemporary sculptors. He described his country home as being like a fifty-year diary, with architectural entries from different periods of his career.

The Glass House, his homage to Mies van der Rohe, sits on a bluff overlooking the lake below, surrounded by what he mischievously called "this beautiful wallpaper" of trees and grass. The eye moves to "an event," the open, white-columned Lake Pavilion (1962), a reference to Lincoln Center, reached by jumping from the bank (or wading through the mud). Underscaled, it requires visitors to stoop under the arches to reach "the living room" where cushions—rather than tables and chairs—were formerly scattered for lounging or picnicking. Further to the left, one glimpses the Kirsten Tower. While eighteenth-century landscape designers usually modeled their viewing towers on medieval architecture, Johnson looked to contemporary

sculptors (perhaps to Fritz Wotruba) to create a zany, totally impractical cubist folly (1985) dedicated to his friend Lincoln Kirsten. Delighting in a sense of danger, he provided no handrails to negotiate the oversized steps leading to various viewing platforms, though today visitors are denied this challenge.

The Ghost House (1984), like a conservatory in the wrong place, creates a visual pause: trees are visible through a structure clothed not in glass but in chain-link fencing—an insider's reference to Frank Gehry's first home in Los Angeles. When smothered in vines, it looks like a hermit's hut. The Library/Study from 1980—cone, cube, and rod—creates an interesting hiccup in the meadow. Perhaps the finest folly is his last, the Orientation Center (1995), which stands by the pines near the arresting monumental entrance gateway (1980). Da Monsta, as he called it, useless for its ostensible purpose, exists as an extraordinary piece of sculpture, with walls and roof that lean and curve, black shapes against barn red. It acknowledges his

friendship with Frank Stella and the latter's architectural model for the Dresden Kunsthalle, and also recalls Le Corbusier's chapel at Ronchamp in France.

The flat area by the house is defined by paths running through the grass, a circular pool (1950s aquamarine) and the windowless facade of the guest house. A path across a small stone bridge (echoing the carefully preserved agricultural stone walls on the property) leads to the underground art gallery (1965)—its collection chosen in consultation with David Whitney, a close friend and a curator at MoMA— with its bermed grass roof adding drama to the tomblike entrance. The sculpture gallery (1970), also on the tour, is equally exciting in a different style, its interior steps reminders of those in Greek villages. Although it presents enormous practical problems of light and temperature and leak control, it was, as Johnson pronounced, "fun." As his own client, he could indulge in these quirky, sometimes perverse but imaginative structures, allowing the landscape to provide the setting, as Nicolas Poussin does in the painting on the easel in the Glass House.

The Glass House is owned and run by the National Trust for Historic Preservation. It opened to the public in 2007.

Also of interest: The Connecticut Trust for Historic Preservation and partners have embarked on a survey of some ninety-one remaining houses in the New Canaan area from the Modern Movement. The pavilion in **Irwin Park**, 848 Weed Street, designed by Landis Gores in 1959, is being restored, and research into the landscaped setting of these structures will surely follow.

Waveny Park, 677 South Avenue (Route 124), New Canaan. Daily, dawn to dusk. Formerly the estate of Lewis H. Lapham, the charming walled garden and its teahouse beside the 1912 Tudor Revival house is looked after by the New Canaan Garden Club. The grounds (now 300 acres) were laid out by Frederick Law Olmsted Jr. and members of the Olmsted Firm between 1902–1938.

16 GLEBE HOUSE MUSEUM & THE GERTRUDE JEKYLL GARDEN

49 Hollow Road, Woodbury, CT 06798
TEL: (203) 263-2855
WEBSITE: *www.theglebehouse.org*
SEE MAPS: pp. 17 & 19

Hours: Garden open during daylight hours year-round for self-guided tours. House open May 1 through December 4, Wednesday–Sunday 1pm–4pm. Admission fee

Location: 87 miles from New York City

Public transportation: Metro-North to Waterbury, taxi 11-1/4 miles; Peter Pan bus to Southbury, taxi 4-1/4 miles

Facilities: Visitor center for garden plan, flyer and other brochures; gift shop with Gertrude Jekyll material; no refreshments; restrooms; picnic tables; house not wheelchair accessible (only parts of garden); dogs on leash

Programming: On history and gardening throughout the year for adults and children

Group garden tours: By appointment, fee

Nearby eateries: Good selection in Woodbury itself

Also of interest: The historic and attractive town of Woodbury, including the Hurd House, open to the public (close by); Van Vleck Sanctuary, 5 Church Road, Woodbury (200 acres), 1 mile; and the Whittemore Sanctuary off of Route 64, toward Middlebury (686 acres), 4 miles

Set in the quiet historic town of Woodbury, the lovely blue-gray, wooden Glebe House, built around 1750, has an interesting history of its own. A "glebe" refers to land yielding revenue to the church or parish minister, and the interiors are furnished to tell the story of the Reverend John Marshall (1743–1789), his family, and two slaves who lived there from 1771 through the Revolutionary War. Church history was made in 1783 when a group of Anglican churchmen met here secretly and elected the Reverend Dr. Samuel Seabury the first Episcopal bishop, thus testing the new nation's stance of religious tolerance and the separation of church and state. Occupied by a jeweler and his family through the mid-nineteenth century, the house and grounds later fell into disrepair until rescued by the Seabury Society for the Preservation of the Glebe House, opening to the public in 1925.

The small garden belongs to twentieth-century lore. It is based on the 1926 designs of the renowned British garden designer and horticulturist Gertrude Jekyll (1843–1932), whose books and articles were extremely influential in both Britain and the United States. Annie Burr Jennings (1855–1939), an admirer of Jekyll, offered to pay for the plans and the installation of a garden. The Seabury Society accepted. Jekyll's approach was simple and unfussy: narrow borders around the house, with such plants as lavender, roses, and rosemary, and long, wide perennial borders, backed by hedges surrounding lawn. The plans reveal her well-known method of planting in interlocking, organically shaped drifts of perennials with a finely adjusted palette of colors; hollyhocks, delphiniums, columbine, peonies, dianthus, veronica, phlox, and flowering shrubs were all in evidence. The garden at Glebe House is one of only three designed by Gertrude Jekyll for American clients, and the only one that remains.

The Jekyll garden was let go over the years, and the 1950s restoration favored the earlier designs of Amy Cogswell (1867–1958), whose quadrant garden by today's front door had been incorporated into Jekyll's plans in 1927. In the late 1970s, however, the discovery of the original Jekyll plans for the Glebe House (at Berkeley) initiated the gradual revival, beginning in 1990, of the Jekyll Garden. This project has been less than successful, but as Judith Kelz, museum director, affirms, "Our goal for the Gertrude Jekyll Garden is to restore by 2012 the entire 600 feet of plantings as close as possible to the original Jekyll design. Over the last twenty years, the plantings have drifted out of their original location and several substitutions of plants were made that are not appropriate."

The six acres are entirely cared for by ten volunteer gardeners and one educational volunteer under the direction of one administrative staff member. Labeling of plants is not used, in keeping with Jekyll's general views. Some 5,000 visitors annually come to the house and garden, which is owned by the Glebe House Museum, with assistance coming from the Seabury Society for the Preservation of the Glebe House, Inc.

17 GOODBODY GARDEN AT FORT STAMFORD

900 Westover Road, Stamford, CT 06902
TEL: None
WEBSITE: *www.stamfordgardenclub.org*
SEE MAPS: pp. 17 & 18

Hours: Garden open daily, dawn to dusk. Admission free
Location: 41 miles from New York City
Public transportation: Metro-North or Amtrak to Stamford, taxi 4 miles
Facilities: No restrooms; picnicking inside and outside of garden; wheelchair accessible on gravel paths; dogs only in surrounding park
Nearby eateries: Many on High Ridge Road off Merritt Parkway

Revolutionary War buffs and local residents in this quiet suburb will know this charming garden created in the early 1900s. Only about an eighth of an acre, it was on the property of the financier Marcus Goodbody (1876–1958). In 1972, after the death of the last owner, the city of Stamford bought seven acres to protect the site of the 1781 fort. The house, left in a dilapidated state, was razed, but the garden clubs of Stamford and Glenbrook took on the responsibility for the rectangular garden. The low stone balustrade that surrounds the garden on three sides and the raised

long pergola on the fourth were restored, and the garden—replanted to the designs of Lucy W. Harriman—was ready for the bicentennial celebrations of 1976. In 2005 it was renovated following the plans of Sharon Slocum. Within straight gravel paths, four large brick-edged beds, lush with perennials, and a few corkscrew topiaries of dwarf Alberta spruce surround an octagonal sunken area defined by boxwood clipped into chunky blocks. A large metal vase with a bold annual display, perhaps of grasses or tropicals, stands in the center. Two areas of lawn fill the remaining spaces with a purple-leafed *Acer palmatum* along the central axis. The pergola, with its climbing hydrangea, offers a shady pavilion area for tea (in the past) and picnics (now). A few crabapples, cherries, and shrubs in the garden relate to the magnolia and tulip poplars just outside and to the encroaching woods beyond the mounds of the fort. A large oak near the less-than-distinctive car park is recorded as having witnessed the Revolution.

The garden is maintained by twenty volunteers from the Stamford Garden Club, who meet twice a month. A steady trickle of visitors enjoy the peaceful atmosphere and the changing seasonal display of colors and fragrances. Native plants have been introduced successfully, and the club is proud of the organic practices it uses 99 percent of the time. Most of the plants are deer-resistant, but the hollies have to be netted during the winter months, and the hostas and a few other plants are sprayed, and protected by dried blood. The club hopes to do some research on the Goodbody family and the early history of the walled garden that they maintain so beautifully on behalf of the city of Stamford.

18 FLORENCE GRISWOLD MUSEUM

96 Lyme Street, Old Lyme, CT 06371
TEL: (860) 434-5542
WEBSITE: *www.florencegriswoldmuseum.org*
SEE MAPS: pp. 17 & 21

Hours: Garden and grounds open daily, dawn to dusk. Griswold House and museum galleries open Tuesday–Saturday 10am–5pm and Sunday 1pm–5pm. Closed major holidays. Rafal Landscape Center, same hours from mid-May through October. Grounds free; admission fee to house and museum

Location: 110 miles from New York City

Public transportation: Amtrak to Old Saybrook, or Amtrak to New Haven and Shore Line East to Old Saybrook, bus to Old Lyme (www.estuarytransit.org, Niantic Shuttle), 4-1/4 miles, or taxi

Facilities: Museum gift store; restrooms; no refreshments; picnicking tables and lawns by river; most areas wheelchair accessible; dogs on leash

Programming: Art gallery talks and events; workshops on sound horticultural practices and organic land care

Nearby eateries: Attractive Old Lyme, within walking distance; Old Saybrook, 4-1/4 miles; and Essex, 6-1/4 miles; list from gallery

Also of interest: Neighboring Lyme Art Association (1921), designed by Charles Platt as an exhibition gallery for the Lyme Art Colony of artists; Thankful Arnold House Museum, 14 Hayden Hill Road, Haddam, 17 miles; Gillette Castle State Park, 67 River Road, East Haddam, 15 miles; Sundial Gardens, 59 Hidden Lake Road, Higganum, 20 miles

The small garden behind the Florence Griswold House is a beautiful example of how a horticultural dimension can enhance a historic site. Close to the picture-perfect Lieutenant River, the yellow house itself is a gem, designed by Daniel Belcher and built in 1817 for William Noyes in a late Georgian style, with a pedimented and Ionic-columned portico. Purchased, with its twelve acres, in 1841 by sea captain Robert Griswold, the once grand home became first a school and then by 1899 a boarding house for summering artists. The Lyme Art Colony, under the leadership of Henry W. Ranger (1858–1916), painted in a French Barbizon style, but with the arrival of Childe Hassam (1859–1935) in 1903 a form of American Impressionism emerged. Willard L. Metcalf (1858–1925), William S. Robinson (1861–1945), and Edmund Greacen (1876–1949) are just a few of the many artists who worked

depended on hundreds of greenhouse-reared plants to create the color bands for the geometric patterns.

Photographs and excavation helped to locate the position of the well (an attractive feature), along with the rectangular garden behind the Griswold House, which features paths on either side of very wide beds intersected by a short cross axis with two additional beds. In 2000, landscape designer Sheila Wertheimer and her "Garden Gang," of thirty volunteers, who meet every Friday, replanted the garden in Miss Florence's luxuriant and seemingly casual style of around 1910, using period plants whenever possible. In 2006, they started a pear and apple orchard, and they also tend other gardens on the eleven-acre property. Only a few trees are labeled, but information can be found at the Rafal Landscape Center, opened in 2009, and there is a planting list for Miss Florence's garden on the website.

Of special note is the greatly expanded Florence Griswold Museum (2003)—where the work of artists who stayed with Miss Griswold, and also their contemporaries, is on display. American Impressionism and one of its sources come together again. Some 63,000 people visit the site annually.

here. The furnishings of the first-floor rooms and hall and the paintings by over thirty boarders on the doors and walls of the dining room immerse the visitor in the period; a small exhibition of photographs and short film clips supplement the presentation.

At the center of this world is the presence of the sea captain's daughter, Florence Griswold (1850–1937), overseeing the meals inside or at the long table on the side veranda and providing makeshift studios for the artists, who also set up easels along the river, on the sound, in the orchard, and in the garden. Paintings of the period often show a garden within a picket fence—a narrow path leading to the house, bordered on either side with overflowing perennials, self-sown annuals, and herbs, with an emphasis on tall hollyhocks, delphiniums, phlox, poppies, and shrub roses, with perhaps an arbor for more roses. It is sometimes referred to as a "Grandmother's Garden," and the style contrasts with Victorian bedding out—which

19 HARKNESS MEMORIAL STATE PARK

275 Great Neck Road, Waterford, CT 06385
TEL: (860) 434-5542; or (860) 437-1523
(FRIENDS OF HARKNESS)
WEBSITE: *www.ct.gov/dep*
SEE MAPS: pp. 17 & 21

Hours: Grounds open daily 8am–sunset. House open weekends and
holidays 10am–2pm, donation requested. Parking charge, pedestrians free
Location: 126 miles from New York City
Public transportation: Amtrak or Shore Line East to New London,
taxi to Harkness, 4-1/2 miles
Facilities: Gift shop (limited hours) in the carriage house; no refreshments;
restrooms by car park; many picnic tables; mostly wheelchair accessible;
dogs on leash
Nearby eateries: Niantic (good selection and boardwalk), 6-1/2 miles, and
New London's Historic Waterfront District, 4-1/2 miles

On a spectacular site with 180-degree views of Goshen Cove and the Long Island Sound, Eolia (named as a tribute to Aeolus, Greek keeper of the winds), was the Renaissance Revival summer home of Edward Stephen Harkness (1874–1940) and his wife, Mary Stillman Harkness (1874–1950). They bought the newly built house, designed by Lord & Hewlett, in 1907, had the interiors and setting redesigned by James Gamble Rogers (1867–1947), acquired more land, and developed the estate as a delightful recreational haven and gentleman's farm. The remnants of the cutting and kitchen gardens and the skeleton of the 1908 Lord & Burnham greenhouses (for orchids, exotic tropicals, and grapes) remain, and one can imagine the golf course, cow pastures, and orchards that the great lawns around

the house once held.

Two formal gardens, on either side of the house, have been restored to reflect the planting of two famous landscape gardeners: Beatrix Farrand (1872–1959) from 1919 to 1935 and Marian Cruger Coffin (1876–1957) in 1949.

The layout of the west, and larger, garden was designed by James Gamble Rogers. A low stone wall surrounds a strong axial layout: straight paths, beds, borders, and lawn—extending from a central fountain—end in a semicircle on the seaward side. A rather magnificent raised, U-shaped classical pergola, with vigorous wisteria providing shade, looks down on the garden—the perfect setting for Mrs. Harkness's afternoon tea. The original Victorian-style planting in 1909 by Walter E. Stiles (1884–1953) featured highly colored annuals and perennials in blocks or lines.

In 1919 Beatrix Farrand was asked to design a smaller, formal garden on the east side (on the site of the former tennis court) to balance the west garden and accommodate a collection of Chinese vases and dogs and Korean sculpture acquired from trips to the Far East. A sunken central section, with a reflecting pool and panels of grass, is surrounded on the higher level by four large beds of low heliotrope edged with catmint and with borders along the low outer walls. It's a quiet, elegant space with beautiful stonework and delicate wrought-iron gates and arches for climbing roses. Recently the planting plans of Marian Coffin, who refurbished the garden in 1949, have been consulted, resulting in some color and plant adjustments and new groupings of the tall, standard heliotropes.

The success of the initial east garden led to Farrand's commission to replant the west garden. Clusters of perennials and annuals in a more sophisticated color scheme (varying shades of yellow complemented by blues; a mix of white, creams, and gray; a restrained use of stronger accents), reflecting her respect for Gertrude Jekyll, introduced more contemporary ideas, while clipped box drew on the much-loved Colonial Revival style. Over the years, returning as a consultant, she added a rather surprising small box parterre garden (with an interesting wrought-iron fence and gate) and, in 1927, a secluded rockery garden with meandering paths among the dwarf evergreens and alpine plants.

In 1952, after the death of Mary Harkness, Eolia and its 234 acres were donated to the state of Connecticut. (Camp Harkness became a separate, adjoining entity for individuals with disabilities.) By the late 1980s the house, gardens, and greenhouses were in a bad state of disrepair. The exciting and ambitious restoration, begun in the 1990s and aided by the Friends of Harkness (formed in 1992), is ongoing. The most recent project, phase 1 of the $2.1 million reinstallation of the Lord & Burnham greenhouses, was completed in 2009; they will be used to propagate the heliotropes and other heirloom plants used by Farrand and Coffin. Currently cared for by two full-time and five seasonal gardeners and a core of twelve volunteers from the Friends, the park attracts some 250,000 visitors annually.

20 HILL-STEAD MUSEUM & GARDEN

35 Mountain Road, Farmington, CT 06032
TEL: (860) 677-4787
WEBSITE: *www.hillstead.org*
SEE MAPS: pp. 17, 22 & 23

Hours: Garden and grounds open daily 7:30am–5:30pm. House open for guided
tours May through October, Tuesday–Sunday 10am–4pm; November through April,
Tuesday–Sunday 11am–3pm. Admission free to grounds, charge for house tour

Location: 115 miles from New York City

Public transportation: Amtrak or Metro-North to New Haven, Amtrak to
Hartford; Greyhound/Peter Pan bus to Hartford; CT Transit bus 66F or 66T from
Hartford to Farmington and Main stop

Facilities: Visitor center with introductory video, brochures, sunken garden plan
and plant list, trail map, and museum shop with *Hill-Stead Plant Book: Beatrix
Farrand's Sunken Garden* (2009) and *Hill-Stead: An Illustrated Museum Guide* (2003)
and topic-related books; restrooms; hot drinks, sodas, snacks, and sandwiches on
weekends; picnic tables; some areas wheelchair accessible; dogs on leash

Programming: Art, architecture, garden, and nature programs for adults and
children, including poetry & music festival in the summer

Garden tours: On weekends, May through October

Nearby eateries: Farmington, 1 mile; list from museum shop

Also of interest: Stanley-Whitman House, 37 High Street, Farmington, 1/2 mile;
New Britain Museum of American Art, 56 Lexington Street, New Britain, 7 miles

Beginning in 1898, Cleveland
industrialist Alfred Atmore Pope
(1842–1913) and his wife, Ada,
bought up ten farms in Farmington,
which would become their retirement
house and 250-acre estate. Their
remarkable daughter, Theodate
Pope (1867–1946), later an architect,
consulted with the well-known
landscape architect, Warren H.
Manning, for the siting of the house
and the layout of the grounds. She
oversaw the building of the house,
completed in 1901, from the plans

executed by McKim, Mead & White
and added the impressive veranda in
1902. An unexpected bonus of the tour
are the superb Impressionist paintings
collected by her parents—early patrons
of Monet, Degas, Manet, Cassatt, and
Whistler—shown along with prints and
Chinese and European ceramics.

A superb driveway with stone
walls (a feature of the property) and
maple trees brings into view a large,
white clapboard Colonial Revival
house at the top of the hill, designed
to look as though it had been there

for generations. Mature elm, spruce, pine, and sugar maple trees dot the lawns, where views of a pond (rather obscured now) and the wooded Litchfield Hills in the distance convey an English parkland look. Theodate Pope's plan included dairy farming, sheep breeding, and a kitchen garden, orchards, and greenhouse to supply produce. Carriage drives provided afternoon outings, and a six-hole golf course catered to her father's pleasure.

Theodate created the Sunken Garden for her mother, placing it in a natural depression to the right of the drive. She designed the central pavilion in 1901, the sundial (which seems misplaced) and, probably, the general layout: a roughly hexagonal space defined by hedges, within a larger space surrounded by a handcrafted wall. The beds were described in 1910 as being filled with an abundance of old-fashioned flowers, such as hollyhocks, phlox, foxgloves and lilies.

After her mother's death in 1920, Theodate invited Beatrix Farrand (1872–1959) to provide new planting plans—though whether these were carried out is unknown—and the area was grassed over in 1940 during the war. When the Connecticut Valley Garden Club and the Hartford Garden Club took up the challenge in 1984 of restoring the Sunken Garden, the Farrand plans were, fortuitously, discovered, and today's planting approximates them as closely as possible. Yew, Japanese holly, and box supply the formal, evergreen elements and two magnolias the height, with thirty-six beds planned in her signature colors of mainly blue, purple, pink, cream, and white with annuals around the center and increasing in height toward the edges with perennials and shrubs.

Hill-Stead was established as a museum by Theodate Pope Riddle at her death and opened to the public

one year later (1947). One part-time garden manager and a core of about fifteen "Garden Gang" volunteers, who meet once a week during the season, look after the Sunken Garden. Some 12,000 people visit the garden and grounds, and 10,000 the house and art collection. The farming component has gone, but contemporary environmental interests are being substituted, along with improved management of the remaining 152 acres. A seasonal farmers' market supports local agriculture. Trails provide short walks through the meadows and connect with the long-distance Metacomet hiking path. Goals include increasing the museum's visibility and the number of engaged supporters, along with diversifying the funding base to support staff and programming.

21 HOLLISTER HOUSE GARDEN

300 Nettleton Hollow Road, Washington, CT 06793
TEL: (860) 868-2200
WEBSITE: *www.hollisterhousegarden.org*
SEE MAPS: pp. 17 & 19

Hours: Garden open May and September, Saturday 10am–noon and 2pm–5pm;
June, July and August, Saturday 8am–10am and 3pm–6pm; plus Garden
Conservancy Open Days (see www.gardenconservancy.org). Admission fee.
House private

Location: 92 miles from New York City

Public transportation: None (or see Glebe House p. 55)

Facilities: Map and brochure from visitor's shed; no refreshments; restrooms;
picnicking for groups by appointment only; partially wheelchair accessible; no dogs

Programming: Biannual garden study weekend

Garden tours: Mr. Schoellkopf (see below) is usually in the garden during
visiting hours

Nearby eateries: Washington Depot, 5 miles; New Preston, 11 miles; Lake
Waramaug, 11-1/2 miles; Woodbury, 6 miles; Litchfield, 13-1/2 miles; list upon request

Also of interest: Falls Village Flower Farm, 27 Kellogg Road, Falls Village, 31 miles

Set in the rolling Litchfield hills, approached by quiet country roads, the Hollister Garden (named after the first owner of the c. 1775 farmhouse) is a superb private garden reflecting the personal taste and eye of George Schoellkopf (born in Texas in 1942). Begun in 1979, it continues to evolve, with old and new areas at different stages as plantings are added, changed, or adapted. It thus reflects the habits of a true horticulturist who is constantly in the garden during the growing season. From the top terrace, one looks out on the garden below, with rooms defined by walls and hedges, connected by steps or short paths. Longer views are across the slow-moving river to the meadow and trees beyond, and behind the cluster of barns and outbuildings, to a backing of woods on steeper slopes.

The visitor wanders through quiet and green spaces or along borders spilling over with perennials and shrubs, delighting in both the interplay of color between the gardens and the specific character of individual spaces. The copper-colored leaves of maples near a rushing stream reinforce the reds of dahlias, day lilies, and crocosmia. The yellow of flowers is echoed in the leaves of such shrubs as spiraea, seen above or through the arches used for vines and roses. The detailing of the paths, pool, and hardscape is richly varied and chosen to reflect the ambiance of the given space. Ceramic pots, a few statues, and interesting artifacts and seats are a reminder of Mr. Schoellkopf's career as an antiques dealer in New York. His appreciation of twentieth-century English gardens such as Hidcote, Sissinghurst, and Great Dixter—with their exuberant planting within a certain formality of layout—is apparent here, and he draws upon them in his own wonderfully quirky, dashing, and knowing way.

Under the auspices of the Garden Conservancy, the nonprofit Hollister House Garden, Inc., was formed in 2005. In time, twenty-five acres of the property, with its five acres of gardens, will be completely transferred to it, to be preserved for future generations. Meanwhile, Mr. Schoellkopf maintains full responsibility for the garden, with input from photographer George Incandela and the help of one full-time gardener and an outside crew who come in to built and interpret the new projects. It is enjoyed by some 850 garden aficionados a year. The Circle of Friends was formed in 2010 to assist the board financially and to promote the appreciation and discussion of fine gardening. There are plans to increase the labeling and to introduce a series of handouts to help locate the plants of special seasonal interest.

22 LAUREL RIDGE FOUNDATION

164 Wigwam Road, Litchfield, CT 06759

TEL: (800) 663-1273 (NORTHWEST CT CONVENTION
& VISITORS BUREAU)

WEBSITE: *www.litchfieldhills.com* (IN SEASON)
or *www.daffodilfestivals.com*

SEE MAPS: pp. 17 & 19

Hours: Grounds open only during the daffodil season (April and early May), daily, dawn to dusk. Admission free

Location: 105 miles from New York City

Public transportation: None

Facilities: None; no restrooms; no picnicking; not wheelchair accessible, though viewing from the road; no dogs

Nearby eateries: Litchfield, 6 miles

Also of interest: Topsmead State Forest, 46 Chase Road, Litchfield (off Route 118), 5-3/4 miles, open daily, dawn to dusk; picnicking, short trails (map in information shed near house); restroom to right of main house, which was designed by Richard Henry Dana Jr. in an English Tudor style, 1925; White Flower Farm, 167 Litchfield Road (Route 63), Morris, 6-1/4 miles

Leaving the road, paths lead down through a shallow valley toward a lake. The narcissi are all around, and they spread up one side of the hill in lovely scatterings and in groups, with breathing spaces of grass and rocks, lines of old stone walls, and trees. From the lake, steps lead up a slope for a view of the two islands, the yellows of the daffodils nicely set against the darks of the conifers on the one furthest away. And if perchance you are reminded of Wordsworth's 1804 poem, "I Wandered Lonely as a Cloud," there, on a bluff, you will find it. Inscribed on a large stone tablet are twelve of its lines, followed by the words, "These daffodils were planted for all to enjoy by Virginia and Rémy Morosani 1941." The original 10,000 have naturalized and been added to, and it is a joyful experience to wander through the twelve acres of early, middle, and late varieties—their subtle perfume infusing the fresh air. One delights in viewing them in their broader setting of rolling hills, woods, lake, and fields of grazing cattle, or examining them one by one. Laurel Ridge Foundation, Inc., a private foundation with Morosani family members still on the board, preserves and maintains this enticing narcissus preserve.

23 GEORGE & OLIVE LEE MEMORIAL GARDEN

89 Chichester Road, New Canaan, CT 06840
TEL: None
WEBSITE: *http://gardencenterofnewcanaan.org*
SEE MAPS: pp. 17 & 18

Hours: Grounds open daily, dawn to dusk (best time is May). Admission free
Location: 45 miles from New York City
Parking: Limited; some on-street parking
Public transportation: Metro-North to New Canaan; taxi or walk 1-3/4 miles
Group garden tours: By appointment, donations encouraged
Facilities: Notice board, maps of the garden in kiosk in parking area; benches; picnicking; no restrooms; not wheelchair accessible; dogs on leash
Nearby eateries: New Canaan, 1-3/4 miles
Also of interest: New Canaan Nature Center, 144 Oenoke Ridge, New Canaan, 2 miles; Silvermine Guild Art Center, 1037 Silvermine Road, New Canaan, 5 miles

Narrow wood-chip paths wind through this 2.7-acre gently hilly woodland garden that lies below the 1940 house lived in by George and Olive Lee. Unable to negotiate the uneven terrain, Olive Lee could sit at the large picture window looking out into the woods of oak, tulip, and beech trees that her husband enriched with azaleas and rhododendrons, spring-blooming bulbs and ephemerals, ferns, hostas, and other plants disposed to the thin, acid soil. He became an avid plant collector in the process. When he died in 1978, George Lee left his house and garden in this quiet residential neighborhood to the Garden Center of New Canaan along with an endowment.

For over thirty years, volunteers have maintained this tranquil spot, using contractors only for such tasks as tree removal after storms. Benches are placed at strategic viewing points and around the wooden hut, the congregating point for the twelve current garden volunteers. Their coordinator, Kathy Lapolla, reports that with the help of a master gardener intern they plan to continue to identify and propagate plants, introduce new varieties, and publicize the garden (now safely enclosed by a deer fence),

in keeping with George Lee's vision. A list of plants is displayed at the hut, and increased labeling is anticipated. Each year some 250 people visit the woodland garden, which is at its best in May when the azaleas are in bloom.

Formed in 1939, the Garden Center of New Canaan, Inc., is dedicated to civic beautification. Along with caring for the Lee Garden, volunteers negotiate with town officials to get permission to design, plant, and maintain thirty-two roadway triangles, arrange for hanging baskets and flower tubs in the downtown section; and look after gardens around public buildings such as the post office, high school, and a church. Without public funding to support its projects, the Garden Center organizes events both to raise money and increase awareness of its attractive town, showing how gardening brings great satisfaction to the beholder as well as the gardener.

THE MYSTIC SEAPORT GARDENS

75 Greenmanville Avenue, Mystic, CT 06355
TEL: (888) 973-2767; (860) 572-5315
WEBSITE: *www.mysticseaport.org*
SEE MAPS: pp. 17 & 21

Hours: Grounds and museum open April through October, daily, 9am–5pm; November through March, Thursday–Sunday 10am–4pm. Museum grounds remain open one hour after closing. Admission fee

Location: 132 miles from New York City

Public transportation: Amtrak to Mystic, walk or taxi 1 mile. Greyhound bus to New London or Peter Pan bus to Mystic, taxi or walk

Facilities: Visitor center with *Map & Guide, Today Sheet,* and *Must-See Seaside Gardens at Mystic Seaport* brochure; restrooms; several gift shops. Two restaurants, a tavern within the grounds, café and bake shop outside; benches and large village green for picnicking; wheelchair accessible; dogs on leash

Programming: Daily; many events

Garden tours: During the Garden Days weekend in the summer and by appointment

Additional eateries: In downtown Mystic; Stonington, 5 miles; New London, 11 miles

Also of interest: Denison Homestead Museum (1717), 120 Pequotsepos Road, Mystic, and the Denison Pequotsepos Nature Center, 109 Pequotsepos Road, both 1-1/2 miles; Bluff Point State Park, Depot Road, Groton (800 acres on the coast), 7 miles

Renowned for its recreation of a nineteenth-century seafaring village— with its tall ships (including the last wooden whaling ship in the world), its museum shipyards, and maritime displays—Mystic Seaport attracts some 300,000 visitors annually. Although not originally known for its gardens, it has responded to the new philosophy since the mid-1970s that has embraced garden history as a natural and necessary aspect of the study of nineteenth-century life. Gardens have therefore been created for two of the houses, the Buckingham-Hall House and the Burrows House. The former is particularly successful, with a charming front garden of heirloom varieties of perennials and annuals, reflecting the 1830s and 1840s, behind the picket fence. The back area is, appropriately, much less manicured and is devoted to period vegetables and herbs, and it includes an orchard, garden shed, and privy. The kitchen draws upon the available produce

outside the door, and, in keeping with earlier garden practices, hay from a neighboring salt marsh is used as mulch. Nancy Spinner, with historical guidance from Rudy J. Favretti and Leigh Knuttel, designed this garden as well as the smaller front and back gardens of the Burrows House, which feature horticulture of the 1860s and 1870s.

Other parts of the Seaport grounds are ornamented by borders—one in dramatic, hot colors, another of cooler pastels—along with planters, grasses, and specimen trees. A final touch is the Children's Museum Zoo Garden, which draws children into the observation of plants through their evocative animal names: elephant ear, spiderwort, hens and chicks, tiger's eye marigold, bee balm, and a host of others. All of these add a layer of enjoyment to the main focus

of maritime history. As Kara Lally, garden supervisor, and Steven Sisk, head gardener, say, "We want to continue educating and preserving our New England horticultural heritage by adding new educational activities, planting additional native and historical trees and introducing a variety of coastal specimens to our collection."

Mystic Seaport, which opened in 1929, has nineteen acres on the banks of the Mystic River, four and a half acres being devoted to gardens or open spaces. The staff of 160 that runs the Seaport includes two full-time gardeners; twenty-one volunteers assist them in maintaining the grounds as well as helping out in the greenhouse. Most specimen trees are labeled, as are many of the plants. For plant lists of the nine gardens, see the website under Museum Gardens.

500 Hawthorne Ave, Derby, CT 06418
TEL: (203) 734-2513
WEBSITE: *www.ct.gov/dep/kellogg*
SEE MAPS: pp. 17 & 20

Hours: Garden and house open May through October, Thursday and Friday 10am–3pm, Saturday 10am–4pm, and Sunday noon–4pm. House by guided tours. Admission: suggested donation

Location: 74 miles from New York City

Public transportation: Metro-North to Derby-Shelton, walk or taxi 2 miles

Facilities: Restrooms in the Kellogg Environmental Center (with nature displays) and picnic tables and gazebo outside; no refreshments; partial wheelchair accessibility; dogs on leash in grounds

Nearby eateries: Ansonia (and historic district); Shelton (and restored nineteenth-century factory buildings)

Also of interest: Osbornedale State Park, main entrance on Chatfield Street, Derby, 3/4 mile

The Osborne Homestead Museum celebrates the life and remarkable career of Frances Osborne Kellogg (1876–1956). Her father, a metal and textile manufacturer and dairy farm owner, acquired the 1840s house in 1870. When he died unexpectedly in 1907, the twenty-four-year-old Frances, his only child, decided to continue his ventures herself. She was successful in various businesses in the United States and in England during her long and productive life, and she set precedents that included becoming the first female vice-president of the Connecticut Forest and Parks Association and the first female bank director in Connecticut. Her husband achieved fame in the world

of agriculture as a breeder of Holstein cattle and the owner of champion milk-producing Jersey cows.

The four-acre grounds provide a pleasant setting for the comfortable house, which she enlarged in the neo-Federal style in the 1920s. One sees lilacs, buddleias, three magnificent weeping redbuds, flowering shrubs, and some good trees in the vicinity of the house, and others on the periphery of the grounds. French windows lead out from the house and conservatory (on the south), where, down a slope, two formal gardens (1911–1912) lie side by side, separated by a white fence with a connecting entrance archway swathed in traveler's joy. The first is the rose garden (of special interest to Mrs. Kellogg) with perennials around the borders, while the second has displays of geraniums, annuals, and dahlias in beds between the brick paths, and a sundial at the end of the axis. The view from above the stone wall is lovely, looking out on the land that she donated for the 350-acre Osbornedale State Park.

It appears that the period gardens will, in the future, be supplemented by new additions, perhaps bringing the various sections into cohesion. A fairly recent small rock garden has interesting conifers with good form and tonal contrasts. In what used to be the trotting horse area, young trees have been planted to obscure the fence. Frances Osborne's Kellogg's final legacy appears in the attractive 1985 Kellogg Environmental Center on the grounds (year-round, Tuesday–Saturday, 9am–4:30pm), where the Department of Environmental Protection, which has owned this property since 1981, runs relevant educational programs.

PARDEE ROSE GARDEN IN EAST ROCK PARK

180 Park Road, Hamden, CT 06517
TEL: (203) 946-8142; (203) 410-1373
WEBSITE: *www.cityofnewhaven.com/parks*
SEE MAPS: pp. 17 & 20

Hours: Garden open dawn to dusk; Pardee Greenhouse open 7am–3pm. Admission free

Location: 81 miles from New York City

Public transportation: Metro-North or Amtrak to New Haven, taxi 3-3/4 miles or CT Transit bus M line from downtown New Haven (Washington and State Streets) to State and Farm Roads, walk one block

Facilities: Restrooms in Pardee Greenhouse; no refreshments; picnicking table; wheelchair accessibility in greenhouse, flat lawn in garden; dogs on leash

Programming: Educational in connection with the greenhouses

Group garden tours: By appointment, fee

Nearby eateries: Not many—State and Ridge Roads or Whitney and Putnam Avenues; many in downtown New Haven

Also of interest: Broken Arrow Nursery, 13 Broken Arrow Road, Hamden, 9-1/2 miles

The Pardee Rose Garden and Greenhouse are tucked away on the edge of East Rock Park. A grand backdrop of trees, rising up into the hills, visually surrounds the garden on three sides. On the fourth, a quiet residential road runs along the side of the rectangular two-acre garden and the handsome, newly renovated greenhouses and education center. The pattern of rose beds is set in a green lawn, with the main axis leading to an amazing brick, three-tiered structure with roses planted at every level and climbers scrambling over the crossed arches of the open dome. Designed for wedding photographs and ceremonies, it offers the bride and groom a place at the top, backed by pink and white roses.

Below, a circle of now very ordinary wooden posts and wire provides support for more climbers, in addition to a double circle of rose beds and two of day lilies.

William S. Pardee (1860–1918), a New Haven lawyer, donated the money for the rose garden to the city of New Haven in memory of his mother. It opened in 1923, with the greenhouse following in 1930–31. The wedding-cake structure was added by Parks Department horticulturist Landon Winchester in the 1970s as part of the rejuvenation and reassessment of the garden. More than 150 varieties of labeled roses are planted throughout, with special beds at the entrance for the twenty All-America trial roses

to supplement the azaleas and other flowering shrubs there and to add more perennials to strengthen the lower level. The long border that runs alongside the road will be cleared and completely replanted with the likes of hardy hibiscus, black-eyed Susans, and spiderwort, with poppy and foxglove seeds scattered to create an informal look. This will help to hide the cheap railing that the climbing roses use there.

The city of New Haven, with the help of the William S. Pardee Trust, maintains the garden and greenhouse.

Also of interest: The 1887 **Soldiers and Sailors Monument** on the summit of East Rock Park is visible from the rose garden (as it is from miles around). The column with the Angel of Peace, and the expansive view, can be reached by foot or by car from various entrances to East Rock Park (the nearest is Farnam Drive off Davis Street, ½ mile). In contrast to the ambiance of the garden, the 426-acre park offers ten miles of trails—through natural woodlands—sports areas, biking roads, playgrounds, and a swimming pool.

that the Pardee receives each year. In summer, annuals are added to mixed roses and perennials along the central walk. Other beds by the entrance now display perennials and grasses, and two have ornamental herbs and vegetables. The visitor senses that although the roses will always be the main focus of the garden, broader planting possibilities are in the air.

In fact, Matthew Naap, who has cared for the garden since 1994 (with a seasonal helper in the summer), intends to gradually replace the weaker hybrid tea roses with hardy varieties for easier maintenance and increased flowering. After getting the outer, wooded edges of the garden under control, he plans

27 RIVERFRONT & LINCOLN FINANCIAL SCULPTURE WALK

Entry points at the following addresses:
- *Mortensen Riverfront Plaza, 300 Columbus Blvd., Hartford, CT 06103, (No parking on site. Use area garages (Morgan Street) or city street parking)*
- *Riverside Park, 20 Leibert Road, Hartford (free parking on site)*
- *Charter Oak Landing, 50 Reserve Road, Hartford (free parking on site)*
- *Great River Park, 301 East River Drive, East Hartford (free parking on site)*

TEL: (860) 713-3131 (RIVERFRONT RECAPTURE)
WEBSITE: *www.riverfront.org/parks/lincoln*
SEE MAPS: pp. 17, 22 & 23

Hours: River walks open 7 days a week, year-round, dawn to dusk. Admission free
Location: 116 miles from New York City
Public transportation: Amtrak to Hartford; Bonanza, Greyhound, Peter Pan, and Chinatown bus lines to Hartford, walk or taxi 1 mile to Mortensen entry
Facilities: Seasonal refreshments at Mortensen Riverfront Plaza; portable toilets except in winter; picnic tables; wheelchair accessible; dogs on leash. Before arrival, download from www.riverfront.org/parks/lincoln the brochure *Public Art in Downtown Hartford*, with maps and the location of the sculptures at Riverfront and downtown
Nearby eateries: Downtown Hartford; see www.hartford.com and click on Feed Me

---

In the 1960s the construction of Interstate 91 cut metropolitan Hartford off from the Connecticut River. Riverfront Recapture, a private, nonprofit organization, has spearheaded the efforts to provide access to—and construct linking parks along—both sides of the river. The downtown entry point, close to the new Science Center, takes you up, by pedestrian staircase or elevator, to Mortensen Riverfront Plaza (constructed over the highway) and magnificent views of the river. An amphitheater stage, topped by a doubled-peaked white tent roof, is used for performances. Boats can dock, and pedestrians can choose to go left toward the boathouse at Riverside Plaza (1.3 miles) or cross Founders Bridge to East Hartford and follow the trail in Great River Park up or down the river on that side. The Lincoln Financial Sculpture Walk (2008), partly financed by the Lincoln Financial Foundation (the charitable arm of the financial services group), has fifteen pieces sited along the way that reflect President Lincoln's legacy—interpreted abstractly by Del Geist's *Equality* (2007), Peter Chinni's *Union* (2006), and Carole Eisner's *Transcontinental* (2006), and more figuratively in sculptures such as Preston Jackson's *Emancipation*.

Riverfront provides recreational facilities and draws visitors to the river through festivals and light displays. Its 148 acres are landscaped in a variety of ways: Mortensen Plaza is an architectural treatment of hardscape, defined areas of grass, formal arrangements of trees, and striking staircases, while along the river side, paths go through quiet woodlands, emerge into open areas of grass, and lead to pocket parks with shrubs, sculpture, and seating. Designated viewpoints provide nicely framed vistas of the river and its bridges. A last link between Charter Oak landing and Mortensen Riverfront Plaza on the city side of the river is in the planning stage. It will cost an estimated $26 million, but the greater goal is to spur on Hartford's economic revitalization and reverse the flight to the suburbs. Riverfront Recapture works in conjunction with local government, federal agencies,

and private-sector partners to put the financial package together and to oversee the development. Marc Nicol, director of park planning, also reports, "In addition to improved signage, Riverfront Recapture and the Greater Hartford Arts Council would like to expand the sculpture walk to include more pieces of art and develop an educational component that can be used by teachers to involve and interest children in the richness of the collection."

28 **ROSELAND COTTAGE**
556 Route 169, Woodstock, CT 06281
TEL: (860) 928-4074
WEBSITE: *www.historicnewengland.org*
SEE MAP: p. 17

Hours: Grounds open daily, dawn to dusk. House open for tours June through mid-October, Wednesday–Sunday 11am–5pm. Admission free for grounds; charge for house tour

Location: 160 miles from New York City

Public transportation: None

Facilities: Visitor center with brochure, restrooms, and shop; no refreshments; picnicking anywhere in the grounds; grounds wheelchair accessible (not house); dogs on leash

Programming: Summer concerts; teas; July 4th festivals; fall arts and crafts festival

Group garden tours: By appointment

Nearby eateries: Few. See brochure from visitor center: Inn at Woodstock Hill, Plaine Hill Road, Woodstock, or Vanilla Bean Café, corner of Routes 44 and 169, Pomfret

Nearby parks of interest: Bowen's philanthropic activities included the purchase and creation of the sixty-acre Roseland Park for the community (on Roseland Park Road near intersection of Routes 169 and 171); Connecticut Audubon Society Center at Pomfret, 189 Pomfret Street (Route 169), Pomfret Center, 6 miles

Also of interest: The Woodstock Green with Woodstock Academy (1801); Prudence Crandall Museum, 1 South Canterbury Road, Canterbury (18 miles); Logee's Tropical Plants, 141 North Street, Danielson (14 miles)

Roseland, the vibrant coral pink Gothic Revival summer "cottage" built for Henry C. Bowen (1813–1896) and his large family, immediately seizes our attention. Designed in the fashionable but—for Woodstock—amazingly modern style by Joseph C. Wells (1814–1860) and completed by 1846, it sits comfortably back from the quiet road, opposite the village green and behind a fence that mirrors the quatrefoil pattern displayed on the verandas. Trees and shrubs were planted on the lawns irregularly, in groupings or as screening, providing the kind of setting advocated by Andrew Jackson Downing (1815–1852). The drive curves around to the front door, and inside one finds more gothic detailing and furnishings as well as later acquisitions of the family whose descendents owned the house until 1968. Beyond, one discovers other architectural gems—the Gothic Revival carriage barn with its long bowling alley and the picturesque grouping of further outbuildings.

The six and a half acres of grounds offer some good mature trees, but maintenance of the outer areas is minimal, while the semicircular parterre opposite the front door, dating from 1850, receives loving attention. It relates rather awkwardly to the house, having lost its lattice fence and entrance arbor, but its strong pattern is appreciated especially from the second floor. A little summerhouse was added between 1910 and 1920—charming but in a classical style.

Initially planted with more roses (a great favorite of the Bowens) and perennials, the garden is now a showcase for dazzling Victorian bedding-out schemes within the twenty-one boxwood compartments. Lines of solid colors, blocks of one or perhaps two contrasting colors, are offset by beds of taller, softer-hued perennials, shrub roses, and hydrangeas. The gardener varies the color schemes each year, selecting heirloom varieties where possible and referring to Henry C. Bowens' original 1850 plant order and later modifications.

Henry Bowen made his fortune in New York as a silk merchant and insurance underwriter. He was also an active abolitionist and the founder of the influential antislavery weekly *The Independent*. His Fourth of July parties at Roseland Cottage—beginning in 1870—attracted celebrities, politicians, and hundreds of family members, friends, and Woodstock residents for twenty-five years.

Historic New England has owned Roseland Cottage since 1970. Some 15,500 people visit the garden each year, and 7,000 of them also take the house tour. The garden and grounds are looked after by one part-time seasonal gardener, helped on a regular basis by about twenty volunteers. The landscape guide is helpful because the policy is not to label. The organization plans to rebuild the entrance rose arbor to the original 1850 design.

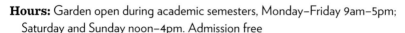

SHOYOAN TEIEN: THE FREEMAN FAMILY JAPANESE GARDEN

343 Washington Terrace, Middletown, CT 06459
(Wesleyan University)
TEL: (860) 685-2330
WEBSITE: *www.wesleyan.edu/mansfieldf/garden/about.html*
SEE MAPS: pp. 17 & 22

Hours: Garden open during academic semesters, Monday–Friday 9am–5pm; Saturday and Sunday noon–4pm. Admission free

Location: 105 miles from New York City

Parking: On the street; then enter through the Mansfield Freeman Center for East Asian Studies, where a brochure with a plan of the garden and its plantings as well as event schedules are available; restrooms; no refreshments; wheelchair accessible

Public transportation: Amtrak to Meriden, or Metro-North to New Haven, Amtrak to Meriden, taxi 7 miles to campus

Programming: Tea ceremonies and garden tours four times a year; tours by appointment.

Nearby eateries: Main Street, Middletown

Also of interest: Wesleyan campus and its Davison Art Center, 301 High Street, and the Ezra and Cecile Zikha Gallery, 283 Washington Terrace; Indian Hill Cemetery, 1850 (and chapel), corner of Washington and Vine, where picnicking is allowed

In a space just 30 by 70 feet on the Wesleyan campus, between the nineteenth-century residence that now contains the East Asian Studies Center and the neighboring house visible through the pines, Stephen Morrell constructed a beautiful little Japanese-style viewing garden (1995), filled with rocks, hillocks, and shaped vegetation. A dry stone river running through it references the nearby Connecticut River and its sharp bend at Middletown. Sitting on the floor of the traditional Japanese tatami room, with its alcove containing perhaps a scroll and an orchid, meditators or participants in ceremonies can gaze quietly at the adjoining garden. Another view from the much larger seminar room looks out on the length of the garden. This garden is important as an educational resource, drawing attention to Japanese planting aesthetics and supplementing the center's gallery and the Meng Reading Room.

Shoyoan Teien is owned by Wesleyan University and looked after by one part-time gardener and two volunteers. Some sixty Wesleyan majors in Asian Studies experience the garden through the seasons, while children from Middletown schools become involved through a range of special cultural programs offered. The Freeman Center's director, Vera Schwarcz, suggests the garden's resonating effects: "May the garden continue to guide and soothe the mind. Here, one can start to understand hidden meanings in the *Tale of Genji*, compose or read haiku poems, or savor subtle shadings of Chinese and Japanese art through various installations and scrolls."

30 HARRIET BEECHER STOWE CENTER

77 Forest Street, Hartford, CT 06105
TEL: (860) 522-9258 ext 317
WEBSITE: *www.harrietbeecherstowe.org*
SEE MAPS: pp. 17, 22 & 23

Hours: Grounds open daily, dawn to dusk. House open June through October, Tuesday–Saturday 9:30am–4:30pm, Sunday noon–4:30pm. November through May, same hours but closed Monday and Tuesday. Admission free to garden; charge for house tour

Location: 118 miles from New York City

Public transportation: Amtrak to Hartford, taxi 1-1/4 miles or CT Transit bus #60 from downtown to Farmington Avenue and Woodland Street

Facilities: Visitor center in carriage house for self-guided garden map and other brochures; shop with *Victorian Blossoms: The Gardens of the Harriet Beecher Stowe Center* (2006), exhibition gallery, and restrooms; no refreshments; picnicking on lawn; garden is wheelchair accessible; dogs on leash

Programming: Book group, salons for discussion of issues related to social justice; ongoing themed and seasonal garden and house tours and celebrations

Nearby eateries: Farmingdale Avenue; West Hartford Center on Farmingdale Avenue and South/North Main Street, 3 miles; Blue Back Square, 65 Memorial Road, West Hartford, 4-1/2 miles

Also of interest: The Mark Twain House & Museum (see next page)

The mission of the Harriet Beecher Stowe Center is to preserve and interpret the writer's home and the historic collections, promote vibrant discussion of her life and work, and inspire commitment to social justice and change. The garden of the beautifully restrained Gothic revival house (1871) that Stowe (1811-1896) moved into with her husband and twin daughters in 1873 and lived in (with sojourns in Florida) for the remaining twenty-three years of her life, plays a small but evocative role in the interpretation of one of America's most famous writers. Although *Uncle Tom's Cabin* (1852) is the most influential of her thirty published books, *The American Woman's Home* of 1869 (written with her sister) has a short chapter on gardening, where they write, "In yards which are covered with turf, beds can be cut out of it, and raised for flowers.... These beds can be made in the shape of crescents, ovals, or other fanciful forms."

In the diminished grounds that now surround the Stowe house (2½ acres), Robert C. Fuoco, the part-time consultant, continues the serious attempt, begun in the 1960s, to tell the story of Stowe's love of flowers and gardens by recreating from photos, writings, and conjecture what was actually there, and complementing these by other period plantings. The Merrill magnolia and the Stowe Dogwood—forming part of the island shrubbery at the back—are thought to have been planted by her. She would recognize the simple wooden fence in front with its finials and a few trees for shade and privacy. The three mounded, shaped beds would amuse her, one representing the Victorian love of tropicals, another the color-themed patterning of bedding-out with annuals, and the third the yuccas that provide the high-textured, strong forms appreciated at the time. The path south of the house is bordered on one side by Victorian favorites planted in an intermingled style and, on the other, by the wildflowers she gathered on her walks beyond the garden. Accommodating the car park, hard surfaces for wheelchairs, irrigation pipes, and modern lighting fixtures is problematic. One wishes there were real Victorian artifacts rather than copies.

The ivy trained around the walls in Stowe's bedroom, the planted terrarium (which in *The American Woman's Home* she described as "the greatest and cheapest and most delightful fountain of beauty"), and her own flower paintings hanging throughout the house add additional contextual meanings. The adjacent good-looking Katharine Seymour Day House (1884), which belonged to Harriet Beecher Stowe's grandniece, is now part of the Stowe Center, and the beds there extend the Victorian range of plants.

Thirty volunteers care for the garden, visited by 15,000 visitors annually. Plans are under way to deepen and expand the mission-focused interpretation of the garden in view of the 2011 bicentennial celebrations of Stowe's birth. An herb and vegetable garden is also being considered. Currently there are few labels, but a publication on the existing plants used is helpful.

Of special interest: Immediately adjoining the Stowe Center is the architectural gem of another of the famous Nook Farm literary residents, Mark Twain. The Victorian conservatory attached to the south end of the house, designed in 1873 by Edward Tuckerman Potter, can be seen from the outside, but a tour of the interiors (by Louis Comfort Tiffany) brings the visitor closer to the planting and the fountain. The **Mark Twain House & Museum**, 351 Farmington Avenue, Hartford, CT 06105, (860) 247-0998, is open Monday–Saturday 9:30 am–5:30pm and Sunday noon–5:30pm. Closed Tuesdays, January through March and on major holidays.

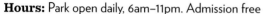

31 WALNUT HILL PARK

184 West Main Street, Vine Street, Hart Street,
and Grand Street, New Britain, CT 06051
TEL: (860) 826-3360
WEBSITE: *www.newbritainct.gov* (SEE LINKS TO ABOUT
    NEW BRITAIN, PARKS) or *www.friendsoftherosegarden.org*
SEE MAPS: pp. 17, 22 & 23

Under renovation.

Hours: Park open daily, 6am–11pm. Admission free
Location: 111 miles from New York City
Public transportation: Amtrak to Hartford and CT Transit bus #41 to downtown
    New Britain, walk or local transit
Facilities: Snacks at the gazebo spring, summer, and fall; restrooms; picnic tables;
    wheelchair accessible; dogs on leash
Programming: Summer concert series, July and August
Nearby eateries: New Britain
Also of interest: New Britain Museum of American Art, 56 Lexington Street,
    on the edge of the park (café inside)

The need for water storage and fresh air, a place for exercise and enriched community life, and a desire for the marriage of art and nature—along with a good dose of public spirit—are often the forces driving the formation of parks. And so it was with Walnut Hill Park, on the outskirts of New Britain. In 1856 ten men purchased most of the current eighty acres, consisting of treeless pastureland and a significant hill, and formed the Walnut Hill Park Company. The hill was transferred in 1857 to the borough of New Britain for the installation of a reservoir, and seventy more acres were added in 1869. The following year Frederick Law Olmsted (1822–1903) was commissioned to design the whole area. The plan reveals his classic recipe for unifying a large space by way of gently curving carriage drives and paths, broad swathes of grass, and different densities of trees to create irregular shapes, control views within the park, and provide a screen around the outside edges. Formal elements—the entrances to the park, a grand fountain area (sadly never built) in the southwest, and the hilltop with the reservoir—were seamlessly integrated into this pastoral landscape (as they were in his 1857 plan with Calvert Vaux for Central Park).

Significant changes have taken place. The Darius Miller Music Shell (1939) has been inserted into a slope and, reflecting contemporary needs, baseball, softball, Little League, and cricket pitches and tennis courts have been accommodated. The dwindling of trees and shrubs and the fragmented planting without a general horticultural plan has produced a certain blandness. But drainage problems, in what Olmsted called The Common, were addressed by the city of New Britain in 2009, with a capital expenditure of some $2.5 million. A fresh approach is found in the little Recognition Garden, situated on the one-mile loop as it crosses the park on the slope. It offers grasses and perennials and imaginative seating, and the memorials are cleverly restricted to the bricks on the approach paths.

The walk up to the top of the hill, the site of the former reservoir, should perhaps be left for last. There, the architectural setting for the impressive ninety-foot, cone-shaped obelisk, a World War I memorial of 1928 by H. Van Buren Magonigle, is fully revealed. The whole ensemble, including the lights designed as vases, is very grand, and the views from the pavilions, especially the southern one to the wooded hills, are magnificent. In 2010 the Friends of Walnut Hill Rose Garden, having raised the funding themselves, planted four quadrants with two borders containing over 800 new roses around the elliptical plateau, with four trellises for climbers. Seventy-five varieties of roses represent, through their color and fragrance, the diversity of the community. As their mission statement says, the rose garden "is part of our pledge of confidence in the City's future. This project will revitalize a piece of New Britain's history, strengthen downtown development and invigorate the community." In addition to the rose garden volunteers, there are four full-time and two part-time groundsmen, sharing an arborist and horticulturist with other city parks. Future plans include planting forty-eight new trees.

32 WEIR FARM NATIONAL HISTORIC SITE

735 Nod Hill Road, Wilton, CT 06897
TEL: (203) 834-1896
WEBSITE: *www.nps.gov/wefa*
SEEMAPS: pp. 17 & 18

Hours: Grounds and gardens open daily, dawn to dusk. Visitor center in the Burlingham House open May through October, Wednesday–Sunday 9am–5pm; November through April, Thursday–Sunday 10am–4pm. Admission free

Location: 59 miles from New York City

Public transportation: Metro-North to Branchville, private taxi service (203) 227-3063, 1-1/2 miles (walk not pleasant)

Facilities: Visitor center for brochures on the garden, farm, and J. Alden Weir. Pick up *Weir Farm Historic Painting Sites Trail* for a map of artists' favorite view points. Restrooms; shop with related material; no refreshments; picnicking, bring a blanket; partially wheelchair accessible; dogs on leash

Programming: Two different guided walks on days visitor center is open. See website. Also other events.

Nearby eateries: Historic town of Ridgefield, 4 miles; list from visitor center

Nearby parks of interest: Weir Preserves, on opposite side of road (110 acres with trails); Lucius Pond Ordway/Devil's Den Preserve, 33 Pent Road, Weston, 5-1/2 miles (20 miles of trails)

Also of interest: Aldrich Contemporary Art Museum, 258 Main Street, Ridgefield, 4 miles

The life and paintings of J. Alden Weir (1852–1919) and family members are celebrated here, along with those of visiting artist friends who sketched and painted outdoors, often choosing the barns and farming activities, the pond, the woods, and the stone walls around the pastures as subjects. Alongside Weir's house and studio stands the studio of Weir's son-in-law, the sculptor Mahonri Young, and their artistic legacy continues in the programs offered today by the Weir Farm Art Center and the artist residencies. The visitor center supplies free art materials, encouraging young and old to draw inspiration from this historic spot.

Although somewhat peripheral to the main story, the small gardens help fill in details about how summers were spent and the properties enjoyed. The visitor center in the Webb Farm was bought by Weir in 1907 and used by tenant farmers until his daughter

Cora Weir Burlingham (1892–1986) made it her family's weekend and summer home from 1931. A keen and knowledgeable gardener, she had Vera Poggi Breed design a sunken garden for her (1932–1940), and in 1969 she asked Friede R. Stege to rethink the planting, with greater emphasis on spring bulbs and early summer bloomers. Within well-crafted retaining walls, a dwarf boxwood hedge in a serpentine design surrounds the lawn. Perennials are planted around the borders, and boxwood columns provide vertical accents. Looked down on from the small terrace, the garden appears intriguingly formal, sharply contrasting with the views of the farm buildings behind. The remnants of the terracing (c. 1947) for the fruit and vegetable garden can be seen across the track.

The second and earlier garden is behind the cluster of buildings connected with J. Alden Weir himself. Acquiring that farm and 153 acres in 1882, he became deeply involved in agricultural plans through his tenant farmer, and as a dedicated fisherman he also dammed the stream for the three-and-a-half acre pond (now in the Weir Preserve across the road), where a pavilion (now gone) on an island provided a destination for family and friends. The vegetable garden and an orchard were always of primary importance. But toward the end of his career, spending more time in the country, an enlarged flower garden (c. 1915) came into being (perhaps for his wife). It became later known as the Secret Garden as it became overgrown during the residency of his daughter Dorothy (1890–1947) and her husband Mahonri Young (1877–1957). This garden (its restoration began in 1995) attracts visitors to its rustic gates and fencing, island beds of bountiful perennials, rocks and spiky yuccas, flowering shrubs and a sundial and fountain—all placed within a loose design with sudden formal elements.

Acquired by the National Park Service in 1990, after a campaign by family and concerned groups to save this significant cultural landscape, the sixty-acre property receives upwards of 17,000 visitors annually. The gardens are looked after by one full-time, one seasonal, and ten volunteer gardeners. Plans are under way to restore the vegetable gardens near the Weir and Young studios.

33 WHEELER FARM GARDENS
171 Bartlett Street, Portland, CT 06480
TEL: (860) 342-2374
WEBSITE: *www.wheelerfarmgardens.com*
SEE MAPS: pp. 17 & 22

Hours: Japanese garden open spring through fall; nursery open May through July, daily, 9am–6pm. Admission free

Location: 115 miles from New York City

Public transportation: Not convenient—Metro-North or Amtrak to New Haven, bus to Middletown, taxi 5-1/4 miles

Facilities: Brochure and map from nursery and garden store; no refreshments; portable toilet during nursery season; benches; picnicking in the teahouse; partially wheelchair accessible; no dogs

Nearby eateries: Quarry Ridge and Portland golf clubs (very close, open to the public); Portland, 3-1/2 miles

The Wheeler Farm Gardens nursery specializes in European alpine geraniums that cascade from balconies and window boxes in glorious colorful profusion. In contrast, the adjoining Japanese garden is a marvel of quiet greens. Winding paths through shade lead to small open spaces where there may be, in season, a dash of color from the irises, balloon flowers, and astilbes,

an occasional haze of azalea blossoms, or a flow of mauve wisteria. Various stopping places to watch the four koi (one white and enormous) from the bridge, listen to the sound of trickling water, or think tranquilly about Japanese practices are provided.

While William and Evelyn Larson have been in the greenhouse and garden center business since 1968, the three-fourths-acre Japanese garden came into being between 2004 and 2007. Based on their reading and on visits to Japanese gardens on the west coast of Canada and the United States, they devised one of their own. Mr. Larson built the wood and bamboo structures and brought in a hundred tons of local stone for the paths, little hills, and stream and pools. Sometimes modern materials intrude, so the strength is in the ambiance and the planting—the varied forms and textures of the pines, cypresses and other conifers (including dwarf varieties) and the accompanying (mostly Asian), deciduous trees and shrubs.

A labor of love, the garden is pruned and looked after by Mr. Larson (b. 1932) (with the occasional help of nursery workers). He plans to encourage more moss to grow and to add plant labels. He is also thinking of extending the garden by building a mound for a new juniper and adding new plantings there and a seat.

34 WHITNEY WATER TREATMENT PLANT & PARK

900–940 Whitney Avenue, Hamden, CT 06517
TEL: (203) 562-4020 (REGIONAL WATER AUTHORITY)
WEBSITE: *www.rwater.com; www.mvvainc.com* (LANDSCAPE DESIGNER);
www.stevenholl.com (ARCHITECT)
SEE MAPS: pp. 17 & 20

Hours: Grounds open sunrise to sunset; treatment plant not open. Admission free
Location: 81 miles from New York City
Parking: Follow sign for CT Historic Trust
Public transportation: Metro-North or Amtrak to New Haven, Whitney Avenue J bus to park
Facilities: None; wheelchair accessible; dogs on leash
Nearby eateries: Five at corner of Putnam and Whitney Avenues, Hamden, 1-1/4 miles; downtown New Haven, 2-1/2 miles

This is a park with a truly contemporary sensibility, merging the utilitarian with the ecologically correct: a long silver stainless-steel tube whose short side has the shape of an electric bulb (or, evidently, an upside down water droplet), high rolling berms of grass that are proudly man-made, and lower areas lushly planted in a naturalistic manner with native trees, shrubs, and grasses around wetlands and a pond that collect excess rainfall from the site. Steven Holl Architects designed the state-of-the-art water purification plant, completed in 2005, and Michael Van Valkenburgh Associates, Inc., undertook the site landscaping (2004–2006), completely reconceiving the existing park. In keeping with the late-twentieth century industrial aesthetic for parks first explored in Emscher Park in the Ruhr Valley, Germany, an enormous tee-and-bend section of pipeline lies like a piece of modern sculpture in the grasses and wildflowers as a historical artifact from the original 1905 Whitney Treatment Plant, which was shut down in 1991.

From many angles there is a very striking contrast of the architecture with the landscape, and the view from the highest berm, reached by a spiral path, looks down on to the vast, 30,000 square feet of the sedum roof nestled in beside the tube or "sliver," over the wetlands with their boardwalk path, and beyond to the surrounding wooded hills. An odd note perhaps are the lines of low hedges of inkberry, *Ilex glabra*, on a plateau, a modernist touch that only works if the shapes are defined by full growth and careful pruning. Handsome benches provide resting points.

Across the street, below the dammed Lake Whitney—whose water is pumped to the water treatment plant—is the Eli Whitney Museum

(915–945 Whitney Avenue), which caters especially to schoolchildren through a variety of water science programs. The Steven Holl building was planned to extend this educational mission by holding classes, lectures, exhibitions within the water treatment center, which itself incorporates high standards for minimal energy consumption. This intention was a casualty of the security concerns that followed 9/11, and now a tall black chain-link fence creates an unattractive appearance, particularly at the entrance to the park from Whitney Avenue. The fifteen-acre site is owned and maintained by the South Central Connecticut Regional Water Authority, whose approach here was innovative and environmentally exciting. The barn and white boarding house (1827) for factory workers were both part of the Eli Whitney armory complex, which mass-produced firearms with water power from the Mill River across the road.

1329 West Middle Turnpike (OPPOSITE DOWNEY DRIVE),
Manchester, CT 06040
TEL: (860) 528-0856
WEBSITE: *www.wickhampark.org*
SEE MAPS: pp. 17, 22 & 23

Hours: Grounds open first weekend in April until last weekend in October, daily, 9:30am–sunset (except in inclement weather)

Location: 121 miles from New York City

Parking: Park in Lot A to begin from the top of the park, or Lot B to start at the bottom. Parking fee

Public transportation: Amtrak to Hartford, CT Transit bus 88M or 88C from Market Street to the park, or taxi 7 miles

Facilities: Brochures, maps, trail guides at entrance and at nature center (with historical section devoted to the Wickhams) and gift shop; concession stand for refreshments on weekends; restrooms in three locations; picnic tables and charcoal grills at various sites; wheelchair accessible; dogs on leash, some restricted places

Group garden tours: By appointment

Nearby eateries: At edge of park, Marco Polo, 125 Burnside Ave, East Hartford, or Buckland Mall, 194 Buckland Hills Drive, Manchester, 3 miles; Evergreen Walk (mall), 75 Evergreen Way, South Windsor, 4 miles

Many former private estates that are now public parks or arboreta are presented in relation to the previous owner's lifestyle and horticultural developments, but Wickham Park wears its history lightly. The main house, The Pines, was torn down in 1964, and a private trust has developed most of the gardens, the many sports areas, and the playgrounds specifically for the general public.

Clarence H. Wickham (1860–1945) followed in his father's footstep as a machine manufacturer. Together, they held over forty patents, including one by Clarence, who became president of the Hartford Manila Co., for the window envelope. He left the bulk of his estate to the Wickham Park Trust for the formation and maintenance of the 130-acre property, which was to become a park upon the death of his wife (1960). Olmsted Associates were brought in to redesign the roadway system and the Oriental Garden. The park opened in 1961.

The view from the house's hilltop site is truly panoramic—over a great sweep of grass and wooded areas (ablaze during the fall foliage season), toward Hartford and the hills beyond. The Nature Center is also in this area, along with two of the themed gardens: the large Sensory Garden (2010), for

wheelchair access and visitors of all abilities, and the Cabin Garden (1994–1996), with a parterre of boxwood and roses, annuals, a pergola, and an arbor (a favorite location for wedding photos and receptions). The rather bedraggled aviary (early 1970s), a throwback to the period when public parks provided zoos, houses an assortment of exotic fowl and injured natives.

Further down the hill, and sheltered by the woods, more themed gardens appear, all rather curious. Bridges, temple gates, and pavilions set the scene for the Oriental Garden (with a delightful duck house in one of the ponds). Some of the sculpture was brought back by the Wickhams from their travels in China. A pergola and two saints define the Italian Shrine Garden, and the English Garden (2003–2005) includes a knot of contrasting barberry and boxwood, clipped hedges, a rose walk, a hydrangea corner, and perennials. Some, like the Lotus Garden (early 1980s) with its little stream and rocks, are thickly planted (lovely Japanese maples and evergreens), while others have definitely been given less attention, though they may come into their own in spring. In a very different vein, a recent boardwalk (2003–2005) through the wetlands at the foot of the hill provides an excellent path for birders and naturalists alike.

Enlarged to 250 acres through a gift, purchase, and land swap, Wickham Park receives some 200,000 visitors a year (many to the sports areas). Only two full-time and three part-time gardeners, assisted by three to six volunteers, look after the grounds, managed by two administrators. Nevertheless, the director, Jeff Maron, who has designed several of the gardens since the mid-1980s, has ambitious plans: "We intend to expand our horticultural collection and labeling process and continue to upgrade our current gardens. We also hope to create a Scottish Garden and an Irish Garden. At that point we will call our collection 'The Gardens of the World.'"

36 YALE UNIVERSITY CAMPUS

149 Elm Street, New Haven, CT (VISITOR CENTER)

TEL: 203-432-2300
WEBSITE: *www.yale.edu/visitor*
SEE MAPS: pp. 17 & 20

Hours: Tours of the campus daily
Location: 77 miles from New York City
Public transportation: Amtrak or Metro-North to New Haven, walk into town, or taxi
Nearby eateries: in downtown New Haven, especially on Chapel Street
Also of interest: Yale Center for British Art, 1080 Chapel Street; Yale University Art Gallery, 1111 Chapel Street

On the northwest side of the sixteen-acre New Haven Green (bordered by College, Chapel, Church, and Elm Streets)—laid out as an open space in 1638 and now a public park of grass and shade trees with three nineteenth-century churches—lie the buildings of Yale University. Intersected by the city streets, the campus, in the tradition of Oxford and Cambridge, is designed around twelve residential colleges with internal courtyards, and larger more communal buildings. The Gothic Revival style, particularly by James Gamble Rogers (1867–1947), dominates, but the Georgian influence is evident, and since the 1950s interesting examples of contemporary architecture have been added.

Recent major upgrading of the colleges has led to the replanting of the courtyards, taking into account the designs and plant palette of Beatrix Farrand (1872–1959), who consulted at Yale from 1922 until 1945 (see also p. 265, Princeton University Campus). Although many of these internal courtyards are closed to the public, Old Campus can be visited, and Farrand's unique moat planting of dogwoods, viburnums, hawthorns, and witch hazels in a groundcover of ivy can be seen on High, Elm, and Grove Streets.

Marsh Botanic Gardens, 227 Mansfield Street (www.yale.edu/marshgardens), once the site of Farrand's nursery and rock garden (some remains) and formerly a popular display garden, is going through a major revision. It caters to the university's science needs but also has extraordinary greenhouse displays. Occasional open houses take place.

NEW YORK

NEW YORK

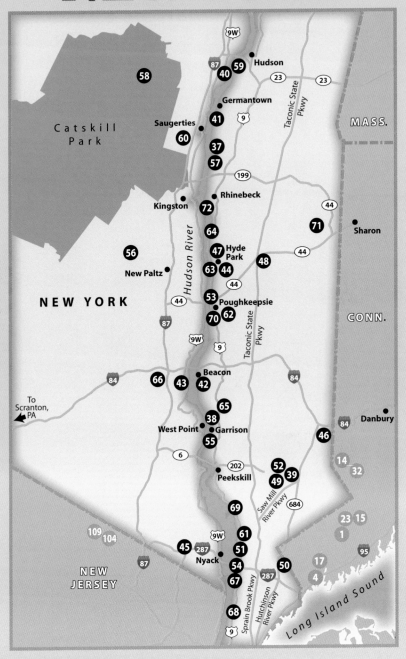

LOWER HUDSON VALLEY

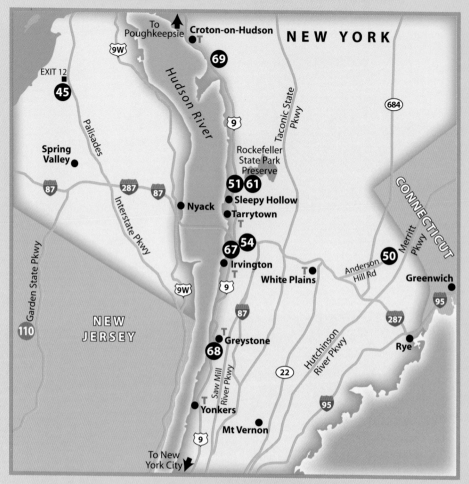

45 The Gardens at Matterhorn, Spring Valley, NY

50 The Donald M. Kendall Sculpture Gardens at PepsiCo, Purchase, NY

51 Kykuit: The Rockefeller Estate, Sleepy Hollow, NY

54 Lyndhurst, Tarrytown, NY

61 Philipsburg Manor, Sleepy Hollow, NY

67 Sunnyside, Irvington, NY

68 Untermyer Park & Gardens, Yonkers, NY

69 Van Cortlandt Manor, Croton-on-Hudson, NY

110 The James Rose Center, Ridgewood, NJ

KATONAH AREA

39 Caramoor Center for Music & the Arts, Katonah, NY
46 Hammond Museum & Japanese Stroll Garden, North Salem, NY
49 John Jay Homestead State Historic Site, Katonah, NY
52 Lasdon Park, Arboretum & Veterans Memorial, Katonah, NY

NEWBURGH/COLD SPRING AREA

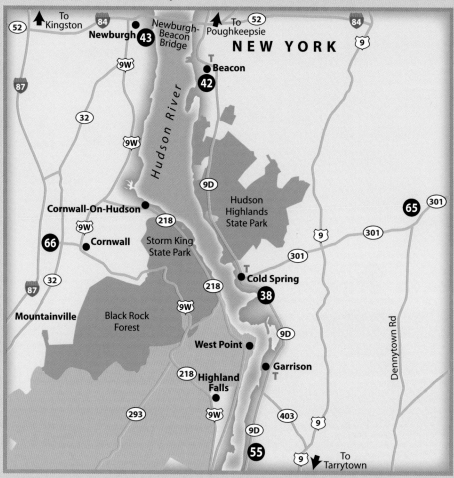

38 Boscobel House & Gardens, Garrison, NY

42 Dia:Beacon, Beacon, NY

43 Downing Park, Newburgh, NY

55 Manitoga/The Russel Wright Design Center, Garrison, NY

65 Stonecrop Gardens, Cold Spring, NY

66 Storm King Art Center, Mountainville, NY

POUGHKEEPSIE/HYDE PARK AREA

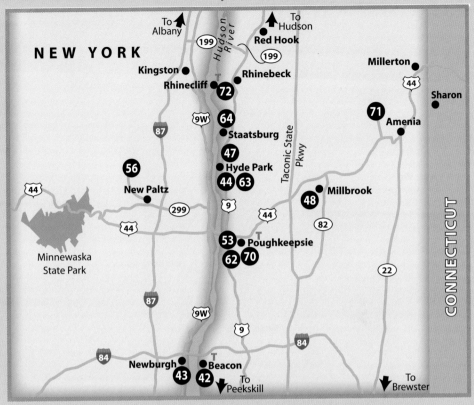

42 Dia:Beacon, Beacon, NY

43 Downing Park, Newburgh, NY

44 Beatrix Farrand Garden at Bellefield, Hyde Park, NY

47 Hyde Park—The Vanderbilt Mansion National Historic Site, Hyde Park, NY

48 Innisfree Garden, Millbrook, NY

53 Locust Grove Estate, Poughkeepsie, NY

56 Mohonk Mountain House, New Paltz, NY

62 Springside Landscape Restoration, Poughkeepsie, NY

63 Springwood: Home of FDR National Historic Site, Hyde Park, NY

64 Staatsburg State Historic Site (Mills Mansion), Staatsburg, NY

70 Vassar College Arboretum & Gardens, Poughkeepsie, NY

71 Wethersfield Garden, Amenia, NY

72 Wilderstein Historic Site, Rhinebeck, NY

SAUGERTIES/RED HOOK/
HUDSON AREA

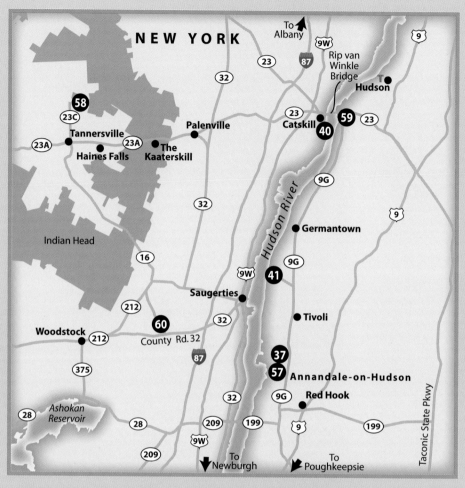

37 Bard College: Landscape & Arboretum & Blithewood Garden, Red Hook, NY

40 Cedar Grove, Thomas Cole National Historic Site, Catskill, NY

41 Clermont State Historic Site, Germantown, NY

57 Montgomery Place, Red Hook, NY

58 Mountain Top Arboretum, Tannersville, NY

59 Olana State Historic Site, Hudson, NY

60 Opus 40, Saugerties, NY

BARD COLLEGE: LANDSCAPE & ARBORETUM & BLITHEWOOD GARDEN

30 Campus Road, Red Hook (or Annandale-on-Hudson), NY 12504
TEL: (845) 758-7179 (ARBORETUM AND HORTICULTURE DEPARTMENT)
WEBSITE: *http://inside.bard.edu/arboretum*
SEE MAPS: pp. 99 & 104

Hours: Open dawn to dusk. Admission free

Location: 99 miles from New York City

Public transportation: Amtrak to Rhinecliff, taxi to Bard College, 8 miles; Metro-North to Poughkeepsie, LOOP, Express A bus to Bard (very few, Monday–Friday only), 24 miles

Facilities: General information and arboretum brochure from Bertelsmann Campus Center or outdoor kiosk at Admission Office (Hopson Cottage), or download brochures, *The Historic Trees of Bard* and *Gardens of Bard,* from http://inside. bard.edu/arboretum/publications/; refreshments (and restrooms) at the cafés at Bertelsmann Campus Center and at Ward Manor Residence; picnicking (tables at Fisher Center for the Performing Arts); limited wheelchair accessibility; dogs on leash

Group garden tours: By appointment

Nearby eateries: Tivoli, 3 miles; Rhinecliff, 8 miles; see www.bard.edu/admission/visiting/dining.shtml

Also of interest: Four miles of hiking trails along Saw Kill Creek and Tivoli Bays

Bard College in its entirety is embraced by the Landscape and Arboretum Program. The 550-acre campus—well wooded at the fringes, and comprising scattered concentrations of buildings within former estates—is linked by roads rather than landscape design. The program, supported by the Friends of the Arboretum, promotes the historic planting in several areas, manages and develops the core collections of oaks, maples, magnolias, redbuds, and dogwoods, and looks after a number of gardens and groves in a variety of styles.

The gardens enhance buildings and mitigate the effects of car parks; some were designed by students and faculty, others commissioned from artists. One such example is *The Parliament of Reality* (2009), by Olafur Eliasson, found opposite the Frank Gehry-designed Fisher Center for the Performing Arts (2003): an open, steel tunnel bridge is linked to an island with rocks in a circular pond. Grasses and twenty-four *Koelreuteria* (golden-rain trees) surround the water, and shaped areas of planted meadow flowers form a transition to the wide, open grassy area beyond.

Horticultural practices are closely related to environmental concerns,

and documentation, monitoring, and research are linked to the academic curriculum. A key concern is the preservation of meadows and woods containing native plants representative of the Hudson River flora, and a student-led movement is under way to make Bard a "bird-friendly" campus. Five full-time and one seasonal gardener look after the Arboretum, assisted by twenty-seven part-time student workers.

Blithewood Garden, Bard College, Blithewood Road. Follow signs to the Levy Economics Institute. Garden open dawn to dusk, May through November. Admission free. Not wheelchair accessible, except for view from above garden; no dogs. Group garden tours by appointment. Available from the campus bookshop at Bertelsmann Campus Center: *Blithewood: A History of Place* (2009) by Bessina Harrar.

Standing on a bluff, with splendid views of the Hudson River and the Catskills, the house, lawns, and garden

(some twenty acres) of Blithewood are now within the grounds of Bard College. The Levy Economics Institute occupies the mansion (not open), designed in an English Palladian style, with porches and extra ornamentation added later, for Captain Andrew Zabriskie by Francis Hoppin of Hoppin & Koen (1903). Magnificent old trees (black locust, red and silver maple) and pines and oak grow on the lawns near the curving entrance driveway, reminiscent of the earlier picturesque style at Blithewood praised by Andrew Jackson Downing in *A Treatise on the Theory and Practice of Landscape Gardening* (1841).

The delightful Italianate garden, also by Hoppin, lies below the house on the west side. In counterpoint to the natural landscape beyond, it is a formal, very defined, rectangular walled space, linked to the house by its central axis. The straight staircase descends to a balustraded viewing terrace, then to a lower level— holding an elegant square pool and small jet of water, another fountain,

and gravel paths crossing at right angles—and finally to an open classical summerhouse with large pergolas to right and left.

These features all speak the language of an architect reveling in knowledge of the past, while the lush planting there today—in what was formerly a rose garden—offers an exuberant contrast: enormous shrub hydrangeas, thick, scrambling wisteria, and beds of surprising shrubs and perennials, grasses, and lavender. Small box hedges define octagonal shapes of grass. Growing on the inner red brick walls (the white on the outside connecting the garden to the house) are hyacinth beans, convolvulus, honeysuckle, wall hydrangeas, and more. As with Prospect Garden at Princeton University (see p. 267), this enclosed space stands apart from the rest of the campus and, with its gentle sound of falling water, creates an especially tranquil spot.

Blithewood and its 825 acres were given to Bard College in 1951 by Andrew Zabriski's son Christian, enlarging the campus some twenty times. The formal garden is maintained by one seasonal gardener and two part-time student workers. Labeling is found on a few significant trees by the house and, in limited form, within the formal garden. "We hope," write the Friends of the Landscape and Arboretum Program, "that Bard's Arboretum will become a destination for individuals to understand and appreciate a nationally significant historical landscape in the Hudson Valley."

38 BOSCOBEL HOUSE & GARDENS

1601 Route 9D (or 1601 Bear Mountain Beacon
Highway), Garrison, NY 10524
TEL: (845) 265-3638
WEBSITE: *www.boscobel.org*
SEE MAPS: pp. 99 & 102

Hours: Grounds and house open April through October, daily (except Tuesday),
9:30am–5pm (last house tour 4pm); November and December, daily (except
Tuesdays, Thanksgiving, and Christmas), 9:30am–4pm (last house tour 3pm).
Admission fee to house and grounds

Location: 55 miles from New York City

Public transportation: Metro-North to Cold Spring, walk 1-1/2 miles, taxi
or Cold Spring Trolley on weekends (www.coldspringchamber.com/trolley.html)

Facilities: Visitor center in the Carriage House for brochure, illustrated book
Boscobel (2005), woodland trail guide, and ticket for house tour; exhibition area,
book and gift shop; honor system for hot and cold beverages, basic snacks;
restrooms; picnicking in designated areas; wheelchair accessibility to grounds only;
no dogs

Programming: Exhibitions in basement gallery area of house; Hudson Valley
Shakespeare Festival; candlelight tours in December

Nearby eateries: Attractive Cold Spring, 1-1/2 miles

Also of interest: Constitution Marsh Audubon Center and Sanctuary (270 acres
of tidal marsh), 127 Warren Landing Road, Garrison, 1 mile south; West Point
Military Academy, West Point, 13 miles; Garrison Art Center, 23 Garrison's
Landing, Garrison, 4 miles

Peerless Boscobel sits on a plateau, its belvedere terrace offering panoramic views over Constitution March to the Hudson River and the Hudson Highlands. The history of this elegant, 1806 Palladian or Federal building is rather tragic, but ends triumphantly. It was built for a site fifteen miles south, in Montrose, by States Dyckman (1755–1806). An accountant in the quartermaster's office in New York for the Royalists, he made a fortune defending his corrupt British superiors in a protracted court case in London, where he lived from 1779 to 1789. There he acquired British tastes and the desire to become the proprietor of an elegant country house. But soon after construction of Boscobel was begun (1803), Dyckman died. Completed by his wife, it was furnished with many of the fashionable objects and books he collected in London, and it remained in the family until 1920, when it became a park and then an unwanted burden on the grounds of a Veterans Hospital.

The house we visit now was rescued from destruction in 1955 by a small group of enthusiasts, dismantled piece by piece, and in 1961 brought to life again on the present site. The project's main patron, Lila Acheson Wallace (cofounder of *Readers' Digest*), favored a beautiful garden rather than a strict historical recreation. Innocenti & Webel devised a formal arrangement: a maple avenue leading to the east facade of the house with a parallel axis that takes visitors from the carriage house through a large, thriving apple orchard, on past the herb garden, and then to the wheel-shaped rose garden. Here one finds a central pool and fountain, weeping cherries, rose displays in summer, and bulbs in spring. Entering the house on the west, the unique decorative swags above the recessed portico are visible.

The Garden Club of Philipstown meets every Tuesday to care for the small decorative herb garden with espaliered pear trees, bobbles of box, and paths lined with lavender. Beds are filled with flowers, herbs, quince, and bay trees, and tunnel arbors run along the sides. The garden sits in front of a brick and glass orangery, designed in a style appropriate to States Dyckman's time, which houses the citrus trees and oleanders in winter.

In the 1970s, the interiors were rearranged with excellent Federal furniture (including pieces by Duncan Phyfe, 1768–1854), fixtures and accessories, along with recovered Dyckman possessions. The boxwoods were removed from the front lawn, leaving an open sweep with a few large

trees (maple, pine, and oak). The upper pond is rather dull, but the one-and-a-quarter-mile woodland trail, developed in 1997, offers additional viewing points of the Hudson, with rustic seats and pavilions along the way.

The mission of Boscobel House and Gardens is to provide memorable experiences of the history, culture, and environment of the Hudson River Valley for the 11,000 visitors to the house and 3,000 to the gardens. Three part-time gardeners care for the forty-five acres, supplemented by the volunteers.

39 CARAMOOR CENTER FOR MUSIC & THE ARTS

149 Girdle Ridge Road, Katonah,
NY 10536
TEL: (914) 232-1253
WEBSITE: *www.caramoor.org*
SEE MAPS: pp. 99 & 101

Hours: Grounds open May through October, Wednesday–Sunday, dawn to dusk.
Admission free to grounds. Rosen House closed for restoration as of publication
Location: 47 miles from New York City
Public transportation: Metro-North to Katonah, taxi 2-3/4 miles
Facilities: Restrooms at the Venetian Theater and the Pegasus Gates; picnicking;
partially wheelchair accessible; no dogs
Programming: Concerts throughout the season
Nearby eateries: Katonah, 2-3/4 miles
Also of interest: Katonah Museum of Art, 134 Jay Street, Katonah, 2-1/4 miles

The gardens of Caramoor act as a gracious setting for more than seventy concerts and musical events that take place in the house and grounds during the season, often preceded by picnics. They also act as a backdrop for weddings, receptions, and photography. The tall, enclosing Tapestry Hedge of arborvitae, hemlock, and cypress is very impressive, with statues of Flora and

Zephyr, attributed to Antonio Bonazza (1698–1763), in their green recesses. However, marquees, cordoned-off areas, and notices, though essential to the main functions, interrupt the flow of the gardens, which include an assortment of styles, spaces and artifacts.

Against a backdrop of trees to the south emerge the intriguing sunken garden (c. 1912) and the "Medieval" Mount, related to each other through a formality of design and variations of green. The mount, with moss-covered slopes and pencil-thin evergreen verticals, looks down on the four box-hedge compartments of the sunken garden, each displaying a carpet of one or two colors of annuals with a tall clay pot in the center. Around the edges, parallel with the low walls covered in climbing hydrangea, are borders of hibiscus, roses, astilbe, and other perennials.

The Spanish-style house (currently closed), courtyard, and outbuildings (1929–1939) were built by the banker Walter Rosen (1875–1951) and his wife, Lucie, who purchased the original building and Italian gardens in 1928. Avid collectors, they filled their country home with furnishings and art works from Europe and Asia and pursued their passion for music. In 1945 they placed their property (about eighty-one acres) in a foundation (which became the Caramoor Center for Music & the Arts). Over the years the music programs have been expanded, the large tent has provided an additional venue, and new borders, artifacts, and a sense garden (1990) have been fitted into the original layout.

40 CEDAR GROVE, THOMAS COLE NATIONAL HISTORIC SITE

218 Spring Street, Catskill, NY 12414
TEL: (518) 943-7465
WEBSITE: *www.thomascole.org*
SEE MAPS: pp. 99 & 104

Hours: Grounds open daily, dawn to dusk; house open May through October, house and garden tours 10am–4pm. Admission free to grounds, charge for tour
Location: 119 miles from New York City
Public transportation: Amtrak to Hudson, taxi 5 miles
Facilities: Visitor center with introductory video, book and gift shop, coffee, tea, and bottled water, and restroom; picnicking tables; wheelchair accessible in grounds and visitor center; dogs on leash
Programming: Particularly related to Hudson River School for adults, families, and schools
Nearby eateries: Main Street, Catskill, 1-1/4 miles; list from visitor center
Also of interest: To visit some of the nearby Hudson River School locations, pick up the *Hudson River School Art Trail* from the visitor center or download it from *www.thomascole.org*; RamsHorn-Livingston Sanctuary (480 acres), Dubois Road, Catskill, 1-1/2 miles

Compared with Olana (see p. 154), this five-acre site is very modest. It celebrates the artist Thomas Cole (1801–1848) who became acquainted with the area in 1825 and then returned to paint in the cottage across the road. He never owned Cedar Hill—then a farm of over a hundred acres. He lived in the yellow 1815 Federal house, with porches on two levels, with his growing family and his wife's relatives until his early death at the age of forty-seven. The view west from the second-floor porch toward the Catskills is still thrilling. One can visit his "old" studio, and plans are under way to rebuild the newer one (used

from 1846 to 1848, but destroyed in the 1970s). The tour and video emphasize his love of his adopted country's natural scenery, his long walks to sketch on the spot, his influence on other artists of the Hudson River School, and his ardent defense of the countryside against the devastation of logging. Revered now for his landscape paintings inspired by American scenery, he himself aspired toward grander historical and allegorical themes in the vein of J. M. W. Turner or John Martin.

The flower garden is just one small aspect of the site—important only as an indication of the modest ways many contemporary lower middle-class families could satisfy their love of flowers and desire for pleasant surroundings. Referring to an 1868 painting, a short double border of perennials aligned with the front door has been partially recreated and filled with hollyhocks, spider flower, bee balm, yarrow, day lilies, and cone flowers. The ladies of the house, uninvolved in farm work,

After much agitating, the Thomas Cole National Historic Site came into being in 1999 as an affiliate of the National Park Service, and it was opened to the public in 2001. Visitor numbers have grown (over 9,000 in 2010), many volunteers assist, and restoration of the buildings and grounds proceeds. The goal is to provide a broad social context relating to the 1840s, with

probably looked after this area, now cared for by three volunteers. Note the delightful privy from around 1815, with classical detailing, and the trees (an enormous honey locust in front of the house is over two hundred years old) scattered throughout the property in the casual style of the period, with some island beds of shrubs in the rear. Groves and woods on the periphery (which evidently included cedars) provided fuel.

The land was sold off bit by bit, and the entire contents of the house were auctioned off in the 1960s, including dozens of Cole's painting. What was left of the property was sold in 1979.

specific plans to bring back the kitchen garden (the mainstay of the household) and restore the stone walls, gates, and carriage drive of the original entrance on Spring Street.

41 CLERMONT STATE HISTORIC SITE

1 Clermont Avenue, Germantown, NY 12526
TEL: (518) 537-4240
WEBSITE: *www.friendsofclermont.org;*
www.nysparks.com
SEE MAPS: pp. 99 & 104

Hours: Grounds open daily, 8:30am–sunset. House open for tours April 1 through October 31, Tuesday–Sunday (and Monday holidays) 11am–4pm; November 1 through December 20, Saturday and Sunday 11am–3pm. Admission free for grounds; charge for house tour

Location: 112 miles from New York City

Parking: Vehicle fee, Saturday, Sunday, and Monday holidays, 11am–4pm

Public transportation: Amtrak to Rhinecliff, taxi 14 miles

Facilities: Visitor center for house tour tickets, cell phone information on Alice's Garden Tour, trail map, introductory video, exhibition on the Livingston family, book and gift shop, and restroom; no refreshments; picnicking tables along the river; gardens partially wheelchair accessible, house first floor; dogs on leash

Programming: Hudson, Livingston family and social history, and more

Group garden tours: By appointment

Nearby eateries: Tivoli, 2 miles; Rhinebeck, 12 miles; Redhook, 8 miles

The siting, just above the Hudson River with views across to the Catskills, is Clermont's greatest asset. Equally remarkable are the deeply undulating lawns that run parallel to the river between the main house and the ruins of "Chancellor" Robert Livingston's 1793 home (destroyed by fire in 1909). Gentler than modern berms, their green waves cast deep shadows that contrast with those contributed by a scattering of black and honey locust trees. Picnic tables await.

The gardens closer to the house are sad remnants of those designed around 1930 by Alice Delafield Livingston (1872–1964). They include—by way of a short walk through the trees—the former kitchen garden, where now there are beds of perennials and some rustic arbors. At the far end is a former greenhouse, the children's playhouse (1910), and their garden plots. Notice boards and cell phone information flesh out the historical period—as at an archeological site. Nearby, magnolias, lilacs, tulip poplars and sugar maples are found, and part of the drive is bordered by pines, recalling the long vistas of avenues remarked upon by A. J. Downing in the 1840s.

Clermont itself was rebuilt by the strong-minded Margaret Beekman Livingston (1724–1800) immediately

after the British had burned the earlier (c. 1730–1750) house in 1777. Later additions were made, and the interior now reflects its 1920s redecoration in the Colonial Revival style. The tour—featuring family portraits, furnishings, and mementoes—immerses the visitor in stories of the seven generations who lived at Clermont over some 230 years. This was a family of great landed wealth and political and social significance, and one member in particular, Robert Livingston (1746–1813), the first Chancellor of New York State, plays a major role in the narrative. He not only helped draft the Declaration of Independence, administered the oath of office to George Washington, served as the first U.S. minister of foreign affairs, and negotiated the Louisiana purchase, but he also worked with Robert Fulton to produce the first steamboat, the *Clermont*, which went from New York to Albany in 1807.

The railway runs just below the house now, cutting off access to the river, but former carriageways and trails (sometimes difficult to follow) provide walks through woods of walnuts and other deciduous trees and meadows, passing some of the estate buildings and the two other houses formerly used by family members. In 1962 Mrs. Livingston deeded most of the family's historic estate to the state of New York, and an additional seventy-one acres were donated by her daughter in 1991. Future plans include finishing the masonry restoration of the walled garden, started in 2005. The Friends of Clermont, formed in 1977, works with the Department of Parks to support and supplement the preservation of Clermont and its programs. Some 90,000 people visit the 500-acre site annually.

42 DIA:BEACON

3 Beekman Street, Beacon, NY 12508
TEL: (845) 440-0100
WEBSITE: *www.diaart.org*
SEE MAPS: pp. 99, 102 & 103

Hours: Grounds and galleries open mid-April through mid-October, Thursday–Monday 11am–6pm; mid-October through mid-April, Friday–Monday 11am–4pm. Admission fee to galleries and inner garden
Location: 63 miles from New York City
Public transportation: Metro-North to Beacon, short walk
Facilities: Visitor center with café, restrooms, and book shop; picnicking in designated area; wheelchair accessible
Programming: Gallery talks, lectures, and performances
Nearby eateries: Village of Beacon, within walking distance

The enormous light-filled galleries in the 300,000 square feet of the former Nabisco box-printing facility contain renowned collections by artists who first became prominent in the 1960s—among others, Dan Flavin, Walter De Maria, Donald Judd, Fred Sandback, and Andy Warhol.

In keeping with Dia's high standards of design, Robert Irwin (b. 1928) was invited, before the galleries opened in 2003, to create a master plan for the surrounding landscape and advise on the light and circulation patterns within. A most rewarding view from the entrance gate looks down on the whole complex, with the Hudson River and the wooded hills in the background. The drive leads down, between graded and shaped slopes—with berberis planted in large blocks and cherry trees in defined earth circles—to the car park, designed as a special feature to mitigate the impact of the usual unattractiveness of such facilities.

An "orchard" of hawthorns and crabapples is set in oval beds (planted with two kinds of ornamental grasses) placed on the diagonal, their flowers and berries (yellow and red) creating splendid contrasts of color in season. The detailing is innovative, although the tarmac is obtrusive. In the museum forecourt the surface changes, and short grass grows through the pattern of some of the paving to green the hardscape a little—a nice touch. Trees are formalized in rows, with, toward the river, a raised cube of tall, and clipped fastigiate hornbeam—a beguiling grove with seating at the end. The view west from there is disappointing, however, lacking any connecting relationship to the Hudson River (because of railroad interference) and with a nondescript dead-end road below.

To the south, the visitor looks down into the totally enclosed sunken garden, which is entered by galvanized metal staircases from the galleries. Here the planting doesn't always cooperate with the minimalist aesthetic of strong horizontals and verticals of color and form, but it's a very tranquil and secluded spot. Two lines of cherries in wide beds, flanked by gray gravel paths, emphasize the length of the rectangular space, with a weeping hemlock at each end. A 'wall' of alternating clipped yew and hornbeam defines the west, with two levels of clipped and contrasting colored hedges on the east. On the short south side, large terraced planters with Japanese barberry lead up to the higher galleries, while wisteria grows profusely on the very tall wall to the north, with yellow-leafed spiraea beneath.

The nonprofit Dia Art Foundation, established in 1974, also maintains site-specific projects in the western United States, in New York City, and on Long Island.

43 DOWNING PARK

North Robinson Avenue, South, Dubois and
3rd Streets, Newburgh, NY 12550
TEL: (845) 565-5559 (SHELTER HOUSE IN THE PARK)
WEBSITE: *www.cityofnewburgh-ny.gov/downing*
SEE MAPS: pp. 99, 102 & 103

Hours: Park open daily, dawn to dusk. Admission free
Location: 67 miles from New York City
Public transportation: Metro-North or Amtrak to Beacon,
   ferry Monday–Friday, or weekend water taxi across the Hudson to Newburgh;
   ShortLine bus to 405 Broadway, Newburgh, walk 1 mile
Facilities: Visitor center in Shelter House (hours usually Monday–Friday 9am–2pm
   and Saturday noon–4pm), light snacks and restrooms; picnicking; wheelchair
   accessible; dogs on leash
Programming: Several concerts, community events, seasonal farmers' market
   (Friday) through the Downing Park Planning Committee
Nearby eateries: Newburgh

Local people enjoy walking around Polly Pond, with its weeping willow trees and duck island, visiting Shelter House (formerly for changing skates) for a snack, scrambling over the large outcroppings of rocks, traipsing to the top of the hill for a view of the Hudson, or gathering for a concert. Garden and landscape aficionados will too, but their visit to Downing Park yields additional resonance, as its creation brought together three generations of American landscape designers.

In 1889 the city of Newburgh asked Frederick Law Olmsted Sr. (1822–1903) and Calvert Vaux (1824–1903), who had collaborated years before on the plan for Central Park (1858), to design a park for the newly acquired thirty-five acres. They offered the designs as a gift on condition that it be named for Andrew Jackson Downing (1815–1852), the eminent horticulturalist, writer, and pioneer of the parks movement, who was brought up in Newburgh, worked in the family nursery, and continued to live there until his unfortunate drowning in 1852. The offer was accepted. Construction began in 1894, overseen by the principals' sons, John Charles Olmsted (1852–1920) and Downing Vaux (1856–1926), and the park opened in 1897.

Unfortunately the observatory tower, a vital feature on the highest point, was demolished in 1961, and the summit of the hill has never been relandscaped. The park was generally not well maintained for many years. However, the spatial characteristics integral to the design remain: wooded slopes, open rolling lawns, and serpentine paths. A number of new structures have been added: the delightful Shelter House (1934), recently restored; the pergola on the hill (1908) (closed); and the amphitheater (1946) where seasonal concerts take place.

Since 1987, the nonprofit Downing Park Planning Committee has partnered with the city of Newburgh to revitalize and restore the park. A master plan was commissioned from Heritage Landscapes in 1989, and although a large infusion of capital is still required, significant projects have been undertaken. Currently there are plans to renovate the Lord & Burnham greenhouses as a revenue-producing garden center (on 2½ acres just north of South Street and Carpenter Avenue) and to expand the community gardening program there.

44 THE BEATRIX FARRAND GARDEN AT BELLEFIELD

4090 Albany Post Road, Hyde Park, NY 12538
TEL: (845) 229-9115
WEBSITE: *www.beatrixfarrandgarden.org*
SEE MAPS: pp. 99 & 103

Hours: Garden open dawn to dusk. Admission free
Location: 70 miles from New York City
Parking: Use 4097 Albany Post Road for parking at Bellefield or at adjoining Springwood (Franklin D. Roosevelt National Historic Site, see p. 162)
Public transportation: See Springwood, p. 162
Facilities: Brochure, restrooms, café, and bookstore at Springwood Visitor Center, April 1 through October 31; picnicking; wheelchair accessible from the portico; dogs on leash
Events: Annual Bellefield Design Lecture
Garden tours: By appointment
Nearby eateries: See Springwood
Also of interest: See Springwood

The house, grounds, and four out buildings of Bellefield have been absorbed by Springwood: Home of Franklin D. Roosevelt National Historic Site, and the boundaries between the two properties are now blurred. A little hard to locate, the Farrand garden—secluded, walled, and hedged—occupies the roughly rectangular space south of the house (presently used by the National Park Service).

Originally built around 1795 in the Federal style, Bellefield and fifteen and a half acres were bought in 1885 by the lawyer and former Democratic state senator Thomas Newbold (1849–1928). McKim, Mead & White, it is believed, remodeled and extended the house for him and his wife, Sarah, between 1908 and 1911, creating the present Colonial Revival home. The property was used primarily in the spring and fall as a family retreat, other periods of the year being spent in Europe, New York, or on the Eastern seacoast.

In 1912, their cousin, the landscape designer Beatrix Jones (1872–1959)—who married Max Farrand in 1916—redesigned parts of the grounds. What is now called the Beatrix Farrand Garden was just one part of the complex, which featured additional ornamental and kitchen garden areas. The entrance drive from the main road still curves gently through lawn and specimen trees to the front entrance and then exits on the other side in a classic nineteenth-century manner.

Bellefield was presented to the National Park Service in 1976 by

Thomas Newbold's grandson, Gerald Morgan Jr. The nonprofit Beatrix Farrand Garden Association took on the responsibility in 1994 for the restoration, preservation, and interpretation of the sadly neglected flower garden.

Beatrix Farrand's concern for detail, in the Arts and Crafts tradition, is seen in her extant drawings of the trellis (used for the restoration), which supports the abundant wall vegetation, the gates with their wrought-iron work, and the stone wall. As no planting lists were discovered, the association used Farrand's plans for the William A. Read house of the same period in Harrison, NY. The resulting display of four themed color borders—pink, white, mauve and purple, and cream and gray, bring to mind Gertrude Jekyll's sophisticated planting schemes. The double borders that line the part of the lawn closest to the house are replaced by single borders in the narrower section just beyond, and then completely give way to the green of the grass, with hemlock hedges defining the sides. Among the many period perennials, a number of old varieties of iris stand out. Never grand or ostentatious, this satisfyingly simple and beautifully maintained space can also be appreciated from the terrace, where the view extends over the long narrow garden to large trees beyond, hinting at further walks and planting.

One part-time gardener—and ten volunteer gardeners who work one morning a week throughout the season—care for the garden, discovered by some 700 visitors a year. No labels are used, in keeping with the tradition of a private garden, but a plant list and plan are available upon request through the website. Anne Symmes, director of the Beatrix Farrand Garden Association, describes the next decade's goals: "We hope to rehabilitate a wild garden which Farrand had designed for the surrounding area and to develop our educational programming, including an audio tour about the garden and its renowned designer."

45 THE GARDENS AT MATTERHORN

227 Summit Park Road, Spring Valley, NY 10977
TEL: (845) 354-5986
WEBSITE: *www.matterhornnursery.com*
SEE MAP: p. 100

Hours: Gardens open April through December, 9am–4:30pm (last entry 4pm). Garden center open April through December, Monday–Saturday, 8am–5pm, Sunday 10am–5pm; January through March, Monday–Friday 9am–3pm, Saturday 9am–4pm, Sunday 10am–4pm. Admission charge to gardens, free to nursery

Location: 35 miles from New York City

Public transportation: Rockland Coaches to Spring Valley, taxi 5 miles

Facilities: Self-serve café; restrooms; garden center and shopping village; no picnicking; limited wheelchair accessibility in the gardens; dogs on leash

Group garden tours: By appointment

Nearby eateries: Nyack, 11 miles; Mt Ivy, 2 miles; Piermont, 14 miles; list from garden shop

Also of interest: Dutch Garden, 1 South Main Street, New City, 5 miles. The entrance is by a path to the south of the splendid Rockland County Court House (1928). This curious little tucked-away garden, designed by Mary Mowbray-Clarke (1874–1963) as a WPA project (1934) with all the hardscape and detailing in brick (teahouse, paths, walls, pergola, bandstand), celebrates the county's early Dutch settlers. It requires more planting, but has the potential to be a lovely garden again.

Enjoying and later reflecting on the attractive Gardens at Matterhorn encourages home gardeners to experiment with new design and planting ideas. Ponds, edged with weeping willows and banks of hostas and connected by wooden bridges, with a pavilion or folly here and there, offer one design possibility. A formal layout of beds of David Austin repeat-blooming roses in grass lawns (2003)—with varieties of old, shrub, climbing, and rambling roses—bordered by a classical colonnade, suggest the calm, floriferous approach. A more open area in the rear showcases an array of conifers of varying hues and shapes (many from Oregon), which are backed by a dazzling hedge of trained Atlas cedar. A small cottage-garden compartment offers different plant and color combinations. Haddonstone furniture and pots have their demonstration area, along with various suggestions for waterworks and patio surfaces.

One's immediate delight is in the richness of planting, in the health and vitality of what grows—which

imparts the impression that these gardens, begun in 2002, are watched and nurtured every day. Good labeling naturally facilitates potential purchasing in the garden center, while the designs act as a showcase for the landscaping side of the business headed by Matt Horn—who has a degree from Cornell University in horticulture and landscape design. From the ornamental gardens (five acres), paths and boardwalks lead through seven acres of woods, used especially in the fall for environmental studies with schoolchildren.

Matt and Ronnie Horn purchased seventeen acres of a former nursery holding area in 1981 and until 1996 were in the wholesale business. Since then, this family-owned business, with their children and now a niece taking their turns, has expanded to some thirty-five acres with a cluster of thirty buildings. Especially attractive are the "green" roofs of colored

sedums, particularly those of whimsical doghouses or gazebos. Racks of seasonal plants, mainly grown and propagated in their upstate nursery in Elmira, NY, under the direction of Noah Schwartz, display many of the plants seen in the gardens, and much more.

The long-term goal of the Horns is to be the best horticultural center in the country, to respond quickly to changing gardening ideas and lifestyles, and at the same time to be innovators in showcasing plant material and demonstrating environmentally responsible practices. One gardener looks after the ornamental gardens with the help of the maintenance and sometimes the administrative staff. The policy is to train all employees to be horticulturally proficient and flexible so that they can deal knowledgably with visitors (10,000 annually) and grow in their careers.

46 HAMMOND MUSEUM & JAPANESE STROLL GARDEN

28 Deveau Road, North Salem, NY 10560
TEL: (914) 669-5033
WEBSITE: *www.hammondmuseum.org*
SEE MAPS: pp. 99 & 101

Hours: Garden and museum open mid-April through November, Wednesday–Saturday, noon–4pm. Admission fee

Location: 54 miles from New York City

Public transportation: Metro-North to Croton Falls, taxi 6 miles

Facilities: Pamphlet with information and map; museum galleries; gift shop; Silk Tree Café, May through October, (914) 669-6100; restrooms; no picnicking; wheelchair accessible

Programming: With Asian and often seasonal emphasis

Nearby eateries: Croton Falls, 6 miles; Ridgefield, CT, 8 miles

Nearby park: Ward Pound Ridge Reservation (4,315 acres), Routes 35 & 121 South, Cross River, 6 miles

Also of interest: Aldrich Contemporary Art Museum, 258 Main Street, Ridgefield, CT, 8 miles; Salinger's Orchard, 230 Guinea Road, Brewster, 6 miles; the Outhouse Orchards, 130 Hardscrabble Road, North Salem, 4 miles

Off a very quiet residential road, one finds the Hammond Stroll Garden, an intimate part of a small Asian complex in Westchester. Dedicated to stimulating interest in the relationship between Eastern and Western artistic traditions, it encompasses a small museum, a café whose menu draws upon both cultures, and a gallery dedicated to featuring artists with an Asian sensibility as well as regional ones.

The centerpiece is the three-and-half-acre Stroll Garden, designed in 1957 by the benefactor Natalie Hays Hammond (1904–1985), the daughter of millionaire mining engineer John Hays Hammond and, in her own right, a set designer, miniaturist, illustrator, and author. The views across the water lily lake, fringed by irises—with a small, rounded island set in its quiet expanse—are lovely. The mostly Asian trees and shrubs—*Chamycyparis, Cryptomeria,* pine, Chinese chestnut, katsura, ginkgo, Japanese larch, maple, azalea, bamboo, and many more—produce exciting shapes and color and variations of height and texture. A lingering stroll reveals individual gardens reflecting the symbolism inherent in the Japanese placement of stones, artifacts, or plants.

It's a pity, then, that the garden falls away at the edges. One side is adjacent to an expanse of lawn and the gray house that was formerly Miss Hammond's. Other sides transition too quickly into unkempt woods. The view onto the car park is also unfortunate. The educational aspect sometimes works well—the opportunity to experiment with raking a dry garden is delightful—but at other times you feel that the garden is trying to say too much, and not well enough. Some of the detailing is well crafted, but elsewhere it is rather cheap looking.

This is an important garden that needs to be supported. Left without an endowment, the privately run trust operates on a shoestring, nevertheless attracting some 8,000 visitors a year, including groups of schoolchildren. The garden is tended by twelve volunteers, while the indoor activities have three administrators. Future plans include regaining the use of the Hammond house (currently rented out) for workshops and classes, and the installation of a traditional Japanese tea room.

47 HYDE PARK—THE VANDERBILT MANSION NATIONAL HISTORIC SITE

4097 Albany Post Road, Hyde Park, NY 12538
(or 119 Vanderbilt Park Road)
TEL: (845) 229-7770
WEBSITE: *www.nps.gov/vama; www.vanderbiltgarden.org*
SEE MAPS: pp. 99 & 103

Hours: Grounds open dawn to dusk; mansion tours daily, 9am–4pm. Admission free to grounds, charge for house tour
Location: 88 miles from New York City
Public transportation: Metro-North or Amtrak to Poughkeepsie, taxi 5 miles
Facilities: Visitor center in the pavilion for park brochure and trail map, book and gift shop, exhibition, restrooms, coffee and basic beverages and packaged snacks; picnic tables north of parking lot and at Bard Rock; partial wheelchair accessibility in mansion and grounds; dogs on leash
Garden tours: On special events days and by appointment, run by the F. W. Vanderbilt Garden Association (contact fwvga@marist.edu)
Nearby eateries: Hyde Park, 1/2 mile

A beautiful Hudson River site, a grand mansion in the restrained Italian Renaissance style, a designed landscape, and a walled formal garden from the period of the last illustrious owners, Frederick W. Vanderbilt (1856–1938), grandson of Cornelius Vanderbilt, and his wife, Louise (1844–1926)—this is Hyde Park. The entrance anticipates these treats: visitors pass the gate house, cross Crum Creek by the elegant White Bridge (1897), continue up the hill, and then curve around on a new road for the first view of the house, with its lawns and venerable trees, including a ginkgo from around 1799.

The Vanderbilts bought the rundown estate in 1895 and poured money into improving its historically important earlier design (1829–1830)—

an English pastoral park for Dr. David Hosack (1769–1835) by André Parmentier (1780–1830), one of the first landscape designers to introduce this style in America. The main farming activities were kept on the east side of the road and remained an important aspect. The 1845 house of the previous owners, Walter Langdon and his son Walter Jr. (1840–1894), was replaced by one in a similar but grander style (1896–1898) by Charles McKim, who also designed the Pavilion (the overflow visitors' quarters) and the gate houses. The house tour suggests the opulence of the new American aristocrats—and their imported European furnishings.

On the west side of the house, pastureland descends toward the

Hudson River, woods defining the important curving lines that edge the valley. Recently, rented goats grazing the steeper areas have replaced the earlier farm animals. Trails lead down to Bard Rock (named after a previous owner) on the river, and others, currently rather overgrown, can be explored.

The formal gardens, along with the tool house and gardener's cottage (1874,) are within the confines of the Langdons' earlier walls, but were enlarged and redesigned by Frederick Vanderbilt with the advice of garden designers James L. Greenleaf (1902–1904), Thomas Meehan and Sons (1910), and Robert B. Cridland (1916–1934). Two of the wide descending terraces—once viewed from extensive greenhouses on the level above—offer wonderful Victorian displays of annuals in patterns of crescent and heart-shaped beds. The long borders of another, overflowing with herbaceous flowers and flanked by cherry trees, lead to a formal pool and the much photographed "Barefoot Kate"

sculpture, a focal point in the pavilion, with a pergola on both sides. Below are the rose gardens (best in June/July) and the early-Renaissance-style teahouse.

Formed in 1984, the F. W. Vanderbilt Garden Association valiantly took on the task of restoring these formal gardens, working in partnership with the National Park Service. The Olmsted Center for Landscape Preservation has recently provided a twenty-five-year plan for the grounds, while the Cultural Landscape Report for the Formal Gardens (2010) has supplied in-depth historical analysis and guide lines for the association. These include bringing back major plantings (such as hedges) and structures where possible, and reintroducing heirloom varieties of the 1930s. Approximately eighty-two active volunteers work in the formal gardens.

After the death of Frederick Vanderbilt in 1938, President Roosevelt was instrumental in the Vanderbilt's niece's decision to donate the house and estate (211 acres) to the National Park Service. It opened to the public in 1940.

48 INNISFREE GARDEN

362 Tyrrel Road, Millbrook, NY 12545
TEL: (845) 677-8000
WEBSITE: *www.innisfreegarden.org*
SEE MAPS: pp. 99 & 103

Hours: Grounds open May 7 through October 20, Wednesday–Friday 10am–4pm; Saturday and Sunday, 11am–5pm. Closed Monday and Tuesday (except legal holidays). Admission fee

Location: 84 miles from New York City

Public transportation: None

Facilities: Map of the garden at the ticket office in the car park; *Innisfree: An American Garden* by Lester Collins (1994) available; two portable toilets; chairs placed for views; picnicking in designated places; limited wheelchair accessibility

Nearby eateries: Millbrook, 5 miles; and deli in Washington Hollow, 2 miles

Also of interest: Cary Institute of Ecosystem Studies, 2801 Sharon Turnpike (Route 44), Millbrook, trails, 2000 acres

"I will arise and go now, and go to Innisfree. . . ." —WILLIAM BUTLER YEATS

Around an irregularly shaped forty-three-acre glacial lake—with promontories and coves, cliffs, and grassy edges, all fringed by woods—appears a simple path. Now descending, now curving, now leveling out, it leads past a series of incidents—arrangements of rocks, water features, and plantings. It's orchestrated to maintain a balance between the seemingly natural and the obviously designed, with a different element achieving prominence along the way. The stroll garden today is the conception of two very different men, while the broad expanse of the lake—a great reflecting mirror of sky and tree

forms and colors—provides the central focus of the ever-changing views.

It all started in 1922, when the artist Walter Beck (1864–1954), son of a German immigrant landscape gardener, married Marion Burt Stone (1876–1959), heiress to the Mesabi Iron Range fortune. By 1930 they had built a large, comfortable summer house, designed by New York architects Robert Carrère and Norman Averill. It was modeled on the Royal Horticultural Society's half-timbered gabled house (1915) at Wisley (Surrey, UK) and sited on a plateau above Lake Tyrrell, within the 950 acres Marion Stone already owned. At first, terracing with straight stone staircases descended toward the water, and regular beds were envisaged for the planting. This

would have been in keeping with the style of the time, which embraced formality around the house while offering longer views of park or lake.

Walter's interest in Chinese landscape painting and garden traditions intervened, however, and until his death in 1954 his life at Innisfree centered around building and maintaining extensive rockeries over and adjacent to the terraces and in the cliff area to the northeast of the house. This necessitated bringing in hundreds of stones from the property, and excavating enormous, finely formed boulders to be placed within his new compositions. A seven-acre reservoir was built above the house, and water pumped from the lake reemerged as little streams and dripping waterfalls— one falling beautifully over the lip of a horizontally placed ledge. His

wife contributed her horticultural knowledge to the project.

After Walter Beck died in 1954, his wife asked the landscape architect Lester Collins (1914–1993) to help her set up the Innisfree Foundation, Inc. While in graduate school, Collins had met Walter Beck (1938) and had visited Innisfree over the years. He became the guiding force after her death in 1959, and Innisfree opened to the public in 1960. The problems were manifold. A garden that had been maintained by a staff of twenty had to be adjusted to new economic realities. In 1972, 750 acres, including the charming gatehouse of Innisfree, was sold to Rockefeller University to create a financial base. The house became an economic liability and was razed in 1982, leaving terraced rockeries and drives relating to an empty space.

and specially fine nozzles. Another addition is the Meadow Stream, of a precisely calibrated width, curving within a close-cut graded lawn, a pattern to be admired from above.

Lester Collins had spent time in China (1939–1940) as a young man and also a year in Japan (1953–1954) on a Fulbright scholarship, and the Asian influence is reflected not in the particular structures (there are no teahouses, pavilions, or pagodas), but in a Japanese sensitivity to the placement of rocks—singly or in groups, among plantings, or like sculpture on the grass. These framed compositions provide a series of "pictures" that draw our eyes in from the lake. In another blending of east and west, the area that used to relate to the house was transformed to great effect through rich plantings of prostrate, upright, and weeping conifers, Japanese maples, rock plants, ferns, and streams.

Since the death of Lester Collins in 1993, his wife, Petronella, and son, Oliver, have continued the mission as the most active trustees. Oliver Collins, trained as an engineer, installed a new misting fountain of upright wood, set among low berms and ginkgos near the cliff at the rear of the former house. Their goal now is to maintain and nurture what already exists rather than to embark on new developments. Some 20,000 to 25,000 visitors (including schoolchildren) find their way to Innisfree annually, where the 150 acres are cared for by nine gardeners, some part-time, during the season.

Collins used a number of bold strategies, based on both a modernist and an Asian aesthetic, to knit the spaces together. Grass berms were constructed to divert cars past the former house site and lead the visitors to a new starting point—a hill from which a great panoramic view of the lake emerges. The path has been extended to form a circuit around the lake. A bubbling fountain (the Air Spring) on the east side and a tall jet fountain on Pine Island—appearing as a plume from across the water— are both unapologetic insertions of the man-made, as is the misting effect in the cliffs at the northern end, dependent on hidden pipes and pumps

49 JOHN JAY HOMESTEAD STATE HISTORIC SITE

400 Jay Street (Route 22), Katonah, NY 10536
TEL: (914) 232-5651
WEBSITE: *www.nysparks.com/historic-sites;*
www.johnjayhomestead.org
SEE MAPS: pp. 99 & 101

Hours: Grounds open daily, dawn to dusk. House tours usually April through November, Tuesday–Sunday; weekends in December; Sundays January through March. Grounds free; admission charge for house tour

Location: 46 miles from New York City

Public transportation: Metro-North to Katonah, taxi 2-1/2 miles

Facilities: Herb garden brochure at the garden or in the museum shop with general material; interpretive exhibitions in the farm buildings; no refreshments; restrooms; picnic tables by the Brick Lot; first floor of house and some areas of the grounds wheelchair accessible; dogs on leash

Programming: Related to the Revolutionary War, abolition of slavery, social context of the house and farm.

Group garden tours: By special appointment

Nearby eateries: Katonah, 2-1/2 miles

New York Governor John Jay (1745–1829) looked forward to retiring "to the house on my farm in Westchester County"—constructed from 1787 on 750 acres. His twenty-seven years of public service included positions as president of the Continental Congress, coauthor of the Treaty of Paris, which ended the Revolutionary War, coauthor of the Federalist Papers, and first chief justice of the Unites States. The narrative and the interiors of the house reflect the years he spent at Bedford House as a gentleman farmer (1801–1829) and the lifestyles of the four further generations (John Jay's son was an ardent abolitionist).

On the horticultural level, what remains from John Jay are the stone ha-ha's to keep the grazing livestock from the pleasure grounds around the house. The front of the house was thus left open to views of the pastures, with just a few shade trees (lindens), the grass lawns, and the drive curving in from the west. Written evidence attests to his pleasure in tree planting and records that his daughter's health was improved by tending to the garden (probably the same site as the current gardens).

The two-story white wooden house, with green shutters and attractive porch, is set on a slight rise way back from the road—its 1924–1926 addition nicely screened by Korean dogwoods. The modest twentieth-century gardens start from the current car park. The first, an exquisite herb

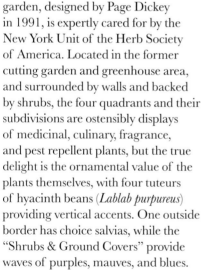

garden, designed by Page Dickey in 1991, is expertly cared for by the New York Unit of the Herb Society of America. Located in the former cutting garden and greenhouse area, and surrounded by walls and backed by shrubs, the four quadrants and their subdivisions are ostensibly displays of medicinal, culinary, fragrance, and pest repellent plants, but the true delight is the ornamental value of the plants themselves, with four tuteurs of hyacinth beans (*Lablab purpureus*) providing vertical accents. One outside border has choice salvias, while the "Shrubs & Ground Covers" provide waves of purples, mauves, and blues.

The trickling of water beckons visitors up into the fountain and sundial gardens—terraces of grass, flowering trees, and perennials, simplified versions of the plantings of the last owner, Eleanor Jay Iselin (1882–1953),

John Jay's great-great-granddaughter. Photo boards help to reconstruct earlier times, as they do elsewhere.

The John Jay Homestead (now sixty-two acres) was acquired for the public in 1953 and is now administered by the Office of Parks, Recreation and Historic Preservation, supported by the Friends of John Jay Homestead, formed in 1977. Plans include developing the landscape around the Ice House and expanding programs for the vegetable teaching gardens (2010). A new visitor center is also in the works. Some 35,000 visitors make use of the grounds, with 6,000 taking house tours. The five gardens (which include the 1920s terrace gardens in front of the house and an herb garden (1990s) at the back) are looked after entirely by fifteen to twenty volunteers from local garden clubs, their work adding to the pleasure of the visit.

50 THE DONALD M. KENDALL SCULPTURE GARDENS AT PEPSICO

PepsiCo World Headquarters,
700 Anderson Hill Road, Purchase, NY 10577
TEL: None
WEBSITE: None
SEE MAPS: pp. 99 & 100

Hours: Grounds open April through October, 7am–7pm; November through March, 7am–5pm. Headquarters not open to the public. Admission free

Location: 30 miles from New York City

Public transportation: Metro-North to White Plains, #12 Bee Line bus opposite station to the entrance, or taxi, 5 miles

Facilities: Visitor center for brochure with map and sculpture locations, vending machine for drinks, and restrooms; picnicking in designated area; wheelchair accessible; dogs on leash

Nearby eateries: To the west on Anderson Hill Road

Also of interest: The campus of SUNY Purchase at 735 Anderson Hill Road is directly across from PepsiCo, where the Neuberger Museum of Art is open Tuesday–Sunday, noon–5pm

This corporation headquarters is exhilarating in its mix of sculpture and horticultural richness set within a designed landscape. The size of the large building is cleverly distributed as low horizontal masses of seven squares linked at their corners around central courtyards in the shape of a Greek cross, open at the north end. Edward Durrell Stone (1902–1978) designed the structure for his client, the beverage and food giant PepsiCo, which moved into its new headquarters in 1970. The architect's son, E. D. Stone Jr., transformed the flat grounds of a former polo club, creating great sweeping lawns in front and to the rear and a large irregular lake. Cars for both employees and visitors are parked out of sight in wooded areas.

Donald M. Kendall (1921), who initiated the move to Westchester, started the sculpture collection in 1965 and, as CEO and chairman of the board from 1971 to 1986, he continued this avocation. It eventually grew to forty-five pieces, ranging from the monumental—works by Henry Moore, Alexander Calder, Isamu Noguchi, and Arnaldo Pomadoro— to the smaller pieces by Henri Laurens, Aristide Maillol, and Jacques Lipchitz, displayed in the intimate settings of the courtyard gardens, where seasonal planting adds color to the groundcover and small trees.

In 1980 the internationally renowned landscape gardener Russell Page (1902–1985) was brought in to adjust the siting of the sculpture and

with Japanese maples, hawthorns, and cherries forming the transition between the park and the formality of the architecture.

Russell was both a superb designer and an extremely knowledgeable horticulturist. Who can forget the line of plane trees trimmed as a hedge on stilts, which echoes the strong horizontal planes of the building, or the delight of coming across the water garden to the west, a modern exercise in geometry bordered by a great bank of perennials? What better siting could be devised for Claes Oldenburg's whimsical forty-seven-foot-high trowel (1976) or George Segal's two women and a man forever sitting on their benches (1979)?

The PepsiCo grounds were the last major project Russell Page worked on before he died. The Belgian landscape designer François Goffinet succeeded him as the garden's consultant and, visiting three times a year, he continues to guard the legacy he has inherited, maintaining the rhythms and occasionally adding new touches such as the azaleas in the west woodlands and the 1990 iris garden. Specimen trees and sculptures are labeled, accentuating their symbiotic relationship.

add horticultural diversity to the 168-acre site. He devised the idea of a "golden path," which loops through the landscape, leading the visitor through sequences of unfolding views and unexpected discoveries: sculpture in secluded spots, and the larger pieces on the lawns experienced from different angles, against a new backdrop, and under changed lighting conditions. The planting plays a major role: a fringing of mixed evergreens and deciduous trees; a cluster of birches on both sides of the path; or the stateliness of a grove of *Metasequoias*. Closer to the corporation headquarters, one finds a Dubuffet sculpture framed by magnolias; a Max Ernst by yew;

51 KYKUIT: THE ROCKEFELLER ESTATE

381 North Broadway, Sleepy Hollow,
NY 10591 (PHILIPSBURG MANOR VISITOR CENTER)
TEL: (914) 631-8200; weekends (914) 631-3992
WEBSITE: *www.hudsonvalley.org*
SEE MAPS: pp. 99 & 100

Hours: House and garden open daily (except Tuesdays), early May through beginning of November, by tour only. See website for the various options and reservations. Pick a tour that includes the garden. Admission fee

Location: 29 miles from New York City

Parking: At Philipsburg Manor and shuttle bus to Kykuit

Public transportation: Metro-North to Tarrytown, taxi 1-1/4 miles

Facilities: The visitor center is at Philipsburg Manor: brochures, guide book, *Kykuit: The House and Gardens of the Rockefeller Family* by Henry Joyce (2005) and related material in the gift shop; café, restrooms; no picnic tables; one tour is wheelchair accessible

Group garden tours: By appointment

Nearby eateries: Sleepy Hollow; Tarrytown, 1 mile; Croton-on-Hudson, 9 miles; Stone Barns Center, 2-1/2 miles (see below). See also www.hudsonvalley.org/content/view/86/151

Nearby parks: Rockefeller State Park Preserve (1,400 acres), Old Sleepy Hollow Road, Pleasantville, 2-1/2 miles

Also of interest: Union Church of Pocantico Hills with Chagall windows, 555 Bedford Road, Pocantico Hills, 2 miles

The hilltop site for Kykuit (Dutch for "lookout") was carefully chosen by John D. Rockefeller, his son J.D.R. Junior, and their advisers. By the beginning of the century, the original four hundred acres of 1893 had grown to more than two thousand. Views to the west extend toward the Hudson, some two miles away, and on to the Palisades; to the east, one looks over the sweeping slopes of a valley to the wooded hills beyond.

The compact six-story stone house in an eclectic semi-Georgian style—with porches on three sides and classical detailing and sculptural decoration—is the result of additions to a smaller house designed by the well-known architects Delano & Aldrich (completed in 1908). These (1911–1913), including the entrance facade, were designed by William Welles Bosworth (1869–1966) in consultation with Ogden Codman (1869–1951), who was responsible for the interiors. It ultimately became the favorite home of the founder of Standard Oil, and he lived here quietly, organizing his significant philanthropic projects, until he died at the age of ninety-seven (1937). His namesake, married to Abby Aldrich, used Kykuit mainly as a spring and fall residence, while their second son, Nelson, inheriting it at the death of his father in 1960, and his family used it as their country base.

Bosworth was also, from 1906, responsible for the conception and realization of the gardens. Terraces were constructed around the house, and in the classic Beaux-Arts tradition, a series of sight lines extending from the house and at right angles to each other tied the layout together. Walls, hedges, pergolas, an alley of lindens, paths, and staircases reinforced the directional flow, with fountains in the middle distance, and perhaps a pavilion or temple to lead the eye on or to form a closure. The influence of European precedents is also seen in the large grotto and in the rockwork with its sculpture and water effects.

Only the staircases and lower terrace on the south side seem inappropriately grand, presided over by Oceanus, a copy of Giambologna's sculpture (c. 1565) in the Boboli Gardens, Florence, who stands high on his fountain bowl, defining the axes of the forecourt. Beyond these garden rooms and terraces lies the green of the golf course—fashioned from the same aesthetic as the English parks of the eighteenth century—and seventy-five miles of carriage roads. A surprising element is the Brook Garden (1908), an early instance of the Rockefellers' interest in Asian culture, which lies to the south and was extended in the 1960s.

Nelson Rockefeller's integration, from 1960, of seventy superb European and American modern pieces of sculpture into the estate adds an exciting and unusual layer. Examples by Maillol, Lipchitz, Moore, Noguchi, Calder, and Meadmore, among others, are brilliantly and distinctively placed in the Inner Garden, with its earlier Italian teahouse and Persian rill, in the Rose Garden, on the terraces, and on the golf course.

The experience of visiting Kykuit is exhilarating, but the constraints of the required group visit make it difficult to absorb its extensive offerings. Just as in the tour of the art gallery in the basement of the house, there is no time to linger or to reflect.

Kykuit is owned by the National Trust for Historic Preservation and is administered by the Rockefeller Brothers Fund. Historic Hudson Valley operates the tours for the approximately 30,000 annual visitors.

Stone Barns Center for Food and Agriculture, 630 Bedford Road, Pocantico Hills, NY 10591, (914) 366-6200. Open Wednesday–Sunday 10am–5pm. Blue Hill Café, Wednesday–Sunday 10:30am–4:30pm; and Blue Hill at Stone Barns restaurant, evening only, reservations.

The mission of this eighty-acre nonprofit farm, established by David Rockefeller in 2004 in the majestic granite structures that had formerly been the dairy and later cattle barns of Kykuit, is to demonstrate, teach, and promote sustainable, community-based food production, a longtime interest of his wife, Peggy Rockefeller. A busy program of adult classes, tours, volunteer opportunities, farmers' market, and summer camps for children serve these purposes. A rectangular garden by Barbara Damrosch at the approach to the main courtyard provides a delightful resting point, and other gardens by Damrosch are found outside the restaurant. The café and restaurant draw upon the produce of the farm.

52 LASDON PARK, ARBORETUM & VETERANS MEMORIAL

2610 Amawalk Road (Route 35), Katonah, NY 10536
TEL: (914) 864-7268
WEBSITE: *www.westchestergov.com/parks*
SEE MAPS: pp. 99 & 101

Hours: Grounds open daily, 8am–4pm. House open only for events. Admission free
Location: 48 miles from New York City
Public transportation: Metro-North to Katonah, taxi 3-3/4 miles
Facilities: Map at entrance to the formal garden or in the visitor center (also the gift and plant shop), open Wednesday–Sunday 11am–3:30pm (except in winter), snacks, cold drinks, and coffee/tea machine; restrooms; picnicking; mostly wheelchair accessible; no dogs
Programming: Horticultural, concerts in summer
Nearby eateries: Katonah, 3-3/4 miles, Somers, 5-3/4 miles, Yorktown, 5-1/4 miles; list in visitor center
Also of interest: Ward Pound Ridge Reservation (4,315 acres), Routes 35 & 121 South, Cross River, 7-1/4 miles; Muscoot Farm and trails, 51 Route 100, Katonah or Somers, 3-1/2 miles

Beyond its varied horticultural features, the 234 acres of Lasdon Arboretum illustrate the ways nature can be redefined for historical and memorial purposes. The arboretum itself—an inner core of thirty-two acres protected by a deer fence—is reached by a gently climbing drive with splendid views over broad pastures and trees. Since Westchester County's purchase in 1986 of Cobbling Rock Farm, the country retreat from 1939 of William and Mildred Lasdon, the layout has been replanned, the visitor now skirting the good-looking avenue of elms leading to the house to arrive at a car park to the east.

New gardens supplement the original three-acre Lasdon plantings around the house. The formal garden, donated in 2001 by Nanette Laitman in memory of her parents, has a splashing fountain of playful boys in the center, colorful seasonal displays in box-edged beds, and a viewing terrace shaded by callery pears. Surrounding it, the synoptic garden displays a good collection of shrubs in alphabetical order, with some special trees interspersed. Beyond, one finds the rain garden, the lilac collection (a bit bare out of season), the orchard, and the conifer collection with mature as well as new specimens, many labeled. Back toward the house, a perennial border, a heather collection, flowering trees, and shrubs provide further interest before one takes a seat outside the former pool house to view

the white Colonial Revival 1940s house sitting above lawns on the hill.

Beyond the deer fence is the Famous and Historic Tree Trail (1991), which, as at Union County College, NJ (see p. 278), features species, grown from the parent tree, that commemorate historic events or famous people. Arranged chronologically, some thriving, some not, each of the thirty-one trees has an informative notice board. We go from the white oak for Columbus to the seed of a sycamore that journeyed on Apollo XIV to the moon and back, with, in between, a white cedar from Fort Ticonderoga, an American beech for Clara Barton (Red Cross), and a redbud from President Roosevelt's home in Warm Springs, GA.

The way leads on through an Asian gateway to the four-acre Chinese Friendship Pavilion and Culture Garden, where the bond between Westchester County and its sister city, Jingzhou, is celebrated. The pavilion, given by the Chinese (1997), sits near the large lake backed by tall spruces, with bamboo, weeping willows, *cryptomerias*, and bald cypresses representing the tentative start of a new Asian collection.

The Trail of Honor commemorates very different events. From the car park a loop leads through sixteen acres of woods, passing memorials to Westchester servicemen and women who served their country, with cairns representing every major American conflict from the American Revolution to Operation Desert Storm. The climax is the Vietnam Veterans Memorial, sited for an expansive view over woods to the hills. Behind the flagpole and the upright black memorial stone, a 1987 sculpture group by Julia Cohen shows a soldier heroically carrying a wounded colleague and nurse reaching out to assist. A veterans' museum by the house is open on weekends

The Lasdon Arboretum shoulders these civic responsibilities along with ongoing research on the American chestnut and dogwoods and the expansion of its horticultural collections. A major goal, led by the Friends of Westchester County Parks, is to build a conservatory. Currently four full-time, one part-time, and four seasonal gardeners look after the gardens and grounds, assisted by twenty volunteers. Lasdon attracts 50,000 visitors annually.

53 LOCUST GROVE ESTATE

2683 South Road, Poughkeepsie, NY 12601
TEL: (845) 454-4500
WEBSITE: *www.lgny.org*
SEE MAPS: pp. 99 & 103

Hours: Grounds open daily, 8am–dusk; house open for tours, May through November, daily, 10am–5pm; weekends in April and December, 10am–5pm. Admission free to grounds; admission charge for house

Location: 82 miles from New York City

Public transportation: Metro-North and Amtrak to Poughkeepsie, taxi 2-1/2 miles

Facilities: Visitor center for self-guided garden and trails brochures, a booklet, *Locust Grove* by Kenneth F. Snodgrass (n.d.), a few basic snacks, gift shop, restrooms, and exhibition gallery; carriage house for permanent and changing exhibitions; picnicking; partially wheelchair accessible; dogs on leash

Programming: Horticultural tours, picnics, wine-tasting, concerts

Garden tours: By appointment

Nearby eateries: Poughkeepsie, 2-1/2 miles; Rhinebeck, 18-1/2 miles; Beacon, 14-1/2 miles

Also of interest: Walkway Over the Hudson State Historic Park (former railroad bridge over the Hudson River), entrance from east side of the Hudson, 61 Parker Avenue, Poughkeepsie; entrance from west side of river, 87 Haviland Road, Highland

The painter and inventor of the telegraph Samuel F. B. Morse (1791–1872) had the greatest influence on the landscaping of Locust Grove. With proceeds from his patents bringing him financial security, he bought the property in 1847 and, steeped in the eighteenth- and early nineteenth-century writings of Thomas Whately and J. C. Loudon, and in tune with the ideas of American Andrew Jackson Downing, he redesigned both house and grounds. Working with the architect Andrew Jackson Davis (1803–1892), he oversaw the transformation of a symmetrical Federal-period house into a delightful villa in the modern "Italian" style (1851–1852): a tower on the west looking out to the Hudson, a veranda on the south, a port-cochere on the east for carriages arriving on the curved drive, and unusual octagonal rooms to the north and south.

Around the house were shaped flower beds with colorful displays, while urns and a fountain added gracious refinement to the lawns and their trees. Black locusts screened the road. To the southeast lay the orchard and the kitchen garden. The rest of the seventy-six acres, although ostensibly a farm, was adjusted through Morse's painter's eye for picturesque effects and views, the Hudson River being the dominant attraction. Paths and carriage trails created circuits, and rustic seats were strategically placed. As he wrote of the property in 1847, "Its 'capabilities' as the landscape gardeners would say, are unequaled. There is every variety of surface, plain, hill, dale, glen, running stream, and fine forests and every variety of distant prospect." Thomas Devoy, as head gardener, managed the gardens and the greenhouses for the Morses, who after 1855 spent winters in New York. Visitors today can still delight in many aspects of this mid-Victorian garden and landscape.

In 1900 the Morse heirs sold Locust Grove to the Poughkeepsie lawyer William H. Young, and the tour features the lifestyle of his family and their eighteenth- and nineteenth-century furniture and possessions. Sensitive to Samuel Morse's place in history, they made few structural changes to the house, except for the addition of the north wing. Avid gardeners, they brought about what is today called the Main Garden—long beds of peonies and dahlias and perennials. Their daughter, Annette Young, committed to preserving the property, left it, along with an endowment, to a private nonprofit corporation (1975).

Views of the Hudson have been blocked by unchecked growth of trees, and Oak Lake, created by the Youngs in 1900, has lost its charm, but the property is still of great interest. About 65,000 visit the grounds annually, while 8,000 visitors take the house tour. The nearly two hundred acres are cared for by one full-time and one part-time gardener, assisted by fifty volunteers. Future plans are restricted by financial constraints, but the maintenance of the ornamental gardens is a priority, and experiments with different combinations of heirloom flowers are ongoing. The Heritage Vegetable Garden, managed by volunteers, makes excellent use of the former kitchen garden, showcasing the kind of produce grown by the four main families of Locust Grove from the eighteenth century to 1946.

54 LYNDHURST

635 South Broadway, Tarrytown, NY 10591
TEL: (914) 631-4481
WEBSITE: *www.lyndhurst.org*
SEE MAPS: pp. 99 & 100

Hours: Grounds open to pedestrians, dawn to dusk (if main entrance is closed, use the path to the old Croton Aqueduct Trail, 100 yards to the north). House open mid-April through October, Tuesday–Sunday 10am–5pm, and November to mid-April, Saturday and Sunday 10am–4pm. Admission charge at times to grounds; admission charge for house

Location: 28 miles from New York City

Public transportation: Metro-North to Tarrytown, taxi 2 miles

Facilities: Visitor center in the carriage house for introductory video and restrooms; also cell phone tour for house and grounds; gift shop in the house; no refreshments; picnicking (bring a blanket); first floor and paved roads of the grounds, wheelchair accessible; dogs on leash

Programming: Craft fair, dog show, and seasonal events

Nearby eateries: Tarrytown, 2 miles, and Irvington, 1 mile

Also of interest: The Croton Aqueduct Trail connects Lyndhurst with Sunnyside, just south (part of the developing Westchester River Walk)

The approach through the park is magnificent: a long, slow drive with views of lawns with great mature trees, a glimpse of the enormous conservatory on the right, and then the appearance of the house with its towers, steeply pointed gables, and medieval-looking windows. Transported into the realm of Sir Walter Scott and the Romantic movement, we sweep up to the entrance. The prospect of the Hudson River, although somewhat obscured by trees, remains.

The architect Andrew Jackson Davis (1803–1892) designed Knoll (1838–1842), a small innovative country villa "in the pointed style," for Philip Paulding (son of William Paulding, former mayor of New York). Unusual at that time in the United States, the interiors and the furniture (all in the Gothic Revival style) were also designed by the architect. Twenty-two years later, Davis was commissioned by the new owner, merchant George Merritt (1807–1873), to expand the villa (the northern tower wing) into the imposing mansion that we see today, adapting the Gothic style to new proportions.

Ferdinand Mangold (1828–1905) worked at Lyndenhurst (named for its

linden trees) from around 1865 for forty years as head gardener, overseeing the layout, drainage, and tree planting, in the English picturesque landscape style, and the horticultural requirements for the 1869 conservatory. He continued under the next owner, the railway magnate and financial tycoon Jay Gould (1836–1892), who acquired the property in 1880, shortening its name to Lyndhurst.

Within a year of Gould's arrival, the Merritt conservatory burned down and was replaced by Lord & Burnham's magnificent E-shaped structure of 19,000 square feet, considered the first primarily iron structure of its time. Today the famous horticultural collections have vanished, but the skeleton of the structure and the informative photo boards suggest the grandeur of the central palm court, the cooler west wing containing the graperies, azaleas, camellias, and bulbs, and the east wing holding ferns, orchids, and carnations, and ending in a rose house for out-of-season blooms.

Helen Gould (Shepard) (1868–1938), daughter of Jay Gould, inherited

Lyndhurst (see p. 228 for her brother's estate, Georgian Court). Around 1911 she added the rose garden (adjacent to the conservatories), now surrounded by a deer fence, and the bowling alley to the west. The last owner, her sister, Anna, Duchess of Talleyrand-Perigord, auctioned off the orchid collection to aid the Red Cross—and sacrificed the conservatory collections to save energy during World War II. At her death in 1961, Lyndhurst, with its overlays of three families, was left to the National Trust for Historic Preservation and opened to the public in 1964. A staff of four, three full-time and one part-time, are responsible for the maintenance of the sixty-seven acres and fifteen buildings. Three garden clubs assist— the Irvington (rose garden), Taconic (fern garden, off the main drive), and Rock (the Carriage House Garden). Of the 65,000 visitors, 25,000 take the house tour, and 40,000 attend the events or use the grounds.

MANITOGA/THE RUSSEL WRIGHT DESIGN CENTER

584 Route 9D, Garrison, NY 10524 (or 22 Old Manitou Road)
TEL: (845) 424-3812
WEBSITE: *www.russelwrightcenter.org*
SEE MAPS: pp. 99 & 102

Hours: Trails open dawn to dusk; house tours by appointment only, April through October, Saturdays and Sundays at 11am and 1:30pm, and on selected weekdays. Admission free to grounds (donation requested); charge for house tour

Location: 50 miles from New York City

Public transportation: Metro-North to Garrison; taxi by reservation (845) 265-TAXI (8294), 3 miles

Facilities: Visitor pavilion for trail maps and brochures, gift shop (open only during tour hours) for Wright merchandise, including *Garden of Woodland Paths* by Russel Wright (1970) and *Guide to Easier Living* by Russel and Mary Wright (1950); no refreshments; portable toilets; picnicking; not wheelchair accessible, dogs on leash

Nearby eateries: Garrison, 3 miles (scattered); Cold Spring, 6 miles

Nearby park: Bear Mountain State Park, Stony Point (off Route 202/9W South), on west of Hudson, 6 miles

The best introduction to Manitoga (Place of the Great Spirit), the house and woods of American Modernist Russel Wright (1904–1976), is the house tour that allows access to the paths surrounding the quarry pool. This inner area, Dragon Rock, is stunning, with the horizontal glass-fronted house and pergola-attached studio, designed by David L. Leavitt, perched on a ledge that looks toward the thirty-foot waterfall and across to the cliff side of the quarry. Trees, mountain laurel, ferns, and plantings in rocky crevices surround the house. The cascade was created by bringing in great boulders, and the quarry dammed to create the pool. This habitation set delicately within nature offers a striking comparison with Frank Lloyd Wright's Falling Water (1936–1939).

Russel Wright, the pioneering industrial designer, was a household name from the 1930s to the early 1960s, with his mass-produced American Modern furniture and household products. He promoted a new, American modern look and relaxed living style, which he and his wife, Mary, presented in their best-selling *Guide to Easier Living* (1950).

In 1942, the Wrights purchased a bungalow on seventy-five acres of nondescript land as a weekend retreat in the Hudson Highlands. The large

trees had been clear-cut some eighty years before, and the quarry (which had provided stone for the New York Public Library) had been abandoned, with boulders and blocks of granite strewn around. After his wife's death in 1952, when their adopted daughter was only two, Wright began spending more time at Manitoga, his main focus for the next twenty-four years.

Paths developed by Wright over the years allowed for movement through the woods to complement the more passive viewing from the house. In this "designed" landscape, he carefully orchestrated views, removing trees and limning up others to frame a feature. He enriched the wildflowers to create a density of color and texture, encouraged areas of moss for a special pause, built bridges over streams, and laid stepping stones over wet patches. The hemlock trees provided the main

canopy, supplemented only with natives along the short (two miles) and longer (four miles) loops.

When Wright died in 1976, he left his New York City house and Manitoga (where his daughter continued to have tenancy) to the Nature Conservancy, an unsuccessful plan. In 1986 the Nature Conservancy transferred ownership to the nonprofit Manitoga, Inc., which tried to deal with the obvious deterioration to structures and landscape, but underfunded, it only became effective in 2000 after buying out Ann Wright, thus qualifying for major grants to public properties. Since then, a great deal has been achieved, including the restoration of the studio (2004) and the pergola (2009), and work on the house and landscape is ongoing. Major challenges remain: woody adelgids have killed many of the eastern hemlocks, deer browsing

eliminates new seedlings, soil erosion has taken place, and many of the carefully nurtured details beyond the immediate house and pool area have disappeared.

Currently some 8,000 people use the trails annually and 2,400 make appointments to see the house. One staff member gives a little time to the grounds, while five volunteer landscape days attract some thirty to forty helpers. Developing a corps of regular volunteers is in the works, and a part-time landscape position is planned. In keeping with Wright's policy, there is no labeling, but interpretive materials that illustrate the native plants used in the designed landscape are being prepared.

56 MOHONK MOUNTAIN HOUSE

1000 Mountain Rest Road, New Paltz, NY 12561
TEL: (845) 256-2152 (GREENHOUSE);
(845) 256-2056 (MEAL RESERVATIONS IN THE HOTEL)
WEBSITE: *www.mohonk.com*
SEE MAPS: pp. 99 & 103

Hours: Garden and grounds open daily, dawn to dusk; greenhouse open daily, 9am–3:30pm. Admission charge to grounds. Hotel for guests and restaurant diners only

Location: 85 miles from New York City

Parking: At entrance gatehouse and shuttle bus during high season

Public transportation: Adirondack Trailways bus to New Paltz, then taxi 7-3/4 miles to hotel, 5-1/2 miles to entrance; Amtrak or Metro-North to Poughkeepsie, taxi 18-1/2 miles

Facilities: Garden visitors' center in the greenhouse: 9am–3:30pm; self-guided garden map, plant shop and displays, gift shop; Picnic Lodge (café) 11am–3pm, and restrooms near the greenhouse; picnicking; limited wheelchair accessibility; no dogs

Programming/events: Annual four-day Garden Holiday, late August/September

Group garden tours: By appointment

Nearby eateries: New Paltz, 7-3/4 miles

Nearby park: The Mohonk Preserve (6,000 acres) with trails surrounding the Mohonk Mountain House land

Also of interest: Apple picking in the fall in nearby orchards; stone houses of New Paltz; Samuel Dorsky Museum of Art, SUNY New Paltz

In 1869 a pair of Quaker educators, twins Albert and Alfred Smiley (1828–1912 and 1903, respectively) bought a small inn and three hundred acres as a summer home in the magnificent Shawangunk Mountains. Over the years they transformed it into a resort offering fresh air, exercise, and healthy living. Developing the garden on the rocky terrain was Albert's joy and special achievement. Cartloads of topsoil, brought in by horses from elsewhere on the property, enriched the terrain close to the hotel. Then, in 1886, the layout of a Victorian ornamental garden was begun in this most unlikely of places—1,200 feet above sea level.

The pattern of beds and their thousands of annuals, grown in the greenhouses and planted at the beginning of June, can best be viewed from the upper level of a wonderful wooden gazebo, thickly covered with wisteria. Every year a new color scheme—Rhapsody in Blue in 2010, Candy Land in 2011, Alice in Wonderland in 2012—emerges, based on the preceding season's experimentation with hardiness and

hue. This is bedding-out at its best, done with great horticultural skill and a zest for fun and display. All the plants that make up the blocks of color have metal tags with Latin and English names. Unusual varieties of coleus are often a feature.

But there is more: a rose garden, the arborvitae maze, a little herb garden, a one-hundred foot perennial blue garden, and a cutting garden. The last, grown in utilitarian lines but with a definite eye on the decorative aspect, supplies the many arrangements of cut flowers in the hotel—supplemented by the orchids, poinsettias, fuchsias, cyclamens, and other indoor potted plants grown in the four greenhouses.

These wonderfully colorful gardens are set within a naturalistic landscape of lawns and specimen trees (notice the weeping, fern-leafed, and copper beeches) and backed by woods. From the hotel (now a greatly enlarged 267-room complex) visitors can walk around the lake through pitch pine, mountain laurel, oaks, and small maples, or join the higher trails for more extensive hikes into the remaining 2,170 acres (and the 4,400 acres of the Mohonk Preserve).

A defining characteristic at Mohonk is the rustic design of the more than one hundred delightfully zany gazebos (called Summer Houses) placed for views and shade, particularly around the lake. A small team of carpenters renews and makes these imaginative structures, as well as all the other woodwork—benches, arbors, fences, railings, and signs throughout the property, forming a connection between the maintained gardens (thirty acres) and the natural landscape. Two full-time and three seasonal gardeners care for the ornamental grounds with two full-time and two seasonal greenhouse staff.

Entrance for day visitors is expensive, so plan on spending the day here. If you have reservations for a meal in the hotel (perhaps breakfast), then access is free. Mohonk Mountain House is still owned by the Smiley family.

57 MONTGOMERY PLACE

River Road, Red Hook, NY 12571 (OFF ROUTE 9G)
TEL: (914) 631-8200
WEBSITE: *www.hudsonvalley.org*
SEE MAPS: pp. 99 & 104

Hours: Grounds open daily, 9am–4pm; house open mid-May to end of October, Thursday–Sunday 11am–4pm, last tour at 3pm. Admission free to grounds; charge to house

Location: 102 miles from New York City

Public transportation: Amtrak to Rhinecliff, taxi 5-3/4 miles

Facilities: Visitor center by parking for *Landscape Guide* and *A Tree Walk* brochures, vending machine for drinks and restrooms; picnicking; wheelchair accessible in main area; no dogs

Nearby eateries: Red Hook, 3-1/2 miles; Rhinebeck, 5-1/2 miles

Also of interest: Produce from the Montgomery Place Orchards is available in season; follow signs from exit for 1 mile on Route 9G. Poet's Walk, River Road (Route 103), Red Hook, 3/4 mile (just north of Kingston-Rhinecliff Bridge), a walk through meadows to scenic views of the Hudson, daily 9am–dusk

Montgomery Place holds a special place in American house and garden history. The influential writer, former nurseryman, and landscape designer Andrew Jackson Downing described it as "second…to no seat in America" in the *Horticulturist* (1847). Another giant of the nineteenth century, Andrew Jackson Davis (1803–1892), designed the elegant open-sided pavilion on the north side, the new south wing, and the west terrace (1841–1844), and supplied the drawings for the four woodcuts illustrating Downing's article. Davis's drawings of additional, delightful rustic structures for viewing points are also extant. These, along with letters and archival material, underscore the new taste that Downing was advocating, which Montgomery Place represented so well.

The summer county seat of some four hundred acres offered a stately approach, mature trees, and well-disposed lawns, with excellent views of the Hudson and the hazy blue Catskills beyond. Walks led to a wilder area of woods containing the dramatic waterfalls of the Saw Kill River and a lake with a boat at the ready. Also described were a good-looking 1839 conservatory for citrus and tender plants, a fine ornamental flower garden surrounded by shrubbery, and carriage rides through some fifty acres of woods at the southern end of the property.

Downing noted a historical layer as well—the original Federal-style house (1804–1805) had been created, along with the working farm, by Janet Livingston Montgomery (1743–1828), the resourceful widow of General Richard Montgomery (1738–1775), an early hero of the Revolutionary War. Later owners, and friends of Downing, were Louise Livingston (1782–1860), the widow of Edward Livingston (1764–1836), who had begun the transformation of the grounds, and her daughter and son-in-law, Coralie Livingston Barton (1806–1873) and Thomas Barton (1803–1869), all keen horticulturalists "whose greatest pleasure seems to be to add, if possible, every year, some admirable improvement."

The gracious house, with further classical adornments on the exterior (1860s) by Davis, decorated with family portraits and furnishings, is open to visitors. Some of the walks on the 360 acres remain, but the seats and pavilions have gone, the lake by the river is surrounded by unchecked growth, the views of the Hudson have been coarsened, and although there are still venerable trees, the horticultural richness has been depleted.

In the 1920s and 1930s Violetta White Delafield (1875–1949), a Livingston descendent, created three new gardens. The "rough" garden of rocks and streams and woodland plants (1929–1932) to the southeast of the house is restored periodically. Narrow stone paths lead to the ellipse (1930–1931)—an oval pool for aquatics surrounded by hemlocks, with some seating, which doesn't quite coalesce. Across the track, one enters the third area (1930s): a rose garden and herb garden, followed by perennial borders (1939), with the potting shed (1929) of the greenhouse acting as a focal

point. It's an attractive, flowery retreat despite the awkwardness of the total design. The Delafields also added the "reflecting" pond—now very weedy— seen from the west terrace, and a sports building.

In 1986 the heir, John Dennis Delafield, transferred the estate (part sale, part gift) to Historic Hudson Valley, which opened it to the public in 1988. Conservation of the house collections is ongoing, while the production of web-based educational programs, trail maps, and brochures is under way—based on the new focus of mankind's relationship to land and land use. One full-time and two part-time staff members care for the 380 acres.

58 MOUNTAIN TOP ARBORETUM

4 Maude Adams Road, Tannersville, NY 12485
TEL: (518) 589-3909
WEBSITE: *www.mtarboretum.org*
SEE MAPS: pp. 99 & 104

Hours: Grounds open daily, dawn to dusk. Admission free
Location: 119 miles from New York City
Public transportation: Adirondack Trailways (800-776-7548) to Hunter,
taxi 7 miles or Adirondack Trailways to Tannersville, 2 miles
Facilities: Brochures and information at the kiosk in the parking lot, and notice
boards at entrances to West Meadow, Woodland Walk, and East Meadow;
cellphone information points for Verizon service; no refreshments; restrooms;
no picnicking; not wheelchair accessible; no dogs
Programming: Environmental awareness, birding, stargazing
Group garden tours: By appointment, on foot or in vehicle
Nearby eateries: Tannersville, 2 miles; list available
Nearby parks: Colgate Lake (East Jewett), 2-3/4 miles

On the way west to the Mountaintop Arboretum along Route 23A, stop to walk to the Catskill Mountain House Site or the Kaaterskills Falls to connect with the Hudson River artists and the nineteenth-century tourists who sought out these magnificent spots of scenic beauty. The Arboretum, much higher up at 2,400 feet, zone 4–5, provides an excellent reason to linger in the area. Its mission is "to provide for the Catskill region a unique and beautiful mountain top environment for a living sanctuary of native and exotic trees and shrubs" and to "offer a diversity of programs for the education and pleasure of the public."

This approach originated with Peter and Bonnie Ahrens, who transferred a portion of their summer home property to Mountain Top Arboretum, Inc., in 1977. The West Meadow, with its concentration of firs, spruces, pines, cypresses, and junipers—local and from around the world—standing against a backdrop of deciduous trees on the surrounding hills is a testament to their interests. It's a designed landscape in the process of maturing, with some very new plantings gradually gaining in stature. A rustic summerhouse provides an inviting viewing point for a berm of dwarf conifers and heathers alongside the exposed Devonian bedrock. By the pond one sees dawn redwoods (Chinese) grouped with bald cypresses (American), and outside the deer fence a large island of dramatic grasses

among small trees and shrubs. Opposite these, a border showcases perennials, hoped to be distasteful to deer.

Two other areas have been added: the two-and-a-half-acre Woodland Walk (fenced in) across from the West Meadow and the East Meadow (a short walk along the private road). The emphasis in both is on native species and the restoration of the diversity that characterized this region before massive logging (for the tanning business), hemlock and chestnut blight, and the overpopulation of deer interfered. Planted wildflowers are encouraged to naturalize, as are the flowering shrubs and trees found in the Catskill forest understory. A delightful fern trail leads through a wood of northern hardwood trees, and a boardwalk extends into wetlands. Such areas within the mountain ecosystem offer opportunities for environmental studies, birdwatching, and plant identification. Finally, past the North American pinetum, one reaches the small nursery of American chestnut trees—a long-term experiment, in conjunction with the American Chestnut Foundation, to breed disease-resistant trees that might once again thrive in the region.

Mountain Top Arboretum, with twenty-three acres, has one full-time and three seasonal gardeners, one administrator, one educational staff member, and twenty volunteers. Their policy is to label many of the trees and shrubs (especially apparent in the West Meadow). Some 2,000 visitors are expected annually. Future plans include strengthening the core collections, continuing the transition from mowed areas to environmentally valuable meadows, and expanding the interpretive trails and outdoor classroom experiences.

59 OLANA STATE HISTORIC SITE

5720 State Route 9G (one mile south of
Rip Van Winkle Bridge), Hudson, NY 12534
TEL: (518) 828-0135
WEBSITE: *www.olana.org*
SEE MAPS: pp. 99 & 104

Hours: Grounds open daily, 8am–sunset; house open for tours, April through
October, Tuesday–Sunday (and holiday Mondays), 10am–5pm (last tour 4pm);
November through March, Friday–Sunday 11am–4pm, last tour 3pm. Admission
free to grounds (parking charge on weekends); fee for house tours

Location: 121 miles from New York City

Parking: At top of the hill by house, or at the Wagon House Education Center
(first right after the lake) to approach the house on foot

Public transportation: Amtrak to Hudson, taxi 4-3/4 miles

Facilities: Visitor center (open on tour days) for map of carriage drives and
brochures, book and gift shop, bottled water and packaged snacks, restrooms;
picnicking; house and immediate grounds are wheelchair accessible; dogs on leash

Programming/events: Ongoing for children and adults at the Wagon House
Education Center/Farm Complex

Grounds tours: By appointment

Nearby eateries: Warren Street, Hudson, 4-3/4 miles; Main Street, Catskill,
3-1/2 miles; list available from visitor center

Also of interest: Greenport Conservation Area (714 acres), 54 Daisy Hill Road,
Greenport, 5-1/2 miles

Visitors to Olana primarily focus on the tour of the house, with its fabled interiors and hilltop setting—allowing for an astounding 180-degree view of the Hudson River, wide as a lake to the south and narrowing further north—with the beauty of the Catskills behind. They seem less drawn to other elements of the master design of Frederic Edwin Church (1826–1900): The middle ground of the descending pasture, the undulating line of the woods, and the ornamental lake (created in the 1860s).

Church, renowned for his paintings of the sublime, purchased 126 acres of farmland in 1860 and engaged Richard Morris Hunt to design a modest board-and-batten house on lower ground, called Cosy Cottage, where the family lived until 1872. Olana, built to be visible for miles around, was created after the summit of the hill (eighteen acres) was purchased by the artist in 1868. Calvert Vaux was the consulting architect for his Persian-style fantasy, but Church, influenced by a trip to the Middle East (1868–1870) and by pattern books, devised the major forms, oversaw every detail, and designed the elaborate internal and external decoration. It was furnished with exotic paraphernalia collected on his travels. A splendid new studio wing was built onto the house between 1889 and 1891. Here and in several other areas of the house, examples of this Hudson River School artist are displayed.

He began planting trees in 1863 in designed sweeps, creating spatial relationships between meadow, water, and woods, and using the landscape as a canvas for a series of carefully thought out compositions experienced from different viewing points around the estate. Close attention was given to the drives approaching the house from the north (Church's preferred entrance) and the south, along with the three ornamental carriage paths (7½ miles) running through the property. The more utilitarian farm roads were integrated into what became an "ornamental farm," as were fields, barns, and sheds. Although the Churches spent time in New York, with winters usually in warmer climes to alleviate Church's arthritis, Olana and its designed landscape figured first in his affections.

At his death, Church's youngest son, Louis (1870–1943), inherited Olana and its farms, and his widow remained there until 1964. The house and its contents and 250 acres were saved from auction by the determination of Olana Preservation, which purchased the estate in 1966, transferring it to the care of the state of New York. It opened to the public in 1967.

Currently the Olana Partnership actively supports the state, appointing a curator, Sarah Price, in 2010 to specifically address the legacy of Church's designed landscape. Major new initiatives are planned, including the restoration of Ridge Road (1884–1885) and the North Meadow; the replanting of hundreds of trees; the clearing of sixty acres of second-growth forest to open up the intended views; the replanting of the orchards; and the revitalization of the Fern Bed. Currently there are three full-time gardeners for the 250 historic acres. The small, attractive Mingled Flower Garden of herbaceous plants (c. 1890) below the house has been restored. Some 135,000 visitors are expected annually.

60 OPUS 40

50 Fite Road, Saugerties, NY 12477
TEL: (845) 246-3400
WEBSITE: *www.opus40.org*
SEE MAPS: pp. 99 & 104

Hours: Open Memorial Day weekend through Columbus Day weekend, Fridays, Saturdays, and Sundays (and holiday Mondays) 11:30am–5pm. Admission fee
Location: 109 miles from New York City
Public transportation: None. Nearest station Rhinecliff, 16-1/2 miles
Facilities: Small visitor center and gift shop; flyer and map of grounds; a short monograph, *Harvey Fite's Opus 40* (1986) by Jonathan Richards; basic snacks and sodas; portable restrooms; picnicking on lawn; limited wheelchair accessibility; no dogs
Garden tours: Occasionally, by appointment
Nearby eateries: Saugerties, 6-1/2 miles and Woodstock, 5-1/2 miles

Opus 40—a designed landscape of stone, handcrafted between 1939 and 1976 by Harvey Fite in an abandoned quarry—takes us by surprise. Ramps and staircases lead to lower pools and terraces and ascend to platforms and walkways, the bluestone arranged crisply to achieve curved and flowing wall forms. A nine-ton monolith, installed at the highest point in 1969, stands tall and stately as the unifying focus of this intriguing, man-made environment. Existing trees and newer additions—growing in areas of soil or in constructed roundels—link this monumental structure to the surrounding woods and the distant views of the Overlook and Roundtop Mountains in the Catskills. Sparsely but carefully sited, a grove of silver birches, dwarf pines, juniper, euonymus, and maples add their notes to the scene.

Harvey Fite (1903–1976) bought the quarry as a source of stone for his sculpture in 1938, and built a house on the east lip. A professor in the Fine Arts division at nearby Bard College (1933–1969), he was invited by the Carnegie Institute in 1938 to do sculptural restoration work in Honduras. Deeply impressed by the dry-stone building methods of the ancient Mayans, he began using the heaps of discarded stone to design an outdoor sculpture gallery in New York for his own work. He formalized the water, already in the quarry from the spring, into large pools, building walls and steps leading downward. Realizing by the late 1960s that the scale overpowered his own figurative sculptures, he moved them out—some to a more domestic setting near the house—and continued working in abstract forms and spaces, refining, rebuilding, and pushing out to the northwest to include an area with high cliff walls, which he called the amphitheater.

He built the Quarryman's Museum in the 1970s to display his collection of tools and artifacts, arranging them in patterns and clusters. Almost as a joke, he called his work Opus 40, suggesting that he would require some forty years to complete it; unfortunately, Harvey Fite was killed in an accidental fall in the thirty-seventh year.

The following year his wife, Barbara, formed Opus 40, Inc., with a small group of trustees. She and then (after her death in 1987) her

the jets of water rarely work. The walls with built-in seats, from the 1990s, constructed around islands of trees and shrubs to the south should be clearly indicated as later additions.

Each year some 5,000 visitors experience the six-and-a-half sculptured acres of Opus 40 and its eight and a half acres of woods. Summer concerts incorporate Fite's vision of integrating cultural events into the site. Financial constraints have restricted all but emergency skilled stonework maintenance, however, and except for once-a-week paid help for grass cutting during the season, most work has been contributed over the

son Tad Richards have shouldered the main responsibility of caring for and managing the site, living in the privately owned home on the edge of the quarry. The integrity of Harvey Fite's achievement has been preserved, although duckweed obscures the reflective qualities of the pools, and

years by the family, or by volunteers during twice-a-year cleanups. Opus 40, Inc., is therefore actively looking for a partner or an appropriate organization that can ensure a future for this important landmarked site.

61 PHILIPSBURG MANOR

381 North Broadway, Sleepy Hollow, NY 10591
TEL: (914) 631-8200
WEBSITE: *www.hudsonvalley.org*
SEE MAPS: pp. 99 & 100

Hours: Grounds, buildings, and animal viewing open April 1 through November 1, daily (except Tuesday), 10am–6pm, last tour 5pm. November 2 through December 27, Saturday and Sunday 10am–4pm, last tour 3pm. Optional guided tours by costumed interpreters. Admission fee

Location: 29 miles from New York City

Public transportation: Metro-North to Tarrytown, taxi or walk 1-1/4 miles

Facilities: Visitor center with gift and book section—see *Philipsburg Manor, Upper Mills* by Margaret L. Vetare (2004), Greenhouse Café (plus outdoor area), open 9am–4pm (daily except Tuesday), and restrooms; picnic tables; wheelchair accessible (except second floor of manor house); no dogs

Programming: Educational programs for schoolchildren

Nearby eateries: Sleepy Hollow, and see entry for Kykuit (p. 135)

Also of interest: Stone Barns Center (see p. 137)

Philipsburg—sitting picturesquely on the millpond formed by the damming of the Pocantico River—has a delightful approach across a wooden bridge. Because its visitor center is used as the starting point for the shuttle bus to Kykuit, it is easily accessible, and even though it features a produce rather than an ornamental garden, it is well worth visiting. The interpretation of the milling and trading complex has been redefined to focus on the lives of the twenty-three enslaved Africans who lived and worked there in 1750 under the supervision of a white overseer.

The enclosed rectangular kitchen garden, with its neat raised beds of herbs and vegetables, and roses scrambling along the wooden fencing, is no longer interpreted as a white man's preserve but as a conjectural plot allocated to a slave. This has led to research on nutrition, diet, and cultural preferences, and changes in the planting to include, for example, more beans and white and sweet potatoes among the more mainstream European preferences of the period. Other considerations include the economics involved in selling the surplus produce to the markets in New York, medicinal practices—possibly a blend of African, Indian, and white knowledge—and questions related to climate adaptation.

The great lumbering oxen, the sheep, cows, and chickens, the functioning

gristmill, the productive orchard, the haymaking and grain growing are all part of the story offered to the visitor, as are the interiors of the buildings with their accouterments of the 1750s. Discussion also centers on the role of the powerful ship-owner and merchant Adolph Philipse (1665–1750), the absentee landlord in New York who was the supplier of slaves and goods for Upper Mills, the promoter of white tenant farmers, and the exporter of the flour, lumber, hardtack, and other produce in his ships that sailed down the Hudson to the markets in New York, the West Indies, and beyond.

The mill and its settlement waned in importance after 1750, when the slaves were sold following Philipse's death and flour from the Hudson lost its commercial edge. It went through a series of owners and changes, and when John D. Rockefeller saved the manor as a historic property in 1940, it had become a large house with tennis court and flower gardens called Philipse Castle, and the actual mill had disappeared. Restored and recreated to represent the colonial period and renamed Philipsburg Manor, it opened to the public in 1943. The twenty-five acres are owned by Historic Hudson Valley, an entity formed in 1987 from Sleepy Hollow Restorations. There is no labeling of plants, but the garden section on the Philipsburg Manor website has a list of market vegetables along with those grown to supplement the slaves' diet.

SPRINGSIDE LANDSCAPE RESTORATION

185 Academy Street, Poughkeepsie, NY 12601
TEL: (845) 454-2060
WEBSITE: *www.springsidelandmark.org*
SEE MAPS: pp. 99 & 103

Hours: Grounds open daily, dawn to dusk. Admission free

Location: 82 miles from New York City

Parking: At entrance on Academy Street

Public transportation: Metro-North and Amtrak to Poughkeepsie and Adirondack Trailways and ShortLine, walk 1-3/4 miles or taxi

Facilities: Self-guided trail guides and brochures at kiosk at entrance; no refreshments or restrooms; picnickers welcome (no tables); not wheelchair accessible; dogs on leash

Group garden tours: By appointment, and some scheduled to coincide with special events

Nearby eateries: Poughkeepsie, 1-3/4 miles; Culinary Institute of America, 1946 Campus Drive (Route 9), Hyde Park, 4-1/2 miles

Also of interest: Poughkeepsie Rural Cemetery (1853), 342 South Avenue, Poughkeepsie, 1/4 mile, open 8am–4:30pm; Maple Grove (1850s), 24 Beechwood Avenue (on St. Simeon Properties), Poughkeepsie, 1-1/2 miles; Walkway over the Hudson, 61 Parker Avenue, Poughkeepsie (east side of Hudson), 3-1/4 miles, or 87 Haviland Road, Highland (west side of the Hudson), 4 miles

This is the place for all those interested in American garden history. In 1984 the battle was won to save from development the twenty-acre pleasure grounds remaining from the estate of Matthew Vassar, which was also a model farm. All but one of the ornamental and utilitarian buildings have gone, and the landscape designed by the leading horticulturist, writer, and tastemaker of the day, Andrew Jackson Downing, from 1850 until his death in 1852, are interpreted through its archeological remains.

The visitor is first struck by the charming 1851 Gothic Revival porter's lodge (privately owned), and then sets off, with an excellent trail guide from the kiosk, along the cleared carriage ways and paths, through the deciduous woods. Notice boards—many with reproductions of 1867 engravings or photos—inspire one to visualize where once were small pavilions, gardens, fountains, ponds, meadows, the flower and the vegetable garden, and the view points. The design made use of knolls and rock outcroppings, supplemented

by appropriate tree planting, and channeled water from springs to compose a landscape with both highly "picturesque" and "beautiful" elements. A rustic seat here and there encourages our inclination to recreate the scenes.

Matthew Vassar (1792–1868), brewer, philanthropist, and the founder of Vassar College (see p. 178), bought the land in 1850 as a site for a rural cemetery. When another area was subsequently chosen, he decided to build his own summer retreat there, which he called Springside. The main villa, designed by Downing and his new partner Calvert Vaux (1824–1895), was never built, the Vassars preferring to live in the ten-room Gothic Revival gardener's cottage. It too has gone, but Springside was so celebrated in the nineteenth century that much is known about it from published descriptions and illustrations, archival material in the Vassar College library, and the three paintings of the estate in 1852 by Henry Gritten (1818–1873) that hang in the Loeb Art Center at Vassar.

Springside Landscape Restoration was organized in 1984 to acquire, protect, and restore Andrew Jackson Downing's historic landscape. The grounds are cleared and new trees are being planted by some ten to fifteen volunteers. Following the Master and Maintenance Plan of 1989 and the subsequent update, the organization tackles projects one by one, the next being to realign historic paths and restore the Jet Vale Fountain, a signature element of the landscape design. They also hope to acquire two critical acres of the original property before they are developed.

63 SPRINGWOOD: HOME OF FRANKLIN D. ROOSEVELT NATIONAL HISTORIC SITE

4097 Albany Post Road, Hyde Park, NY 12538
TEL: (845) 229-9115
WEBSITE: *www.nps.gov/hofr*
SEE MAPS: pp. 99 & 103

Hours: Grounds open dawn to dusk; house open seven days a week, 9am–5pm (except Thanksgiving, Christmas, and New Year's Day). Admission free to grounds; charge for house tour

Location: 88 miles from New York City

Public transportation: ShortLine bus to Hyde Park; Metro-North or Amtrak to Poughkeepsie, then taxi, 5 miles. Or Metro-North, May through October, to Poughkeepsie and then Roosevelt Ride, shuttle service. See www.nps.gov/hofr, or call National Park Service at (845) 229-5320

Facilities: Henry A. Wallace Visitor and Education Center, where tickets, tours, brochures, trail maps, exhibits, an introductory film, and restrooms are available; also Nesbitt Café, open April 1 through October 31, with additional seating within a garden of Russian sage, roses, and grasses; New Deal bookstore; picnic tables by the car park and on the south side of the visitor center; buildings and central site are wheelchair accessible; tram from the Wallace Center to the FDR house for docent-led tours; dogs on leash

Programming: Ongoing, particularly on Roosevelt and American history

Nearby eateries: Hyde Park village; Culinary Institute of America, Hyde Park south on Route 9, 2 miles; list at visitor center (see also www.dutchesstourism.com)

Other gardens: The Beatrix Farrand Garden is on the grounds (see p. 120)

Also of interest: The FDR Presidential Library and Museum on the grounds; the Eleanor Roosevelt National Historic Site, Val Kill (www.nps.gov/elro), Eleanor Roosevelt's private retreat—accessible by shuttle from Springwood and on foot (1-1/2 miles) using the Roosevelt Farm Lane Trail, which starts opposite the FDR entrance

Standing on a bluff above the Hudson River, Springwood is the 1915 enlargement for Sara Roosevelt (1854–1941) and her son Franklin Delano Roosevelt (1882–1945) of the house bought by Sara's husband, James Roosevelt (1828–1900), in 1867, along with 110 acres. Its best features, by Francis L. V. Hoppin, are the serene, symmetrical neo-Georgian entrance facade and the south-facing terrace where stunning views of the

Hudson and the mountains beyond were once to be seen. The bedrooms of Sara, Franklin, and his wife, Eleanor (1884–1962), on the second floor also benefited from this prospect.

The large country seat also included other estate houses; a designed landscape with carriage drives, orchards, and meadows; an ornamental garden, greenhouses, and kitchen garden; agriculture and livestock; woods and forests.

The Rose Garden, in the former large fruit and vegetable garden of the 1880s, adjacent to the main house and surrounded by walls and a hemlock hedge, has the main floricultural display. Designed in 1912 for Sara Roosevelt, it contains beds of vibrant annuals in blocks of color, day lilies, and peonies, and the rose garden itself at the east end with a thriving array of floribundas and tea roses. There in a band of grass lie the graves of both Franklin and Eleanor Roosevelt, the large white marble memorial simply stating their names and dates. The two dogs, Fala and Chief, are buried behind. As Eleanor later wrote, "The place he looked upon as the most beautiful was the rose garden, in which his mother always, up to the last few years of her life, picked her own roses, and this was where he wished to be buried."

The greenhouses (1907), which provided additional roses along with potted plants for the house, can be visited. The cone-shaped tower of James Roosevelt's stables (1886;

vernacular adaptation of Queen Anne style) makes a felicitous backdrop to the ensemble. The picturesque Carpenter's Gothic of the gardener's cottage (c. 1845–1850) is seen at the edge of the car park.

The interest in managing the estate was passed on from James Roosevelt, the gentleman farmer from old-stock landed gentry, to his son, FDR. Together they had purchased trees in Europe in the 1880s, and many varieties were subsequently planted. FDR increased the acreage of the estate significantly (at one point to 1,200 acres) and while his mother managed the house and its immediate grounds he developed sound wood, farm, and land practices. His experiments at Springwood fed national policies in forestry, agriculture, and the environment during his presidential years (1933–1945).

Despite his mother's emphasis on their landed gentry roots, Franklin Roosevelt left Springwood to the American people, with lifetime rights for Eleanor and their children. When these rights were waived, the house and some thirty-three acres were transferred in 1945 to the National Park Service. The Presidential Library and Museum had already been set up in 1941.

Accommodating the 126,000 visitors a year has necessitated many changes, such as new entrance drives and larger car parks. Now, with the reacquisition of land to 500 acres, a General Management Plan (draft 2010), directed toward the next twenty years, is taking up the challenge of broadening the scope of the interpretation. Opening up the views of the Hudson River, using heirloom varieties of plants in the flower garden, and introducing and showcasing management strategies for the woods are a few of the items under discussion, all with a view to revealing more fully the Roosevelts' relationship with their property.

64 STAATSBURG STATE HISTORIC SITE (MILLS MANSION)

Old Post Road (or 75 Mills Mansion Drive),
Staatsburg, NY 12580
TEL: (845) 889-8851
WEBSITE: *www.nysparks.com; www.staatsburg.org*
SEE MAPS: pp. 99 & 103

Hours: Grounds open dawn to dusk. House usually open April 1 through October 31, Wednesday–Sunday 11am–4pm, special hours in December. Call to confirm. Admission free to grounds, charge for house

Location: 98 miles from New York City

Public transportation; Metro-North or Amtrak to Poughkeepsie, taxi 11 miles, or Amtrak to Rhinecliff, taxi 6-3/4 miles

Facilities: Brochure/trail map in museum shop in the basement, also books and gifts, tickets to house, restroom; no refreshments; restrooms also on the waterfront; picnicking (bring a blanket); first floor of house and carriage drives wheelchair accessible; dogs on leash

Programming: The Friends of Mills Mansion sponsor events in conjunction with the Office of Parks, Recreation, and Historic Preservation

Group garden tours: By appointment

Nearby eateries: Rhinebeck, 5 miles north

Also of interest: The 998 acres of the Mills-Norrie State Park is made up of the two connecting parks and the Dinsmore Golf Course, open to the public

This imposing mansion, a product of the Gilded Age, sits well on the bluff with graded lawns sweeping down to small bays and grassy banks. Staatsburgh is the only Hudson River mansion not to have access to the water cut off by the railroad. Designed for Ogden (1857–1929) and Ruth Livingston Mills (1855–1920) by Stanford White in 1894 (shortly before his partner, Charles McKim, created the nearby Hyde Park for the Vanderbilts), it was based on the great Palladian British houses of the eighteenth century. Mr. Mills's wealth, inherited from his father's banking, railroads, and metal mining interests, and his wife's family's prominence allowed the couple to greatly expand the existing house she had inherited. Owning houses in New York, Newport, San Mateo, California, and Paris, they used Staatsburgh primarily for periods between September and January.

The entrance drive, with good views of grassy dales edged by mixed woods, ascends to the large porticoed entrance of the white stuccoed house. Thought to be the model for Edith Wharton's Bellomont in *The House of Mirth*,

Staatsburgh, with its public rooms of ample proportions and its opulent furnishings (still in place), summons up visions of house parties and large-scale entertaining. Palms in Chinese pots, ferns, and many floral decorations, although artificial, cleverly suggest how the Edwardian interiors were once decorated with flowers and plants from the estate's large state-of-the-art greenhouses.

Ogden Livingston Mills (1884–1937) inherited the estate from his parents, and it then passed to his sister, Gladys Phipps (1883–1970), who donated the house and 192 acres to the state of New York in 1938. The Friends of Mills Mansion, founded in 1988, helps run the house tours and is involved in the ongoing restoration projects.

The enormous cost of preserving the house and its interiors has left the grounds neglected. Maples and underbrush have invaded carriage roads, pools, and paths. In an overgrown area, photo boards help identify the location of the former greenhouses. A tree planting program is replacing some of the dead, diseased, and overmature specimens, and the Office of Parks, Recreation, and Historic Preservation hopes eventually to clear the network of paths. Perhaps the wall along the road will be restored one day. Some 25,000 people visit the house annually, and more enjoy the views, the river walk, and the existing trails, maintained by the staff of the Mills-Norrie State Park.

 STONECROP GARDENS
81 Stonecrop Lane, Cold Spring,
NY 10516
TEL: (845) 265-2000
WEBSITE: *www.stonecrop.org*
SEE MAPS: pp. 99 & 102

Hours: April through October, gardens open Monday–Friday, as well as the 1st and 3rd Saturdays, 10am–5pm. Open until dusk on Fridays, May through September. House not open. Admission fee

Location: 62 miles from New York City

Public transportation: Metro-North to Cold Spring; taxi 6-1/2 miles

Facilities: Visitor center in the Potting Shed—collect map, brochure and plant list; wear sensible shoes; no refreshments; two portable toilets in car park, two restrooms in Horse Barn; discreet picnicking in specified areas; limited wheelchair accessibility; no dogs

Programming: Horticultural, yoga

Group garden tours: By appointment

Nearby eateries: Cold Spring, 6-1/2 miles; list available in the Potting Shed

Nearby: Fahnestock State Park, 1498 Route 301, Carmel, 4 miles

Stonecrop—with twelve acres of display gardens surrounded by fifty-one acres of fields and pastures—is now a destination garden for both the horticulturist and the general garden visitor. It began as a summer retreat for Frank and Anne Cabot: a new hilltop house by Polhemus & Coffin built in 1957–1958 on thin and rocky pasture land, 1,100 feet above sea level, and technically in zone 5. The Cabots fenced off an area for perennials and vegetables, but their first love was, appropriately, alpines. They hired the specialist Rex Murfitt in 1960, and Stonecrop Nurseries came into being (its greenhouses and exterior beds remain). The mail order business lasted only six years, but the collections and

display of alpines increased and are still one of the great attractions.

Over the years, particularly from 1975 onward, thanks to great quantities of new soil, compost, and mulch, old gardens were enlarged, new ones developed, and water (offering yet more possibilities for plantings) became an important and delightful component. Within "rooms" and courtyards—sheltered by the house, catching a southern exposure, or shaded by trees and shrubs—a multitude of microclimates serve the gardens. The 1997 conservatory, partly suspended over the pond, broadens the displays with tropicals, Mediterranean plants, nonhardy evergreens, the Australian collection, and succulents.

Not to be missed is the Flower Garden, redesigned in 2003 by Caroline Burgess, director since 1984. In spring it provides an exuberant display of bulbs in the irregular pattern of beds, while in high summer the lush semihardy perennials, tropicals, and unusual annuals take over. The beds are color-themed; many of the plants are very tall, and the four steeple trellises carrying annual and perennial vines rise up even higher. Colors are repeated here and there, creating a sense of cohesiveness.

After the stunning views of meadows and hills from the front of the house, the Lake and Hillside Garden offers a totally different experience. Below a wide rock ledge, the former fifty-foot drop has become a rocky terrain of little streams and pools and meandering paths with crevices and ledges and soil-filled pockets for alpines, thymes (and other Mediterranean plants), dwarf conifers, shrubs, and aquatic plants. The garden, orchestrated by Sicilian mason Cono Reale in the 1980s, is a feat of sensitive rock placement and water manipulation, and the view to the lake below—its two parts connected by the flintstone bridge and backed by Metasequoia Grove—is picture perfect. The walk continues to the Systematic beds of 2003 (planted by families)—an interesting project, but difficult to do well—or to the Woodland Garden, developed in the 1980s, where spring ephemerals are the special draw, with specimens trees incorporated, as they are elsewhere.

In 1992 the Cabots moved to Canada, and the gardens were opened to the public by the newly formed Stonecrop Gardens, Inc. A horticultural internship and a developing School of Practical Horticulture help to carry out its educational mission of promoting the highest standards of horticultural practice, while for the general public, temporary labels with numbers (identified on the list provided) highlight a seasonal selection of plants. The gardens are cared for by six full-time and five part-time gardeners and two administrators. About 7,000 people visited in 2009.

66 STORM KING ART CENTER

Old Pleasant Hill Road, Mountainville,
NY 10953
TEL: (845) 534-3115
WEBSITE: *www.stormking.org*
SEE MAPS: pp. 99 & 102

Hours: Open April 1 through October 31, Wednesday–Sunday 10am–5:30pm; and November 1 through approximately November 14, Wednesday–Sunday, 10am–5pm. Also open 10am–5:30pm on the holiday Mondays of Memorial Day, Independence Day, Labor Day, and Columbus Day. Admission fee

Location: 60 miles from New York City

Public transportation: ShortLine bus (800) 631-8405 to Storm King

Facilities: Map/guide and daily events flyer at admission booth and also at visitor center in the museum building with accoustiguide for rent and bookshop (see *Earth, Sky and Sculpture: Storm King Art Center*, 2000); beverage vending machines; Storm King Café (near north parking area) on weekends; restrooms in various places; picnicking in designated areas; wheelchair accessible; trams run regularly through the grounds and visitors may board and disembark at various stopping places; no dogs

Programming: Daily docent-guided walking tours and a wide variety of weekend programs

Nearby eateries: Cornwall, 2 miles; list available from visitor center

Storm King Art Center features monumental sculpture in great open spaces, as well as more modestly scaled pieces in intimate settings. Here the manmade meets the strength and beauty of the Hudson Highlands in harmonious or provocative interplay. A museum—formerly a country house—on the brow of the hill offers changing exhibitions.

It started small in 1958, the vision of Ralph E. (Ted) Ogden (1895–1974) of the Star Expansion Company (bolts and engineering), and then of his son-in-law and business partner, H. Peter Stern (b. 1928). Originally thirty-two acres, with a focus on Hudson River School artists and small scale semifigurative European sculpture, it has increased to 500 acres, its magnificent views carefully protected by an additional 2,100 acres donated to the Open Space Institute.

The sculpture, which was clustered around or near the house, has grown in scope and size, now reaching farther into the landscape, itself regraded, replanted, and realigned to accommodate exciting additions of a later generation of artists. Mark di Suvero's urban pieces made of industrial material look superb in this rural setting, as do those by Alexander Calder, Alexander Liberman, and Robert Grosvenor. Other artists have been invited to create site-specific sculpture: the precision of Richard Serra's *Schunnemunk Fork* (1990–1991) holds its own on ten acres; Andy Goldsworthy's meandering wall (1997–1998) curves around trees, disappears into the pond, and reemerges to end at the thruway; Maya Lin's waves (2007–2009) create a dialogue with the silhouettes of the hills.

William A. Rutherford Sr.—the landscape architect for Storm King from 1960 until his death in 2005—designed the specially constructed hillock near the museum for the Noguchi (1977–1978), the remarkable site for the Kenneth Snelson (1974), and the area for the David Smith sculptures. He also planted the avenues of trees (maple and pin oak) and started reducing the acres that require mowing by establishing wide paths between large shaped areas of longer grass—thereby enhancing some middle-ground views as well.

Since 1996, landscape designer Darrel Morrison has extended these practices in a most exciting way. Using a variety of native grasses and a legume, partridge pea, he composes on a very large scale. Just as the trees present startling changes in color through the seasons, so these shapes evolve, making bold statements and creating a dynamic setting for many of the sculptures. The goal is to replace eighty of the two hundred acres of formerly mown grass with these new compositions. The woods beyond provide a setting for smaller art works and offer nature trails in their furthest reaches.

Storm King is a nonprofit, privately sponsored foundation welcoming some 75,000 visitors annually. The future plans of David R. Collens, the director since 1974, include reviewing and expanding visitor services and programs, commissioning new site-specific work as funds become available, and dealing with the ongoing conservation and maintenance of the outdoor sculpture in an evolving landscape.

67 SUNNYSIDE

3 West Sunnyside Lane, Irvington, NY 10533
TEL: (914) 631-8200; 914-591-8763 (WEEKENDS)
WEBSITE: *www.hudsonvalley.org*
SEE MAPS: pp. 99 & 100

Hours: Grounds and house usually open April 1 through October 31, daily (except Tuesdays), 11am–5pm, last tour 4pm; November through December, Saturday and Sunday 10am–4pm, last tour 3pm. Separate admission for house and grounds; 45-minute tours with costumed guides, approximately every 30 minutes

Location: 29 miles from New York City

Public transportation: Metro-North to Tarrytown, taxi 2-1/2 miles

Facilities: Visitor center for brochure with plan of grounds; gift shop with good book section; restrooms; picnic tables; no refreshments; wheelchair accessible, except second floor of house; no dogs

Group garden tours: By appointment

Nearby eateries: Irvington, 1 mile; Tarrytown, 2-1/2 miles. See also extensive list at www.hudsonvalley.org/content/view/86/267

Washington Irving (1783–1859) had already achieved international fame as a writer when, after seventeen years abroad, he sought a property along the Hudson River. In 1835 he purchased a small Dutch farmhouse in Tarrytown, NY, and with the help of a friend, the artist George Harvey, he remodeled it, creating stepped, gabled Dutch (or Scottish) additions, dormer windows, tall chimneys, a long porch with gothic detailing overlooking the river and, in 1847, a "Spanish" tower providing guest and servants' quarters.

His Sunnyside—though an eclectic mixture of styles and historical periods and cultural associations—formed a picturesque whole. Except for a four-year period in Spain (1842–1846), he remained in his "cottage," his "little snuggery," writing, among other books, his five-volume *Life of George Washington*, entertaining a stream of visitors, and, as a country gentleman, indulging with great pleasure in his modest farm (at one point twenty-seven acres). Animals, the poultry house, the orchard, and vegetable gardens helped supply the produce for his household of relatives, and the cutting garden produced flowers for the house. Horses grazed in the meadow or were kept in the stables.

The landscape was also carefully considered—trees were cleared for river views, and other features included a little cascade and a stream, a small pond, a short path circling through the

woods, and, much to his delight, roses and honeysuckle climbing profusely over the porch and ivy (from Melrose Abbey in Scotland, with its Sir Walter Scott associations) on the walls. Well-spaced trees stood on the lawn, and on the north side a squat icehouse, designed to look like a little chapel, lent a bit of whimsy. Sunnyside was an idyllic retreat, but already touched by the coming of the railroad in 1847. Irving bitterly regretted that he had sold his water frontage, and today the modern electric cables slicing through the views further diminish the charm.

The fame of Sunnyside and its landscape spread during Irving's lifetime through prints, illustrations and descriptions in books and magazines, and even advertisements that appropriated the symbolism of the cozy American cottage and its naturalistic setting. The great garden proselytizer Andrew Jackson Downing (1815–1852) gave it his stamp of approval as early as 1841, using it as an illustration in his *Theory and Practice of Landscape Gardening*. Irving, never very well off, encouraged the publicity to promote his books.

Years later, when John D. Rockefeller Jr. bought the property from an Irving descendent (1945), the 1850s were taken as the defining period for the interiors of the house and the landscape. Later additions were removed (except for the stables and the gardener's cottage) and early sections rebuilt.

Sunnyside, with its fifty-five acres, is owned and run by Historic Hudson Valley, set up by Rockefeller in 1951. The grounds are maintained by three part-time gardeners. Docent-led tours and programs for children are the main educational events, with the site attracting 26,650 people in 2009. Sadly, an out-of-scale car park, overbuilt stone bridges, intrusive culverts, and a green pond interfere with its picturesque qualities. But a small cutting garden (including a selection of nineteenth-century favorites), with vegetables alongside, and some fruit trees in the orchard continue to charm.

68 UNTERMYER PARK & GARDENS

945 North Broadway, Yonkers, NY 10701
TEL: (914) 377-6450
WEBSITE: *www.yonkersny.gov; www.untermyer.com*
SEE MAPS: pp. 99 & 100

Hours: Grounds and gardens open 8am–dusk; garden hours may vary. Admission free
Location: 18 miles from New York City
Public transportation: Metro-North to Greystone, walk or taxi 1 mile,
or Metro-North to Yonkers, Bee-Line bus #6 or taxi 2-1/2 miles
Facilities: Restrooms at the community center at entrance; no refreshments;
picnicking in the park; wheelchair accessible; no dogs
Programming: Occasional concerts in the summer
Nearby eateries: Yonkers, 2-1/4 miles
Also of interest: Pier at foot of Main Street in Yonkers and the downtown
waterfront renovations; Hudson River Museum, 511 Warburton Avenue,
Yonkers, 1 mile

The extraordinary Untermyer Park and Gardens were bequeathed, without an endowment, by Samuel Untermyer (1858–1940) to the city of Yonkers. The sixteen acres were part of the 150-acre country-house estate of the well-known attorney, businessman, and democrat who in 1899 bought the house, Greystone, from the estate of Samuel J. Tilden (1814–1886), whose bequest helped form the New York Public Library.

Untermyer hired the architect Joseph H. Freelander (d. 1943) to remodel the house (no longer extant) and William Welles Bosworth (1868–1966) to design the gardens (see also Kykuit, p. 135) and refurbish the greenhouses. The engineer Charles Welford Leavitt (1971–1928) masterminded the

fountains. The site is superb—on a bluff above the Hudson River looking west to the Palisades. Today, seeing what has been saved and restored after years of neglect is exhilarating, while the task of ending further deterioration and managing land thickly overgrown and eroded is more than daunting.

The visitor is drawn irresistibly to a portal in a high, fawn-colored castellated brick wall, where through the shade of weeping beeches a long, narrow canal appears, running like a reflecting ribbon to a shallow amphitheater, heralded by sphinxes on double columns. Water also forms the cross axis, traversed by stone bridges and bordered by such brightly colored summer bedding as cannas and geraniums, with green pyramids of cypress. Currently the fountains in the canals are still. Classical columned tower pavilions (no longer accessible) stand high on the four corners of the walls, and a few more trees add height within. Known as the Grecian Garden, it draws on formal European and Mogul gardens in an eclectic and fanciful way.

From the circular temple structure on the open west side, a view of the grand lower balustraded terrace with its large (now dry) mosaic pool extends over a jungle of vine encased trees to the river. Descending the Vista Staircase to the north allows for a further viewing point defined by a balustrade and more classical pillars. Across the lawns to the south, in what is now a scruffy woodland area, one discovers a temple gazebo with a filigreed roof perched on large boulders with a grotto below—suffering, unfortunately, from neglect and graffiti.

The Yonkers Parks Department owns the Untermyer Park and Gardens, now increased to thirty-three acres, which are looked after by its general maintenance staff. A grant of $100,000 in 2005 from New York State and another of $65,000 in 2009 helped to save some of the garden's hardscape, but more funds are required to complete the restoration of the mosaic pool. Plans will next address the carriage trails for better pedestrian access to the outer areas. The Untermyer Performing Arts Council is seeking a more permanent structure for the summer concerts in the park.

69 VAN CORTLANDT MANOR

500 South Riverside Avenue,
Croton-on-Hudson, NY 10520
TEL: (914) 631-8200; (914) 271-8981 (WEEKENDS)
WEBSITE: *www.hudsonvalley.org*
SEE MAPS: pp. 99 & 100

Hours: Grounds and house open late May through early September, Thursday–
Sunday (and Monday holidays) 10am–5pm; last tour of house at 4pm. October,
open for Blaze evenings only. November through late December, Saturdays
and Sundays 10am–4pm; last tour of house at 3pm. House tour approximately
every 30 minutes by costumed guides. Admission fee to grounds, or house
and grounds

Location: 38 miles from New York City

Public transportation: Metro-North or Amtrak to Croton-Harmon; taxi 3/4 mile
(walk is not pedestrian-friendly)

Facilities: Visitor center, brochure with map; gift shop; no refreshments; restrooms;
picnic tables; not wheelchair accessible on second floor of Manor House or Tenant
House; no dogs

Programming: Family events; schools programs

Nearby eateries: Croton-on-Hudson, 2 miles; see website for list, under
"Welcome"

On the banks of the Croton River,
close to where it flows into the Hudson,
lies Van Cortlandt Manor—restored
and recreated to represent the period
following the Revolutionary War,
1790–1814. Distinctive wooden
porches surround the stone house on
three sides, with a double staircase
leading up to the main floor. The
property (including the ferry house
and various outbuildings) celebrates
the life of the energetic land owner,
patriot, and political leader Pierre
Van Cortlandt (1721–1814), his wife,
Joanna, and their family.

Inheriting 1,225 acres in 1748,

Pierre moved his family to Croton the
following year, built the house, acquired
a further 3,138 acres, and proceeded to
manage and develop his lightly settled
property—building sawmills and
gristmills and sending his cash crops
of wheat and meat down the Hudson
to the markets. The elegant interiors
of his house, which was renovated and
enlarged after suffering damage during
the Revolution, contain colonial and
federal furniture, family paintings,
Chinese export porcelain, and other
telling objects, many original and
others acquired. The airy kitchen on
the ground floor features eighteenth-

herb and vegetable patches offer the produce the household would have required. If the old varieties are kept, this exercise in garden history will be both an educational tool and an attractive display. Elsewhere are lilacs, dogwood, catalpa, linden, and general wooded areas.

After being owned for 257 years by the Van Cortlandt family, the manor was sold out of the family in 1945. John D. Rockefeller acquired it and the remaining five acres in 1953, buying additional land soon after. The research staff from Colonial Williamsburg (an earlier JDR project) was enlisted to decide on its

century cooking equipment, and the guides discuss cooking methods, baking, recipes (for food and medicine), homemade alcoholic drinks, imported foods and garden produce, and the role slaves played.

The conjectural reconstruction (in the 1950s) of some garden areas represent, in microcosm, the plants and flowers grown both for ornamental and utilitarian purposes during the New Nation period. A "Long Walk" of brick extends from the manor toward the Ferry House, with pretty borders on each side featuring bulbs, perennials, and annuals such as tulips, borage, iris, foxglove, St. John's Wort, and columbine. Above this walk appears the orchard, with a few apple, quince, plum, and peach trees. Below,

interpretation. Nineteenth-century buildings were removed, and Van Cortlandt Manor was opened to the public in 1959 as a property of Sleepy Hollow Restorations, the forerunner of present-day Historic Hudson Valley. It currently has thirty-six acres. Only herbs are labeled, but a list of plants found on the Long Walk and in the herb and vegetable gardens is available.

70 VASSAR COLLEGE ARBORETUM & GARDENS

124 Raymond Avenue, Poughkeepsie, NY 12604
TEL: (845) 437-5686
WEBSITE: *http://vcencyclopedia.vassar.edu/buildings-grounds*
SEE MAPS: pp. 99 & 103

Hours: Grounds open dawn to dusk. Admission free
Location: 80 miles from New York City
Parking: Check in at main gate, obtain visitor's pass for designated spaces
Public transportation: Metro-North to Poughkeepsie, taxi 3-1/2 miles
Facilities: Guide and map from College Center (to the rear of main building) with the Retreat café and restrooms; restrooms also in main building; picnic tables in the Shakespeare Garden and by Sunset Lake (1912); most areas wheelchair accessible and main campus can be toured by vehicle; dogs on leash
Group garden tours: By appointment with college horticulturist
Nearby eateries: Arlington business district, immediately to north of the campus
Also of interest: Frances Lehman Loeb Art Center on campus to right of main entrance. Three paintings (1852) by Henry Gritten show Springside, Matthew Vassar's home (see p. 160). There is also a sculpture garden. Walkway over the Hudson, 61 Parker Avenue, Poughkeepsie, 3 miles, or 87 Haviland Road, Highland (on west side of the Hudson), 5-1/2 miles

Vassar College has been linked with trees since its founding. The school was established in 1861 for the education of women by Matthew Vassar (1792–1868), who owned the local brewery. The large brick Main Hall (1861–1865), still the center of the campus, was designed by James Renwick in a French Second Empire style. Its treeless, flat site—formerly the Dutchess County Racetrack—must have inspired Vassar to lay out the first plantings himself in 1865, and (almost) each graduating class since 1868 has ensured the ongoing renewal of the collection by donating or adopting a tree. The formal creation of the arboretum and a sustaining fund was the prescient initiative of the class of 1875.

Some 230 species and hundreds of individual specimens grow throughout the main campus. White pine, Norway spruce, and red oaks line the entrance drive, and single trees or groups are scattered on the open lawns: a mixture of natives and nonnatives— yellowwood and purple European beech, sycamore and golden raintree, some venerable, others still to realize their mature forms. Many of them are labeled in this area.

To the rear of Main is the conifer collection, with patterned beds of annuals and tropicals creating a vivid contrast (as they do elsewhere on the campus). Happily, the commitment to green spaces and plantings has encouraged the siting of car parks on the periphery. The addition of many new buildings over the years has been accompanied by careful attention to landscape design, circulation, new environmental concerns in consultation with Sasaki Associates, Diana Balmori Associates, and currently Michael Van Valkenburgh Associates, which, in 2010, drafted a new Master Plan.

The Shakespeare Garden, created in 1916, has gone through several incarnations, most recently in the late 1980s. Entered (no signs) through a latticework arch for roses from the parking lot beneath Olmsted Hall or by a path leading from Sunset Lake, it's a tranquil, flower-filled

spot (with seating). A sundial at the main intersection of brick pathways within the rectangle is surrounded by brick-edged beds containing an array of perennials. Up the slope, beds of annuals and tropicals provide further color. Just two beds of herbs at the top of the garden continue the link to Shakespeare, as many others failed to survive. The three squat little sculptures in the garden belonged to a set imported by Vassar from Italy in the 1850s for Springside (see p. 160)

One hopes that the ubiquitous presence of trees leaves all of the 2,450 students with a lasting appreciation of this legacy. In addition, the Vassar Farm and Ecological Preserve (550 acres), reached from Hooker Avenue, directly involves students through classes in natural history, ecology, botany, and earth science classes. Student assistants also help the two

full-time gardeners with the care of the eighty-acre central campus.

The Vassar Arboretum Index: A Portable Guide to the Trees of Vassar Campus is under way and will include some fifty notable tree species with descriptions and photographs.

WETHERSFIELD GARDEN

214 Pugsley Hill Road, Amenia, NY 12501
TEL: (845) 373-8037
WEBSITE: None
SEE MAPS: pp. 99 & 103

Hours: Garden open June through September, Wednesday, Friday, and Saturday noon–5pm; house and Carriage House open by appointment, June through September. Call for information. Admission charge to grounds and tours

Location: 95 miles from New York City

Public transportation: None

Facilities: Brochure and garden map outside restrooms in car park; *The Wethersfield Garden* by Henry Hope Reed (1998) and *The Wethersfield Carriage Collection* by Jeanne Stalker with Maurice St. George (2003) available for purchase; no refreshments; picnic tables in grove; wheelchair accessible on gravel or grass paths; no dogs

Garden tours: By appointment

Nearby eateries: Millbrook, 10-1/4 miles; Amenia, 7 miles; list on request

Also of interest: Dutchess Wine Trail (*www.dutchesswinetrail.com*)

A beautiful approach with open views of cattle and horses grazing in wooden fenced fields leads past the home farm and climbs up the drive to Weathersfield—sitting on the ridge of a hill behind a shelter belt of white pines and Norway spruce. Chauncey D. Stillman (1907–1989), philanthropist, conservationist, gentleman farmer, and National City Bank (now Citibank) heir, initially bought forty-seven acres and in 1938 built a red brick Georgian-style country house, designed by Bancel LaFarge.

The garden draws upon the classical vocabulary of formal Italian gardens and their interpretation through the early twentieth-century Beaux-Arts style (see also Kykuit, p. 135). Every shape and form is exactly calibrated in this marvel of harmonious geometry that extends both horizontally by long axes, north to south and east to west, as well as vertically, through clipped hedges and trees of varying heights, breadths, and colors.

The self-guided tour suggests a route through garden rooms and along terraces, taking in vistas that terminate at a sculpture, an urn, a belvedere, and a fountain, or lead the eye out to sweeps of pasture land and hills, with a Palladian-style arch placed in the middle distance. Yew is used for large cones and balls and low hedging; arborvitae for an arch and the amazing alley of twenty-four-foot-high "walls"; linden for another hedge; and European beech for a long pleached tunnel. Shaped weeping beech adds tall accents, and viburnum and European dwarf cranberry serve for low delineations. Softer forms come from lilacs, magnolias, and Korean dogwoods and accents of strong color from Mr. Stillman's fuchsias ('Black Prince'), still propagated in the greenhouses.

Landscape architect Evelyn N. Poehler worked with Mr. Stillman from 1947 to 1976, designing all the gardens and pools except for the Inner Garden, created by Bryan J. Lynch when Wethersfield was built. Within this enclosed space bordered by perennials, a narrow Persian rivulet canal runs parallel to a shady pergola of vines, backed by katsura trees. On an upper terrace, four patterned compartments of bedding-out introduce a new note, with three great cut-leafed beeches beyond.

Another feature, rather bizarre, is the wilderness that lies outside the three acres of tended gardens. Carriage drives loop through the woodland, with classical characters, sculptured by Peter Watts and Josef Stachura (late 1960s and 1970s), displayed along the way—a throwback to an earlier period.

As Mr. Stillman got older, he turned from hunting to carriage driving and breeding topclass Hackney horses. His guests were treated to two-hour drives along his twenty miles of carriage roads—a link to the customs of the British eighteenth-century gentry. The superb Carriage Collection can be visited, as can the house itself (separate reservations).

Wethersfield and its 1,200 acres are owned by the Homeland Foundation, Inc., which manages the house, garden, and farms. The ten-acre garden and wilderness (the section open to the public) is cared for by two gardeners, one arborist, and two groundskeepers (all full-time), and three or four seasonal employees under the supervision of a full-time administrator. Some 3,000 people visit the garden each year, and 600 the house. There is no labeling, but the book, *The Wethersfield Garden*, is helpful. Preservation of the original sixty-year-old garden remains the goal.

72 WILDERSTEIN HISTORIC SITE

330 Morton Road, Rhinebeck, NY 12572
TEL: (845) 876-4818
WEBSITE: *www.wilderstein.org*
SEE MAPS: pp. 99 & 103

Hours: Grounds open daily, 9am–dusk. Self-guided trail guide available from gift shop during tour hours and from the Wilderstein website. House tour: May through October, Thursday–Sunday noon–4pm; also weekends Thanksgiving through December

Location: 109 miles from New York City

Parking: Enter through main gate during tour hours; use designated trails parking area at rear gate at other times

Public transportation: Amtrak to Rhinecliff, walk or taxi 2 miles

Facilities: Basement gift shop during tour hours with Suckley/Hudson Valley books, introductory video on Margaret Suckley, restrooms; no refreshments; picnicking; house partially wheelchair accessible, grounds not; dogs on leash

Group house and garden tours: By appointment

Nearby eateries: Rhinebeck, 4-1/2 miles and Rhinecliff, 2 miles; information from docents

Also of interest: Poet's Walk, River Road, County Road 103, Redhook, 7 miles

The pumpkin-colored Victorian Queen Anne house (set off by plum, green, and cream trim), with its asymmetrical skyline, beckoning veranda, and porte-cochère, is the star attraction at the moment. But the restoration of the grounds—long neglected and overgrown—has tremendous potential to reconnect the house with its original landscape, designed by the renowned Calvert Vaux and his son in 1890, and to convey more fully the outdoor activities and interests of the Suckley family.

The forty-acre Hudson River site was bought in 1852 by Thomas Holy Suckley whose fortune came from the family export trade and real-estate investments. His Italianate villa was enlarged and remodeled for his son, Robert Bowne Suckley, and his wife by Arnout Cannon in 1888. This house—little changed and last inhabited by Margaret (Daisy) Suckley (1891–1991), a distant cousin and confidante of Franklin D. Roosevelt—is the one we visit today.

Vaux's romantic picturesque style epitomizes the kind of landscaping many wealthy American families desired at the time. Developed in the 1840s, it remained popular for many decades: open lawns with specimen trees around the house, a curved

gardener and some two hundred volunteers. Events throughout the year, such as the Daffodil Tea and Fala Gala (a doggy event named after the Scottie given by Margaret Suckley to FDR), help bring in the public and attract supporters.

Gregory J. Sokaris, executive director of Wilderstein Historic Site, describes the major landscape challenges: soil erosion exacerbated by both the runoff etching gullies in the steep southwestern river slopes and the dense second-growth tree canopy; and damage, brought on by periodic flooding and decades of neglect, to the drainage culverts protecting the road to the river. In the next five years, these problems—to be treated through professional engineering and vegetation management—will be addressed as part of the restoration to the Vaux & Company planting plan.

approach and network of drives, walks, and trails throughout the property to carefully sited prospect points, rustic gazebos and garden seats, and, at a discreet distance from the house, the greenhouses and produce and cutting garden. The carriage house and the gatehouse lodge are also important architectural features, while a summerhouse for afternoon tea and a tennis court were later accommodated.

The house and grounds declined as Margaret Suckley lived on, in genteel poverty, at Wilderstein (the "wild man's stone," referring to the Indian petroglyph by the river) until the age of ninety-nine. In 1980 she arranged for the property to become an independent, not-for-profit site after her death. Wilderstein Historic Site first tackled the restoration of all aspects of the house, but is now turning its attention to the grounds, which are cared for by one part-time, seasonal

LONG ISLAND

LONG ISLAND

NASSAU COUNTY

74 Bayard Cutting Arboretum, Great River, NY

75 Farmingdale State College, Department of Ornamental Horticulture Teaching Gardens, Farmingdale, NY

76 John P. Humes Japanese Stroll Garden, Mill Neck, NY

79 The Nassau County Museum of Art at the William Cullen Bryant Preserve, Roslyn Harbor, NY

80 Old Westbury Gardens, Old Westbury, NY

81 Planting Fields Arboretum State Historic Park, Oyster Bay, NY

82 The C. W. Post Community Arboretum, Brookville, NY

SUFFOLK COUNTY

🜂73 Bridge Gardens, Bridgehampton, NY

🜂77 LongHouse Reserve, East Hampton, NY

🜂78 Madoo Conservancy, Sagaponack, NY

36 Mitchell Lane, Bridgehampton, NY 11932
TEL: (631) 537-7440
WEBSITE: *www.peconiclandtrust.org/bridge_gardens*
SEE MAPS: pp. 185 & 187

Hours: Garden open beginning of April through October, Saturday 10am–5pm, Sunday noon–4pm; also from Memorial Day to Labor Day, Wednesday and Thursday noon–5pm and Friday noon–dusk. Admission fee

Location: 95 miles from New York City

Public transportation: LIRR to Bridgehampton, then short walk; Hampton Jitney and Hampton Luxury Liner to stop on Montauk Highway, Bridgehampton, then short walk

Facilities: Brochure and map near entry gate; restroom; no refreshments; picnicking (1 table); limited wheelchair accessibility; no dogs

Group garden tours: By appointment

Nearby eateries: Close by, Bridgehampton; Sag Harbor, 5-1/2 miles and Water Mill, 3-3/4 miles

Also of interest: Morton National Wildlife Refuge (187 acres), 784 Noyack Road, Sag Harbor, 2-1/2 miles

The attorney Harry Neyens (b. 1942) and medical writer and editor Jim Kilpatric (b. 1938) bought the land in 1988 and developed the gardens incrementally. The 1991 house, designed by Steven Levine, pays homage to the barn it replaced. It sits on a slope, with excellent views of the expanse of the inner garden from under the wisteria-clad pergola on the terrace. Below, one is drawn to the distinctive pattern of the parterre garden: five circles (filled with white shells) of red berberis bordered by lavender and box clipped into the form of twisted strands of rope. Surrounding this display are four beds filled with a wonderful array of herbs of all sizes

and textures, divided into sections: culinary, medicinal, textile, and miscellaneous. A seat backed by a rose hedge is placed for the best view, back across a circle of thyme and the herb parterre to the multiwindowed, two-story house, with espaliered apple trees on the lower level adding crisply to the linear effect.

In the west, a scattering of conifers (*Cryptomeria* and five native junipers) break up the expansive lawn with their dark forms, while to the north a perennial border and a courtyard garden, with a rectangular pool bordered by grasses, topiary, and potted plants, relate directly to the house. Around this large Inner Garden, which

includes additional sections, such as the maze garden, made of low lines of ivy in gravel with a bank of daylilies behind, run the double privet hedges, one of the glories of the garden, with wavy-edged tops. A walkway passes between them, with exits and entrances and portholes to peer through. One section was radically pruned in 2009, but it will reemerge in a few years. Finally, the bamboo grove that screens the railway line can be explored, a favorite for children.

On the other side of this hedge, further to the west, lies the outer garden. It's a difficult space, as the individual parts—a rose garden (arranged on a wheel-shaped parterre) with three adjacent white arbors, the lilac shrubbery, the whimsical topiary garden at the top of the slope, and the lavender and thyme parterres—don't come together in a cohesive whole at the moment. But this is a garden to watch, as Rick Bogusch, the garden

manager, plans, on behalf of the Peconic Land Trust (which was gifted the garden in 2008) and the Bridge Garden Advisory Committee, to "increase, diversify, and label plant collections, reduce the amount of lawn by planting trees and shrubs, establish an ornamental vegetable garden, and add visitor amenities." With about 1,000 visitors a year, the five acres of Bridge Gardens are cared for by one full-time and two part-time gardeners, along with two volunteers.

74 BAYARD CUTTING ARBORETUM

440 Montauk Highway, Great River, NY 11739,
or Union Boulevard & Montauk Highway
(NY-23A), both East Islip, NY 11730
TEL: (631) 581-1002
WEBSITE: *http://bayardcuttingarboretum.com; www.bcahs.net*
SEE MAPS: pp. 185 & 186

Hours: Grounds and first floor of house open April 1 though October 31, 10am–
5pm; November 1 through March 31, 10am–4pm, except main winter holidays.
Admission: car fee, April through October

Location: 54 miles from New York City

Public transportation: LIRR to Great River and walk 1/2 mile (or taxi)

Facilities: Information brochure with map in the house, with Hidden Oak Café,
Tuesday–Sunday 11am–4pm, (631) 277-3895, and gift shop; download tree and
shrub lists from the website in advance; restrooms; no picnicking; main areas
wheelchair accessible

Programming: Organized by the Bayard Cutting Arboretum Horticultural Society,
www.bcahs.net; concerts

Garden and house tours: By appointment and on listed days

Nearby eateries: East Islip, 1 mile; Oakdale, 2 miles; Sayville, 5-1/2 miles

Also of interest: Heckscher State Park, Southern State Parkway (1,469 acres of
trails, beach, picnicking), 3 miles

A drive fringed by oaks leads to Westbrook, an 1886 Tudor Revival house designed by Charles Haight (1841–1917) for New Yorkers Mr. and Mrs. William Bayard Cutting. Its site, laid out by the Frederick Law Olmsted firm in 1887, is incomparable. Extending from the front entrance, the great lawn of Oak Park displays some fourteen species of mature and younger oaks, spaced for good growth and form and edged by the rhododendron collection, which can be visited along meandering paths to the south. On the far side of the house, a large open lawn runs down to the Connetquot River, with an enormous weeping beech on the right and a shrubbery collection on the left. From the café (occupying the living room, library, and porch), one can relish the views and imagine the busy rounds of tennis, bowling, sailing, golfing, croquet, riding, fishing and swimming that took place on this thousand-acre country estate in its heyday. Large kitchen and flower gardens, greenhouses, and a dairy herd led the estate toward self-sufficiency.

The Pinetum, lying to the north of the carriage house, reflects an early passion of William Cutting (1850–1912), and today attracts specialists and the general public alike. A hard-surface path winds through this impressive collection, arranged in a naturalistic way with both small and medium sized groupings and single specimens. Begun in the 1890s with advice from Charles Sprague Sargent of the Arnold Arboretum, it received new additions after a devastating hurricane of 1985. The visitor, thanks to excellent labeling, can identify some of the many species and cultivars of fir, spruce, *Chamaecyparis*, cedar, pine, *Cryptomeria*, juniper, hemlock, yew, and box. Asian, European, and native are all represented: boldly upright, drooping, weeping, prostrate, compact, or spreading. Soft- needled or spiky, they come in silver, blue, and every shade of green, and are offset by deciduous conifers, attractive broadleafed trees, and shrubs, as well as a collection of hollies.

The 690 acres also encompasses long stretches of the river, with walks leading to inlets and connecting ponds where the planted areas give way to woodlands and wetlands—a paradise for bird lovers, botanists, and naturalists. Notice boards also draw attention to Idle Hour, the William K. Vanderbilt mansion on the opposite side of the river, now part of Dowling College.

William Bayard Cutting's financial interests included railroads, New York ferries, land development, banking, insurance, and sugar-beet refineries. He was also a significant philanthropist, supporting social and cultural endeavors. The Bayard Cutting Arboretum was donated in stages, beginning in 1936, to the Long Island State Park Region by Bayard's wife and their daughter, Olivia James. It was fully transferred in 1952, "to provide an oasis of beauty and quiet for the pleasure, rest, and refreshment of those who delight in outdoor beauty; and to bring about a greater appreciation and understanding of the value and importance of informal planting." Upwards of 150,000 visit the arboretum, which is operated by New York State, with support from the Cutting endowment. Five full-time and five to ten part-time groundskeepers are assisted by volunteers from the Bayard Cutting Arboretum Horticultural Society. The site hopes to add a horticulturist to the staff in the near future.

75 FARMINGDALE STATE COLLEGE, DEPARTMENT OF ORNAMENTAL HORTICULTURE TEACHING GARDENS

Farmingdale State College, 2350 Broadhollow Road (ROUTE 110), Farmingdale, NY 11735
TEL: (631) 420-2133 (DEPT. OF OH); (631) 420-2111 (CAMPUS POLICE)
WEBSITE: *www.farmingdale.edu/horticulture*
SEE MAPS: pp. 185 & 186

Hours: Garden open April 1 through December 1, daily, 10am–5pm. Admission free

Location: 34 miles from New York City

Parking: On campus, follow directions to university police building, pick up free permit and park in student lot #2 for close access to the gardens

Public transportation: LIRR to Farmingdale, taxi 3 miles, or N95 LIRR Shuttle to inside campus grounds

Facilities: Download brochure with plan before visiting; First Stop Café in Campus Commons (limited hours); restrooms in greenhouse during business hours, Monday–Saturday, or in university police building; no picnicking in actual garden; mostly wheelchair accessible; no dogs

Programming: Annual garden festival in June

Group garden tours: By appointment

Nearby eateries: Along Route 110 business corridor

Also of interest: Walt Whitman House Museum (his birthplace), 246 Old Walt Whitman Road, Huntington Station, 5 miles

"Horticulture," the entrance gate proclaims, written large in wrought-iron letters. And indeed visitors are drawn from the boring expanses of the car park toward an exuberance of planting, outside the garden walls, indicative of what is found within. A central grass axis is flanked by long beds of dramatically patterned annuals in blocks and lines of color. Each year the color combinations will change—in these beds and in others—for this is a teaching garden of Farmingdale State College. The six full-time members of the Department of Ornamental Horticulture offer a four-year program in General Horticulture or in Landscape Development leading to a Bachelor of Technology; a two-year Associate in Applied Science, and a shorter Ornamental Horticulture Certificate program. From this school come the much-needed horticultural professionals who will fan out into private residential work, landscape contracting, parks departments, greenhouse work, and related areas. When the original agricultural program ended, this section was saved—with the backing of the Long Island nurseries, which need a supply of trained horticulturalists.

The challenge in this approximately four-acre enclosed garden, designed beginning around 1930 by members of the department, has been to provide numerous styles of gardens for the students and a great array of plant combinations in suitable microclimates, and at the same time to create a harmonious flow from one area to another. Instead of the dreaded "low maintenance" look, complexity and horticultural skill have been embraced, and very dramatic and striking color combinations, often with big-leafed, strongly formed tropicals, are part of the show. Perennials in long beds, planted for a succession of color from May through November, have their place, as do parallel beds highlighting grasses and shrubs, a rose garden, a quiet silver/gray garden, an ornamental herb garden,

The white cupola of a c. 1898 Lord & Burnham conservatory acts well as a focal point, and although without its glazing since Hurricane Gloria in 1985, it offers displays of traditional conservatory plants, including *Plumbago* and hanging baskets of pendant sedum. A couple of adjoining greenhouses, off limits to the visitor, overwinter all the tropicals and, with the nursery, provide more training areas. Beyond, in four acres that are less intensively gardened, lies the pinetum, merging with campus grounds.

Owned by the State University of New York, the eight acres, cared for by six summer interns, have some 10,000 visitors a year (7,000 to 8,000 during the fundraising Garden Festival period). As for future plans, Michael Veracka, chairman of the Department of Horticulture, reports, "Within the next three to five years we plan to

and various others. Hedges surround compartments, and the rich collections of specimen shrubs and conifers on the sides provide intermediate layers that blend with the taller trees beyond.

develop 'The Sustainable Garden' in an area currently used as a nursery. It will address contemporary issues such as resource conservation, recycling principles, and product development."

JOHN P. HUMES JAPANESE STROLL GARDEN

347 Oyster Bay Road (ENTRANCE ON DOGWOOD LANE),
Mill Neck, NY 11765
TEL: (516) 676-4486
WEBSITE: *www.gardenconservancy.org/humes.html*
SEE MAPS: pp. 185 & 186

Hours: Open late April through mid-October, Saturday and Sunday 11:30am–4:30pm (last admission 4pm). Admission fee

Location: 29 miles from New York City

Public transportation: LIRR to Oyster Bay, taxi 2-1/2 miles or Locust Valley, walk or taxi 1-1/2 miles

Facilities: Brochure from attendant; restroom; no picnicking; not wheelchair accessible; no dogs

Programming: Tea ceremonies and Japanese related cultural events

Group garden tours: By appointment

Nearby eateries: Locust Valley, 1-1/2 miles; Bayville, 4 miles; Oyster Bay, 3-1/2 miles; list available from attendant

Also of interest: Bailey Arboretum County Park, 194 Bayville Road, Locust Valley, 1 mile

In 1960 the lawyer John P. Humes (1921–1985) and his wife were inspired by a visit to Japan and the gardens of Kyoto to create their own meditative garden. Between 1960 and 1964, Japanese landscape designer Douglas DeFaya and his wife, Jean, transformed two acres of the woodland below the house, and a traditional Japanese teahouse was imported to be a destination point near the pond. While Mr. Humes served as U.S. Ambassador to Austria between 1969 and 1975, the garden suffered from neglect and became very overgrown. On his return, he decided not only to rehabilitate it, but also to increase its size to four acres and to plan for its transition into the

public domain. Stephen A. Morrell, the current director, began working full-time in 1982, designing the new area according to the principles, techniques, and symbolism of the Japanese stroll garden. Within the deciduous woodland, Japanese maples were planted, and throughout the stroll garden a further blending of native and Asian plants of the same species was introduced (witch hazel, holly, sweetspire, iris, skunk cabbage, pine, violet, ferns, and others), along with the signature Japanese trees, shrubs and groundcovers, including *Cryptomeria*, katsura, *Stewartia*, ginkgo, and *Skimmia*.

From the parking lot, with its great stand of bamboo, we pass through a

Japanese wooden, roofed entranceway to start the journey. Flanked at first by azaleas and rhododendrons, we cross the bridge and begin the ascent with its symbolic implications. Pausing at the top, we discover a beautifully crafted path, which, like a stream, finds its way down the hillside with twists and turns. The arrangement of stepping stones, the placement of the rocks, and the small areas of moss are exquisite. As in Japan, all materials are natural, and bamboo is used for delicate fences, as a water pipe, and for the teahouse at the bottom, as well as for plantings. A weeping willow bends over the pond which is edged by primulas and irises, and the waterfall creates a visual resting place.

Owned by the Humes Japanese Garden Foundation (set up by John P. Humes in 1980), the garden has been operated by the Garden Conservancy since 1993. To help screen it from the residential roads on two sides, the sound of traffic, and the threat of development, the garden was expanded in 2009 to five acres. It is cared for by three gardeners, assisted by three to seven volunteers, and is visited by some 2,500 people annually.

LONGHOUSE RESERVE
133 Hands Creek Road, East Hampton,
NY 11937
TEL: (631) 329-3568
WEBSITE: *www.longhouse.org*
SEE MAPS: pp. 185 & 187

Hours: Grounds open late April through mid-October, Wednesday and Saturday
2pm–5pm; July and August, Wednesday–Saturday 2pm–5pm. Admission fee

Location: 105 miles from New York City

Public transportation: LIRR to East Hampton, walk or taxi 1-1/2 miles; Hampton
Jitney to East Hampton, taxi 2 miles

Facilities: Information, maps at the gatehouse, and small shop and plants;
restrooms by house; no refreshments; no picnicking; motorized wheelchair
accessibility (call in advance); no dogs

Programming: Horticultural, visual and performing arts, educational for children
and adults

Group garden and house tours: By appointment

Nearby eateries: East Hampton, 1-3/4 miles

Also of interest: Guild Hall Museum, 158 Main Street, East Hampton,
2 miles; Pollock-Krasner House & Study Center, 830 Springs-Fireplace Road,
East Hampton, 5-1/2 miles

Always amazing, still developing, LongHouse Reserve was begun in 1975 as a private house and garden by the textile designer Jack Lenor Larsen (b. 1927) on sixteen acres of land. On the cusp of new design trends in the late-twentieth century, and the product of an aesthetic taste honed by international travel, it reflects Larsen's friendships with artists and craftsmen and his ingenuity in designing with nature.

From the discreetly placed car park, with sand and wood-chip surfaces, visitors reach the gatehouse entrance via a wooded area, or along the great *Cryptomeria* allée. The bronze gong

(2003) by Toshiko Takaezu introduces an ode to the dunes and the East Hampton coastal topography, as the path wends its way between waves and then climbs up mounds of sand sculpted into forms and planted with grasses, a few trees, and the prostrate conifer *Microbiota decussata*. From this direction, the second-floor entrance to the house (closed, except to special tours) is dramatic. With the deep eaves and emphatic beamwork reminiscent of the seventh-century Shinto Outer Shrine at Ise in Japan—a design feature picked up elsewhere on the property— the house (designed by Charles Forberg in 1986) is, nonetheless, thoroughly modern, with long windows looking over the grounds and generous skylights. A veranda at ground level offers lovely views across Peter's Pond.

As in his own business, Mr. Larsen works here with both subtle and bold effects, the loosely natural and the highly designed, and creates sophisticated spatial and horticultural transitions between them. Central to this experience are the contemporary sculptures: placed on expansive lawns, silhouetted against a backdrop of water, framed by hemlock hedges, or forming the finale of an axis that extends from a narrow rectangular pool. Either collected by Jack Lenor Larsen or on loan from galleries or from the artists themselves, they form an ongoing and carefully orchestrated dialogue with the landscape: the glass *Cobalt Reeds* (2000) by Dale Chihuly rise up from a long border of grasses;

Fly's Eye Dome (1998) sits triumphantly on the Second Lawn. The designer benches invite visitors to savor these sights, while the enclosing grass slopes of the amphitheater (carved out of the debris from excavating the pond) offer a meditative repose.

In addition, seasonal sculpture exhibitions (contemporary or ethnographic) are shown in the sculpture court or in the grounds. The annual invitational "Planters: On and Off the Ground," featuring variations on the theme of containers and planters, assembles highly creative designers to continue Jack Lenor Larsen's tradition of dedication to interweaving horticulture, art, and design.

LongHouse Reserve, a nonprofit foundation begun in 1991, is cared for by four full-time gardeners and a volunteer horticultural director.

the density of *Floating Rain* (2001) by Takashi Soga hovers on its stalk above the scree garden; the *Reclining Figure* by Willem de Kooning (1969–1982) plays off a trained horizontal weeping blue atlas; and Buckminster Fuller's

Active committees assist the four administrative staff members in raising funds and obtaining grants. Visitors number some 9,000 annually. Sculpture is labeled, but few of the plants are currently.

78 THE MADOO CONSERVANCY

618 Sagg Main Street, Sagaponack, NY 11962
TEL: (631) 537-8200
WEBSITE: *www.madoo.org*
SEE MAPS: pp. 185 & 187

Hours: Garden open May 15 through October 15, Fridays and Saturdays noon–4pm. Admission fee

Location: 97 miles from New York City

Parking: On street

Public transportation: LIRR to Bridgehampton, taxi 3 miles; Hampton Jitney or Hampton Luxury Liner to Bridgehampton, taxi 3 miles

Facilities: Kiosk at entry with brochure; no refreshments; restrooms; no picnicking; not wheelchair accessible; dogs on leash; see publication *Notes from Madoo: Making a Garden in the Hamptons* by Robert Dash (2000)

Programming: Summer and winter lecture series

Group garden and house tours: By appointment, fee

Nearby eateries: Bridgehampton, 2-3/4 miles

Also of interest: Parrish Art Museum, 25 Jobs Lane, Southampton, 9 miles; The Dan Flavin Art Institute, Corwith Avenue (off Main Street), Bridgehampton, 3 miles

Madoo (Scottish for "My Dove") is a garden to linger in. Just two acres, but a warren of different spaces, going from deep shade to dappled light and then on to broader, open spaces, with a richness of planting that reflects the skills of a thoroughly knowledgeable gardener. Paths, always of well-considered materials with effective transitions, suggest a variety of possible explorations, and often their narrowness focuses attention on tree trunks and the texture of the bark.

The artist Robert Dash (b. 1934) purchased the property in 1966—a collection of sheds and a large barn dating from the 1740s, which formed the basis of the summer and winter studios and houses. The garden has developed over time with new sections added and details refined, and it now extends out to the edge of the potato fields. It would be impossible to design a garden like Madoo in one fell swoop—it's too quirky, too individualist. The myriad aesthetic choices reveal an instinctive response to what thrives and what new possibilities present themselves within the height, hue, and density of previous plantings. What appear to be found objects—pots, sculpture, and other artifacts—have been wittily incorporated, while the deliberately strong colors of painted doors, wooden arches,

window frames, a ladder, or a chimney provide startling and exciting forms or frames.

A sophisticated mingling of styles and a commentary on garden history are often apparent: a "Japanese" bridge—with modern oval, painted hoops inside—relates to a pool, whose spraying metal fountain recalls the famous one that existed at Versailles in the seventeenth century and, in turn, inspired the one at Chatsworth in Britain. Elsewhere "normal" proportions are thrown to the wind, with little bobbles of cypress placed in gravel below the much taller fastigiate ginkgos. Pruning and pleaching and limning produce strong shapes within a looser fullness, while distinctive forms and colors (such as the yellows of the tall chamaecyparises) are picked up and amplified above the hedges, linking various parts of the garden together. Although Mr. Dash wrote in 1992 that "what is here now is mainly a green garden"—and he has tended toward subtle colors, extending his interest to grasses and planted meadows— fulsome displays of climbing roses appear in season, and a new tunnel arbor, with a long Persian-like rill, has been constructed for them.

Madoo was first opened to the public in 1993, and in 1994 the Madoo Conservancy was formed to plan for its preservation. But meanwhile the garden will doubtless evolve, color selections for the furniture and garden structures may suddenly change on whim, and future plans include staining the 1744 Summer House in the manner of a Russian dacha or Swedish country house. At least 1,000 people visit the garden annually, and 400 the house and garden (in tours). Mr. Dash, who has always gardened organically, has the help of one full-time gardener and three seasonal workers. There is no labeling, but Mr. Dash is often on hand to assist.

1 Museum Drive, Roslyn Harbor, NY 11576
TEL: (516) 484-9337
WEBSITE: *www.nassaumuseum.org*
SEE MAPS: pp. 185 & 186

Hours: Grounds open daily, 9am–5pm; museum open Tuesday–Sunday 11am–4:45pm. Admission fee to museum

Location: 23 miles from New York City

Parking: Charge on weekends

Public transportation: LIRR to Roslyn (closer) or Manhasset (more trains), and taxi 2 or 4 miles

Facilities: In the museum, sculpture maps and trail brochures; the Café Musée (sit-down service) Tuesday–Sunday noon–4pm, and gallery shop; restrooms in main museum and in children's museum during regular hours; picnicking but no tables; grounds and garden partially wheelchair accessible; no dogs

Programming: Centered around the art museum

Group garden tours: By appointment, (516) 484-9338 x12

Nearby eateries: Roslyn, 2 miles

Also of interest: Cedarmere, 225 Bryant Avenue, Roslyn Harbor, 2 miles, the house and partial grounds of William Cullen Bryant (1794–1878); grounds open, house renovation started 2009

A museum of nineteenth- and twentieth-century American and European art with changing exhibitions, a children's museum, a formal garden, and outdoor sculpture now occupy the 145 acres of Clayton, the former estate of Childs Frick (1883–1965). Bought by his father, Henry Clay Frick, in 1919 as a wedding gift, the original 1900 Ogden Codman Jr. house (built for Lloyd Bryce, who acquired acreage from William Cullen Bryant) was redesigned by Charles Allom for the Fricks to become the three-story Georgian Revival mansion. A long drive, with expanses of lawn studded by sculpture (not always in pristine condition) and defined by the curving edges of woods, brings one to the house.

In 1925 Mrs. Frick, an avid gardener, hired the pioneer woman landscape architect Marian Cruger Coffin (1876–1957) to redo the enclosed formal garden, which is found adjacent to the car park (once the polo grounds). An independent entity, but linked by a path to the house, the "Georgian Garden" was restored to Coffin's conception in phases, beginning in 1995, based on photographs and blueprints. From the arched entrance in the privet hedge, one sees the straight lines of box hedges, brick paths, and the geometry of the lawns. Four distinct sections emerge, arranged around a central area with a fountain pool and beds of perennials. Within this calm and restrained space, the long main axis leads to an oval area with a wonderful teak, trellised sitting construction by Milliken-Bevin (1931, restored 1989), reminiscent of the seventeenth-century one at Het Loo in Holland. The planting, though now simplified, retains the spirit of this important period garden: two compartments have their intricate box and gravel parterres, with rose or perennial beds and borders. A third now features grass and cherry trees, and the fourth has attractive contemporary planting on stone-raised beds.

On a much larger scale are the magnificent lawns around the house—all with arresting sculpture and mature trees: magnolias (south), conifers (north), and to the east a fine prospect of the ponds (in overgrown surroundings) and the edges of woods. Wide grassy paths lead from one open meadow to another, with the three pieces of a Richard Serra sculpture (1983) spanning the intervals. Of the eight short nature trails opened in 2006, perhaps #8, Tuliptree Forest, and #7, the Frick Pinetum, are the most appealing. The latter, a particular interest of Mr. Frick in the 1920s—he collected conifers from around the world—has, with advice from Professor Andrew Greller, been cleared of undergrowth and invasives, and within

the depleted collection the forest-floor ferns are returning. On the west, the view of Roslyn Harbor has been lost to trees, which detracts from the siting of the house, but the sound is glimpsed along the Jerushua Dewey trail. This path passes by the about-to-be-restored guest cottage, built by William Cullen Bryant in 1862 and of architectural significance.

Nassau County acquired the estate in 1969 from the Frick family and in the late 1970s opened it as an art museum and preserve. The Nassau County Museum of Art, privatized since 1989, is a nonprofit institution supported by federal, state, and county grants, membership, and donations. The garden and grounds are cared for by two full-time, one seasonal, and six volunteer gardeners and overseen by one administrator. Future plans include the ongoing process of restoring the Coffin garden, identifying and labeling more of the trees, shrubs, and flowers throughout the estate, and creating interpretive materials to make this information available to the public— some 225,000 visitors annually.

80 OLD WESTBURY GARDENS

71 Old Westbury Road, Old Westbury, NY 11568
TEL: (516) 333-0048
WEBSITE: *www.oldwestburygardens.org*
SEE MAPS: pp. 185 & 186

Hours: Open late April through October, daily (except Tuesdays), 11am–4pm; grounds open 10am–5pm. Also special weekends in November and for two weeks in early December. Garden tours daily (except Tuesday). Admission fee

Location: 23 miles from New York City

Public transportation: LIRR to Westbury, taxi 2-1/2 miles

Facilities: Brochures in various languages and maps at ticket booth and in house; light refreshments in the Café in the Woods; restrooms by car park and in house; gift shop in house with publications on Old Westbury; seasonal plant shop; picnicking in designated area; house is wheelchair accessible; no dogs

Programming: Horticultural and fine arts talks, concerts, craft workshops for all ages

Group garden tours: By appointment

Nearby eateries: Westbury, 2-1/2 miles, and Roslyn, 3 miles

The approach and the siting of Old Westbury immediately impress. One enters through magnificent eighteenth-century gates and proceeds along a double avenue of linden trees to broad views of open lawn and a house framed by rhododendrons and trees. An axis from the north—an avenue of beeches initially—continues to the front door and through the house, where the south terrace offers a splendid view of the third avenue. Emerging from a large grassy area defined by hemlock hedges, it proceeds south toward another set of wrought-iron gates and continues between lindens. The proportions are grand, and the world beyond screened out.

To the west and east are bodies of water: a large naturalistic lake—and its path to the eye-catching eighteenth-

century-style classical gazebo—and the smaller West Pond, seen from the terrace of the striking West Porch. A Corinthian colonnade behind a formal reflecting pool (both added in 1928 by White, Allom & Co.), and the billowy shapes of clipped boxwood close the shorter axis.

The house, interiors, and grounds, on 175 acres of formerly Quaker-owned farms, were designed by the Englishman George Crawley (1864–1926) for John (Jay) Shaffer Phipps (1874–1958), who benefited from the fabulous wealth of his father, Henry Phipps (1839–1930), finance manager of Carnegie Steel. His British wife, Margarita Grace (1876–1957), brought up in Peru, had developed a fondness for country-house living when she lived in England as a young woman. The compact red-brick manor house

(1904–1907), reminiscent of the Charles II period of the seventeenth century, is furnished in a predominantly eighteenth-century style, with British paintings from that time, along with several family portraits (one by John Singer Sargent).

Tours of the garden, self-guided or with a docent, begin on the west terrace at the giant American beech. The walled garden is a favorite destination. The detailing here is exquisite. Designed by Crawley as an "Italian garden" on two levels, it has two charming corner summerhouses, attractive balustrading, a central fountain in the lower section, and a larger pool at the south end surrounded by a semicircular pergola covered in wisteria. The borders, now generously

garden (with David Austin varieties). Then one approaches the charming miniature Thatched Cottage and its colorful garden, created for their daughter Peggy, and the plainer cabins built for her brothers. Crossing the main axis, on the way to the East Lake, reveals a splendid view of the house and its terrace reached by grand staircases from this level.

Publications suggest that although the Phipps owned five other houses, Westbury was a much-loved home, filled with family and friends, and offering riding and polo, tennis, golf, and swimming, as well as orchards, greenhouses, vegetable gardens, and a dairy. After the death of Jay and Dita Phipps, the main house and 100 acres (now 200) became the nonprofit

planted for three seasons of interest, are always meticulously maintained. Crabapples, weeping cherries, Irish yews, and climbing roses lend vertical interest, while the north wall has an array of espaliered trees and shrubs.

A path from one of the filigreed wrought-iron gates leads to rooms defined by hedges (sometimes incorporating garden sculpture), a short hemlock allée, and a large rose

Old Westbury Gardens, opened to the public in 1959. About 60,000 people visit annually, and plans include increasing the concerts, programs, book signings, etc., to continue to draw in more visitors. Six full-time gardeners are supplemented in season by five international interns and several part-timers. A sampling of trees are labeled, as well as plants in the walled garden.

PLANTING FIELDS ARBORETUM STATE HISTORIC PARK

1395 Planting Fields Road, Oyster Bay, NY 11771
TEL: (516) 922-8678
WEBSITE: *http://plantingfields.org*
SEE MAPS: pp. 185 & 186

Hours: Grounds open daily (except December 25), 9am–5pm. House open for self-guided tours, April 1 through September 30, daily, 11:30am–3:30pm. Also guided tours. Main greenhouse and Camellia Greenhouse open daily 10am–4pm. Admission free

Location: 31 miles from New York City

Parking: Fee on weekends and holidays

Public transportation: LIRR to Oyster Bay, walk or taxi 1-1/2 miles; or (more trains) LIRR to Locust Valley, taxi 3-1/4 miles

Facilities: Arboretum Center for pamphlets and maps, vending machines, and restrooms; also visitor center in the Hay Barn (hours vary) with café (seasonal weekends), gift shop, exhibition area, and restrooms; picnicking; wheelchair accessibility; no dogs

Programming: Lectures and concerts, school groups

Nearby eateries: Oyster Bay, 1-1/2 miles

Also of interest: Sagamore Hill, 12 Sagamore Hill Road, Oyster Bay, home of Theodore Roosevelt from 1885–1919, 3-3/4 miles; Joseph Lloyd Manor, Lloyd Lane and Lloyd Harbor Road, Lloyd Harbor, a 1766 house on Long Island Sound, 12-1/2 miles

Planting Fields includes a house, garden, landscaped grounds, woodlands, and unique conservatories set in 409 acres. They reveal the lifestyle and the horticultural interests of former Gold Coast estate owners, as well as providing a range of activities adapted to contemporary visitors. The name stems from the local Matinecock Indians, who called this fertile area set back from the coast and on a rise their "planting fields."

William R. Coe (1869–1955), who had immigrated from England in 1883 with his family of modest means, became a successful marine insurance executive and financier. His wife, Mai H. Rogers, the daughter of one of the founders of Standard Oil, was independently wealthy. The Coes rented and then bought the estate in 1913 from James Byrne, who assembled several farms and built a country house in 1906 designed by Grosvenor Atterbury (1869–1956), with gardens (from 1904–1910) by James Greenleaf (1857–1933). The Green Garden Court, the circular pool, and the tunnel arbor for roses stem from this period.

William Coe immediately expanded the formal gardens near the house. The firm of Lowell & Sargent designed the Italian Garden (1918) and its delightful teahouse, the children's playhouse, and the greenhouses—constructed for Mr. Coe's new collections, which included the famous camellias brought from England in 1916. Walker & Gillette built the handsome new outbuildings and, after the destruction of the house by fire in 1918, was retained to design a new sixty-five-room Elizabethan-style manor (1918–1921). The Coes collected and imported European furniture, paintings, and furnishings to produce a comfortable "olde" country house, employing contemporary craftsmen to fill in the missing features.

The Olmsted Brothers were hired from 1918 to create an appropriate setting in their signature English country house park style—including the broad sweeps of the east and west lawns with their mature specimen trees (the enormous weeping silver linden remains). In 1926 the firm also designed and landscaped a drive, with carefully orchestrated views, starting at the new entrance fitted with the splendid 1712 Carshalton Gates (no longer used by visitors) imported from Britain.

William Coe continued to enrich the planting on the estate, and to build up his collections—particularly of magnolias and imported rhododendrons and azaleas. He also increased the range of greenhouses, which miraculously survive. While

February is the peak time for the camellias, ongoing seasonal displays, along with the permanent plantings, are year-round attractions.

Coe Hall was bequeathed to the state of New York at the death of William Coe in 1955 "to promote training in agriculture and horticulture." It was used briefly by SUNY between 1957 and the early 1960s, and the very special five-acre Synoptic Garden (arranged alphabetically by family) stems from this period, its attractive walk leading to the holly, dwarf conifer, and heather gardens and the conifer trail. With the help of the Planting Fields Foundation, formed in 1979 by William R. Coe II, the house has been refurnished and the gardens restored—including the Italian Garden, returned to its original planting in 2010. Thirteen full-time gardeners care for the arboretum, with five part-time seasonal helpers and a hundred volunteers. About 160,000 people visited in 2009.

82 THE C. W. POST COMMUNITY ARBORETUM

Long Island University, 720 Northern Boulevard, Brookville, NY 11548
TEL: (516) 299-3500.
WEBSITE: *www.liu.edu/arboretum*
SEE MAPS: pp. 185 & 186

Hours: Open daily, dawn to dusk. Group garden tours by appointment. Admission free

Location: 25 miles from New York City

Public Transportation: LIRR to Greenvale, campus van shuttle on weekdays or taxi, 2-3/4 miles. For additional options see www.liunet.edu/cwpost/about/visit/directions

Parking: At Hillwood Commons

Facilities: Hillwood Commons (restrooms and cafeteria); picnicking; wheelchair accessible; dogs on leash

Opened to the public in 2002, this arboretum features thirty particularly good trees and labels them clearly. Download the *Visitor's Guide and Map* before arriving and proceed on a self-guided walk through the C. W. Post campus of Long Island University. It is located on the former estate of cereal heiress, businesswoman, collector, and socialite Marjorie Merriweather Post. The university, which bought the property in 1951, has been careful to leave the views from the Great Lawn of the striking 1921 Tudor Revival house, Hillwood (now Winnick House) unimpeded.

Marian Cruger Coffin (1876–1957) designed the garden and terraces to one side of the house in 1922, also bringing in a range of trees for the grounds. Although rather basically maintained now, with sections in disrepair, the formal layout has survived. The flower garden within a beautifully crafted brick and stone wall remains. Interesting built-in brick benches create a central diamond shape, and the clipped box and yew bobbles stand tall above a scattering of roses and perennials. The terrace above still has a few magnolias but has lost its box hedges, while the third, formerly the tennis court, has a labyrinth laid out in the grass by the students (2001). A long brick pergola with climbing hydrangeas (formerly roses) proceeds up the hill and fizzles out in an unkempt circle with an exedra.

The difficulties of a college shouldering the cost of maintaining a historic garden are evident, but the unusual Coffin water garden (a stream that emerges from beneath the 1929 "cottage") has been restored, though perhaps without the emphasis on the flowers that once lined its banks.

NEW JERSEY

83 Acorn Hall, Morristown

84 Bamboo Brook Outdoor Education Center, Far Hills

85 Lewis W. Barton Arboretum & Nature Preserve at Medford Leas, Medford

86 Branch Brook Park, Newark

87 Leonard J. Buck Garden, Far Hills

88 Sister Mary Grace Burns Arboretum of Georgian Court University, Lakewood

89 Colonial Park Arboretum, East Millstone

90 Cross Estate Gardens, Bernardsville

91 Deep Cut Gardens, Middletown

92 Drumthwacket, Princeton

93 Duke Farms, Hillsborough

94 The Frelinghuysen Arboretum, Whippany

95 Greenwood Gardens, Short Hills

96 Grounds For Healing at the Robert Wood Johnson University Hospital, Hamilton

97 Grounds For Sculpture, Hamilton

98 Hereford Inlet Lighthouse Gardens, North Wildwood

99 Hudson River Waterfront Walkway

100 Laurelwood Arboretum, Wayne

101 Leaming's Run Gardens, Cape May Courthouse

102 Macculloch Hall Historical Museum & Gardens, Morristown

103 Morven Museum & Garden, Princeton

104 New Jersey State Botanical Garden at Skylands, Ringwood

105 Peony's Envy, Bernardsville

106 Presby Memorial Iris Gardens, Upper Montclair

107 Princeton University Campus & Prospect House Garden, Princeton

108 Reeves-Reed Arboretum, Summit

109 Ringwood Manor, Ringwood

110 The James Rose Center, Ridgewood

111 Rutgers Gardens, New Brunswick

112 Sayen Botanical Gardens, Hamilton

113 Union County College's Historic Tree Grove & Arboretum, Cranford

114 Van Vleck House & Gardens, Montclair

115 Well-Sweep Herb Farm, Port Murray

116 Willowwood Arboretum, Far Hills

45 The Gardens at Matterhorn, Spring Valley, NY

117 Ambler Arboretum of Temple University, Ambler, PA

118 Andalusia, Andalusia, PA

125 Highlands Mansion & Gardens, Fort Washington, PA

126 Hortulus Farm Garden & Nursery, Wrightstown, PA

130 Meadowbrook Farm, Meadowbrook, PA

132 Pennsbury Manor, Morrisville, PA

135 St. Mary Medical Center Healing Gardens, Langhorne, PA

137 Tyler Formal Gardens at Bucks County Community College, Newtown, PA

See Garden State Gardens: A Consortium of New Jersey's Public Gardens: *www.gardenstategardens.org*

NEW JERSEY

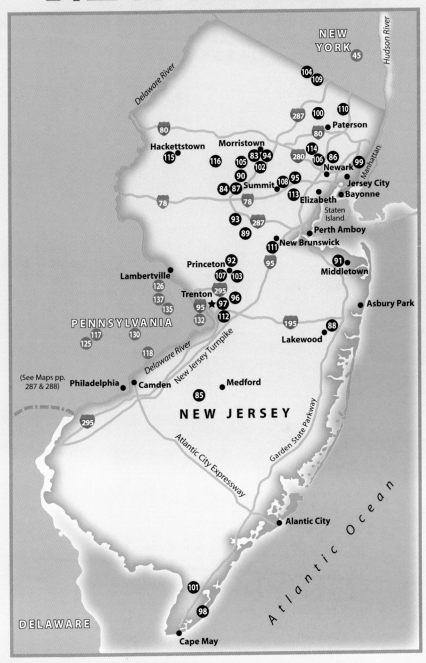

HUDSON, ESSEX & UNION COUNTIES

NEW JERSEY

287

80

80

46

287

Upper
Montclair 106

114
Montclair

280

3

Fort
Lee 99

80

Orange

95

99 Hudson River

495
99
Weehawken

99
Hoboken

Short Hills 95

86

South
Orange
Newark

280

99

24

19

139

Summit 108 Milburn

Jersey
City

78

22

78

99

113
Cranford

95

78

22

Bayonne

Upper
Bay

Garden State Parkway

New Jersey Turnpike

To
Philadelphia

Staten
Island

NEW
YORK

Manhattan

86 Branch Brook Park, Newark, NJ
95 Greenwood Gardens, Short Hills, NJ
99 Hudson River Waterfront Walkway, NJ
106 Presby Memorial Iris Garden, Upper Montclair, NJ
108 Reeves-Reed Arboretum, Summit, NJ
113 Union County College's Historic Tree Grove & Arboretum, Cranford, NJ
114 Van Vleck House & Gardens, Montclair, NJ

NORTHEAST NEW JERSEY

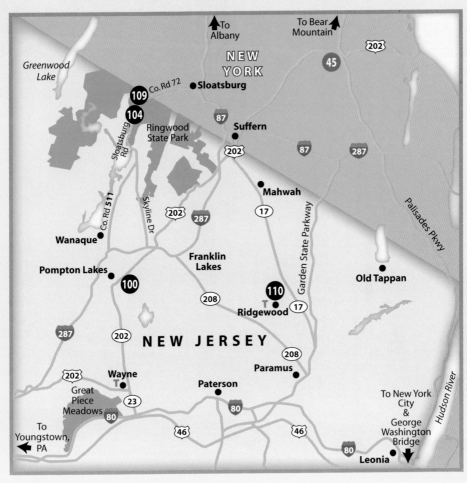

100 Laurelwood Arboretum, Wayne, NJ
104 New Jersey State Botanical Garden at Skylands, Ringwood, NJ
109 Ringwood Manor, Ringwood, NJ
110 The James Rose Center, Ridgewood, NJ

45 The Gardens at Matterhorn, Spring Valley, NY

MORRISTOWN AREA

83 Acorn Hall, Morristown, NJ

84 Bamboo Brook Outdoor Education Center, Far Hills, NJ

87 Leonard J. Buck Garden, Far Hills, NJ

90 Cross Estate Gardens, Bernardsville, NJ

94 The Frelinghuysen Arboretum, Whippany, NJ

102 Macculloch Hall Historical Museum & Gardens, Morristown, NJ

105 Peony's Envy, Bernardsville, NJ

116 Willowwood Arboretum, Far Hills, NJ

ARROW TO:

93 Duke Farms, Hillsborough, NJ

SOMERVILLE/
NEW BRUNSWICK AREA

PRINCETON / TRENTON AREA

92 Drumthwacket, Princeton, NJ

96 Grounds For Healing at the Robert Wood Johnson University Hospital, Hamilton, NJ

97 Grounds For Sculpture, Hamilton, NJ

103 Morven Museum & Garden, Princeton, NJ

107 Princeton University Campus & Prospect House Garden, Princeton, NJ

112 Sayen Botanical Gardens, Hamilton, NJ

CAPE MAY AREA

To Swainton

To Atlantic City

Great Sound

NEW JERSEY

Delaware Bay

47

Cape May Courthouse

9

Jenkins Sound

619

47

101

Cape May County Park South

147

N. Wildwood Blvd

Stone Harbor

47

9

Grassy Sound

Hereford Inlet

98

North Wildwood

Richardson Sound

47

S. Wildwood Blvd

Wildwood

Garden State Pkwy

Sunset Lake

Wildwood Crest

Atlantic Ocean

9

To ferry

Jarvis Sound

Diamond Beach

Cape May Harbor

Cape May Inlet

Cape May

98 Hereford Inlet Lighthouse Gardens, North Wildwood, NJ

101 Leaming's Run Gardens, Cape May Courthouse, NJ

PRINCETON AREA

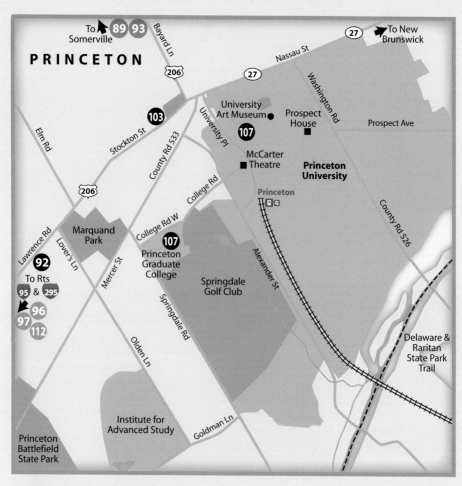

92 Drumthwacket, Princeton, NJ

103 Morven Museum & Garden, Princeton, NJ

107 Princeton University Campus & Prospect House Garden, Princeton, NJ

ARROWS TO:

89 Colonial Park Arboretum, East Millstone, NJ

93 Duke Farms, Hillsborough, NJ

96 Grounds For Healing at the Robert Wood Johnson University Hospital, Hamilton, NJ

97 Grounds For Sculpture, Hamilton, NJ

112 Sayen Botanical Gardens, Hamilton, NJ

83 ACORN HALL

68 Morris Avenue, Morristown,
NJ 07960
TEL: (973) 267-3465
WEBSITE: *www.acornhall.org*
SEE MAPS: pp. 209 & 212

Hours: Grounds open dawn to dusk. House open Mondays and Thursdays
10am–4pm, Sundays 1pm–4pm. Admission free to grounds; fee for house
Location: 33 miles from New York City
Public transportation: NJ Transit to Morristown, walk or taxi 1-1/4 miles
Facilities: Gift shop in the house; no refreshments; no restrooms on grounds, but in
the house for tour visitors; picnicking; house not wheelchair accessible, but garden
can be viewed from a few points; no dogs
Nearby eateries: Attractive downtown Morristown, 1 mile; list available
Also of interest: The walk from the bottom of the garden to the Frelinghuysen
Arboretum (1 mile) through woods and pastures

A Victorian house with period
furnishings requires the setting of a
Victorian garden, and this is what the
Home Garden Club of Morristown
strives to provide for Acorn Hall.
The 1853 Italianate villa—yellow
with chestnut-maroon trim—has a
picturesque octagonal tower and a
front porch with elaborate wooden
decoration. Except for a few modern
improvements (bathrooms and
electricity), the house has remained
essentially the same as it was around
1860.

Built in 1853 for Dr. John
Schermerhorn, the fully furnished
house was sold in 1857, after the
death of his wife, to Augustus Crane
(1816–1906), a New York importer of
Asian goods who became a Morristown
banker. Remaining in the Crane family
until 1935, it eventually passed to a

grandniece, Mary Crane Hone. She
donated the house and its contents to
the Morris County Historical Society in
1971, and was delighted at the way the
volunteers of the Home Garden Club
of Morristown transformed a neglected
garden to a style appropriate to the
period of 1853–1888.

Drawing upon archival photos
and nineteenth-century garden and
landscape books, the club drew up a
list of bulbs, ferns, perennials, roses,
shrubs, vines, trees, and wildflowers
and, following the 1971 designs of
Alice Dustan Kollar, replanted the
garden in the five acres remaining from
the original eight.

The area in the front of the house
has hardly changed: its short U-shaped
drive is still set within lawns and tall,
irregularly spaced specimen trees, both
deciduous and coniferous. The black

oak, the source of the name of the house, survived until 2003. Only the large ornamental bed is missing.

The restoration of the rear gardens (no photographic evidence available) is based on hypothetical evidence: oval or circular beds of flowers—visible from the veranda (against views of the Ramapo Mountains in the distance)—islands of trees and shrubs, and a picket fence, bordered by perennials, dividing the ornamental garden from the large kitchen garden and orchard.

Instead of the produce garden, one finds the circular formal parterre of 1996 (more in the style of a Colonial Revival garden) behind the picket fence, which is planted with roses and clematis. A gazebo (1976), designed in the Victorian style by James V. Balsamel, nicely incorporates some cast-iron trellis with acorn and oak decorations, salvaged from a home

of the same period on Macculloch Avenue. Magnolia, quince, forsythia, and other flowering shrubs and small trees, especially lovely in the spring, are backed by locusts and spruces within the woods to the north—also screening out neighboring properties on the east and west.

Between four to six volunteers help out every Wednesday for two to three hours. Gardening has been especially challenging lately, as the lack of a deer fence has resulted in many losses. Plans include coming up with more deer-resistant varieties while preserving the overall Victorian ambiance. About 2,000 people visit the garden annually and 1,600 visit the house. The Morris County Historical Society hopes to publish an updated brochure on this attractive property whose garden holds such potential.

84 BAMBOO BROOK OUTDOOR EDUCATION CENTER

11 Longview Road, Far Hills, NJ 07931
TEL: (973) 326-7601
WEBSITE: *www.morrisparks.net*
SEE MAPS: pp. 209 & 212

Hours: Grounds open 8am–dusk. House not open. Admission free
Location: 49 miles from New York City
Public transportation: NJ Transit to Gladstone, taxi 2-3/4 miles
Facilities: Brochure/trail map at front of house; portable toilets only;
 picnicking—bring blanket; limited wheelchair access; no dogs
Garden tours: By appointment, ask for superintendent of education
Nearby eateries: Chester, 5-1/2 miles

The best way to arrive at Bamboo Brook is from Willowwood, taking the one-mile walking trail through meadows and woods. Known originally as Merchiston Farm, Bamboo Brook was the home of the landscape architect, author, and garden lecturer Martha Brookes Hutcheson (1871–1959) from the year after her marriage to William Hutcheson in 1910 until her death.

The restoration in 2010 of the impressive garden (completed in 1940) that she designed to the side of the house—which links up at right angles to the earlier, quiet terraces of boxwood, shrubs, and perennials to the rear—has brought her career into the spotlight again. One of the first women to enroll in the landscape architecture program at MIT (1900), she supplemented her courses with studies at the Arnold Arboretum and travel abroad—the gardens of Italy and France particularly influencing her work. Her practice was initially in Boston, and then, after 1906, in New York. *The Spirit of the Garden*, published in 1923, contains essays on her design philosophy for gardens of the Country Place era.

Although Martha Brookes Hutcheson and the Tubbs brothers at Willowwood were good friends, their different conceptions are striking: the emphasis here is on the large statement and the formal organization of space, defined crisply by the central geometry of four stone and grass staircases converging on a large circular reflecting pool—all seen to great advantage from the top of the garden, with its more fluidly shaped pond. Water is the connecting link, and it descends in a stream, disappearing and reappearing, going under the "Little House," flowing into a succession of attractive stone pools before disappearing into the woodland. The planting was still sparse

for the new garden in mid-2010, and some of the detailing rough, with utility covers in full view, but the challenge taken on by Morris County is much to be admired. This is a garden to be watched and revisited. Gardeners at Willowwood also look after Bamboo Brook.

Parts of the twenty-three-acre grounds are currently surrounded by deer fences, necessary but upsetting in their relationship to the house. The latter, a shingle-covered central block with wings, dates to 1720, but was enlarged and renovated by the Hutchesons between 1911 and 1940. It is now the headquarters of the New Jersey Conservation Foundation.

In 1974, the Hutcheson's daughter, Martha Hutcheson Norton, and her husband donated the property with its 100 acres to the Morris County Park Commission. The county of Morris plans an updated brochure on the garden and trails for 2011.

85 LEWIS W. BARTON ARBORETUM & NATURE PRESERVE AT MEDFORD LEAS

1 Medford Leas Way, Medford, NJ 08055
TEL: (609) 654-3000
WEBSITE: *www.medfordleas.org*
SEE MAPS: pp. 209 & 287

Hours: Grounds open 9am–dusk. Admission free
Location: 86 miles from New York City
Parking: By the Community Building
Public transportation: None
Facilities: Brochures for arboretum and pinetum from office in the community building, also restrooms; no refreshments; picnicking—bring a blanket. All the courtyard gardens and the pinetum are wheelchair accessible; dogs on leash
Nearby eateries: Medford Village, 1 mile; chain restaurants along I-295

The landscaped grounds, courtyard gardens, pinetum, wildflower meadows, natural woodlands, and wetlands are all considered part of the arboretum at the Medford Leas Retirement Home, reflecting its belief in the relationship between nature and well-being. The name commemorates Lewis W. Barton, one of the Quakers who helped found the community in 1971; the arboretum itself was established in 1981.

The core one-story residences (interesting modern wooden-clad, barnlike structures) are built around thirty-three courtyards of gardens with connecting glass and brick corridors. Each space has been distinctively designed by the Morris Arboretum in conjunction with the Medford Leas staff, the staff themselves, or by local landscape architects—with input from the residents encouraged. Quiet green ground covers with conifers and accents of deciduous

trees alternate with gardens of mixed flowers and shrubs; lush displays contrast with minimal plantings and rocks, suggesting a Japanese aesthetic. Beyond this area, separate houses often have patios or pergolas and small areas for private gardening, while more specimen trees, with good labeling, grow on the connecting lawns.

Close to the main courtyard is the compact pinetum, with some fifty-six interesting specimens arranged singly for optimum form, but also creating visual clusters with intermingled deciduous trees. The self-guided brochure is helpful here. Trails run through the property, and the beginnings of a New Jersey conifer collection can be seen in one of the meadows.

Four full-time and four seasonal gardeners care for the 168-acre arboretum, with the staff at the Morris Arboretum supplying advice and technical assistance. At least twenty residents are also involved in working in the gardens and greenhouse, while others have taken up birdwatching, wildflower cataloguing (see the website), group walking expeditions, and nature and environmental programs.

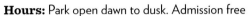

86 BRANCH BROOK PARK

(Access by car from Lake Street, South Branch
Brook Drive, Middle Branch Brook Drive, etc.)
Newark, NJ 07194
TEL: (973) 268-2300 (BRANCH BROOK PARK ALLIANCE)
WEBSITE: *www.branchbrookpark.org*
SEE MAPS: pp. 209 & 210

Hours: Park open dawn to dusk. Admission free

Location: 15 miles from New York City

Public transportation: PATH train to Newark, Penn Station, NJ Light Rail to
Park Avenue (Southern Division), Bloomfield Avenue (Middle Division), Davenport
Avenue (Northern Division), and Heller Parkway, or Franklin Avenue/Branch Brook
Park (Extension Division). Buses: NJ Transit #11, 27, 28, 29, 41, 72, 74, 90, 92, 93, 99,
and 108. See www.njtransit.com

Facilities: Maps at eight kiosks and visitor center; restrooms (or portable toilets)
in each division; limited refreshments (three hot dog vendor vans); picnic tables;
some areas wheelchair accessible; dogs on leash

Nearby eateries: Bloomfield Avenue, east and west; Heller Parkway/Franklin
Street, west

Also of interest: Newark Museum, 49 Washington Street, Newark, 2–3 miles

Branch Brook Park is to Newark
what Central Park (1859–1873) is to
Manhattan and Prospect Park (1866–
1873) to Brooklyn. Longer (almost
four miles) but skinnier (averaging only
a quarter-mile), and with 360 acres
(including extensions) as opposed to
843 (Central Park) and 585 (Prospect
Park), it had, like many other public
spaces, a slow start. Frederick Law
Olmsted and Calvert Vaux, the
designers of the two New York City
parks, were consulted in 1867/68,
but no real progress was made until
1895 when money was allocated for
a county park.

The land consisted of an existing
1871 reservoir in the south and a
swampy, unhealthy area northward.
The Morris Canal, opened in 1831,
ran along the western edge. The
firm of John Bogart and Nathan F.
Barrett was hired first, followed by the
Olmsted Brothers, with John Charles
Olmsted (1852–1920), stepson and
nephew of Frederick Law Olmsted,
becoming the partner responsible for
the redevelopment of the designs.
Unique to Branch Brook is the string
of lakes and the connecting stream that
run through the Southern, Middle,
and Northern divisions. The southern
section featured shrubberies and
flowers within a formal layout (now
mostly gone), which then gave way to
open meadows and woods, with drives

and paths running throughout the whole property.

The Olmsted general plan of 1901 remains the guiding force as this tarnished jewel is gradually being polished up again. The Branch Brook Park Alliance, formed in 1999, has partnered with the Essex County Department of Parks to help stem the tide of deterioration and gradually restore the park to its former glory, and significant achievements have been made. The Alliance also commissioned Rhodeside & Harwell, in 2009 to produce *The Cultural Landscape Report, Treatment, and Management Plan*, an analysis of the entire park, its history, and future prospects, and indicating shifting requirements, such as sports facilities.

By 2004, almost half of the original 1,985 cherry trees given in 1928 by Caroline Bamberger Fuld had

gone. The goal of planting 3,000 more by 2010 became a publicity strategy to heighten awareness of the park, attracting large numbers of visitors during the two week annual Cherry Blossom Festival in April. This monoculture planting allows for superlatives (the largest, best, and most diverse collection of cherry trees in the whole United States) and will give Essex County Executive Joseph N. DiVincenzo Jr. the momentum to develop a more complex approach. Those interested in the legacy of parks initiated by Frederick Law Olmsted and Calvert Vaux will recognize the challenge to Newark and be heartened to see how Branch Brook Park is emerging again.

87 LEONARD J. BUCK GARDEN

11 Layton Road, Far Hills, NJ 07931
TEL: (908) 234-2677
WEBSITE: *www.somersetcountyparks.org*
SEE MAPS: pp. 209 & 212

Hours: Grounds open April through November, Monday–Friday 10am–4pm, Saturday 10am–5pm, Sunday noon–5pm; December through March, Monday–Friday 10am–4pm; closed on major holidays. Admission fee. Garden tours on Sundays at 2pm April and May (excluding holidays)

Location: 42 miles from New York City

Public transportation: NJ Transit to Far Hills, walk or taxi 1 mile

Facilities: Visitor center for map, bloom list, and brochures; restrooms; no refreshments; picnicking in designated areas; partially wheelchair accessible (use lower parking lot); no dogs; wear sturdy shoes

Programming: Horticultural, birding, art, and photography

Group garden tours: By appointment

Nearby eateries: Far Hills (café in railway station), 1 mile; Bedminster, 1-1/2 miles; Gladstone, 4-3/4 miles; list available in visitor center

No distractions of house or layers of human history here—just the glorious immersion in the beauty and richness of woodland, stream, and rock planting, set within a small valley. The garden was brought into existence through the horticultural passion of Leonard J. Buck (1893–1974) and the eye and knowledge of the consultant Zenon Schreiber (1904–1989), who was known as the premier rock garden designer in the United States.

The twenty-nine acres of rocky ravine, purchased as part of his property in 1937, was of special interest to Mr. Buck, a geologist and president of his own import and export business of minerals and chemicals in Morristown. Beginning in the early 1940s, clearing and blasting and chipping and layering had exposed seven outcroppings of rocks by 1953, and five others followed. The Moggy Hollow stream was dammed to create a small lake, and one of the first intriguing views is of the shaped green of the valley floor with the serpentine stream running through it. Massive dawn redwoods from 1948 are combined with younger specimens.

The rocks, as "islands" or as part of the valley walls—some tapering into the lawns—are planted naturalistically, according to the different microclimates. Scree, or pockets, ledges, and plateaus of soil

hold drifts or small groups of alpines, dwarf conifers, succulents, heathers, thymes, ferns, and mosses. The outcroppings are offset by "Planting Beds" of azaleas, rhododendrons, and flowering shrubs and perennials, which in turn merge with the rich plantings of the woodland filled with natives and exotics.

Paths wend past the rocks to Japanese primroses and other damp-

loving plantings, across a bridge canopied by wisteria, around the lake edged by irises, and up into the woods—where views of the rhythmic flow of the garden are appreciated from different heights and angles. It's a glorious sight in April and May— with the spring ephemerals and the magnolias, dogwoods, Chinese fringe trees, and other flowering trees, but lovely in all seasons, and the songs of birds and the very special atmosphere of the valley seem to muffle the noise from the nearby road.

Donated to the Somerset County Park Commission in 1976 by Helen Buck (1899–1997), the garden was renamed for her husband. Since then the planting and development has continued. The F. Gordon Hardy Foster Fern Collection was added in 1987, containing over fifty species of

native and exotic ferns interspersed among shade perennials. The Helen R. Buck trail (opened in 2008), winds down the hillside, completing a circular path from the Scenic Overlook. A rustic pavilion in Azalea Field provides a refreshing pause. Site improvements from the 2003 Master Plan include further wheelchair accessibility, expanded parking, and the creation of a space for hosting larger events.

A horticultural manager with a garden foreman, three full-time gardeners, two or three seasonal gardeners, and an interpretive gardener care for the collections, which are visited by some 10,000 people annually. Three to four volunteer gardeners assist, as well as ten to twelve active docents. The policy is to label extensively and sensitively.

88 SISTER MARY GRACE BURNS ARBORETUM OF GEORGIAN COURT UNIVERSITY

900 Lakewood Avenue, Lakewood, NJ 08701
TEL: (732) 987-2373
WEBSITE: *www.georgian.edu/arboretum*
SEE MAP: p. 209

Hours: Open daily, 8am–dusk. Admission free

Location: 60 miles from New York City

Parking: Ample; use parking lot A or C

Public transportation: NJ Transit bus to 9th Street on Route 9 in Lakewood (2 blocks from the arboretum)

Facilities: Download color map from website before visit, and pick up color guidebook for self-guided tours at the Cunningham Library, #5 on map, or from the security office. See also *Georgian Court: An Estate of the Gilded Age* by M. Christina Geis (2003), available online or from the University Finance Office (732) 987-2240; restrooms in Cunningham Library; refreshments in Raymond Hall Dining Hall or Court Café during the semester; picnicking; mostly wheelchair accessible, except for Sunken Garden; no dogs

Group garden tours: By appointment, small fee

Nearby eateries: Route 9 in Lakewood and Howell (1–5 miles north of arboretum)

Other parks nearby: Lake Carasaljo Municipal Park, Route 9 (River Avenue), Lakewood (adjacent); Ocean County Park (former Rockefeller Estate), 659 Ocean Avenue, Lakewood, 2-1/2 miles.

The arboretum at first takes second place to the extraordinary remnants of the pseudo-Italianate gardens designed in the late 1890s by the architect Bruce Price (1845–1903) to complement the Georgian-style winter home (hence the name) he built for George Jay Gould (1864–1923), the millionaire son of railroad tycoon Jay Gould (see Lyndhurst, p. 142).

From an enormous marble and bronze fountain (1902) designed by the Beaux-Arts sculptor John Massey Rhind, Apollo (as at Versailles) spurs on his team of winged horses accompanied by mermaids and putti.

Three avenues radiate out in a patte d'oeil lined by pedestals, many holding nothing, others with great urns for flowers or concrete gods and goddesses (painted white), and rather the worse for wear. A large wrought-iron eagle with wings outstretched and fierce demeanor (1900) presides where the axes cross. The trimmed green hedges strengthening the formal design have gone, but to the north two awkward columned "pergolas" remain.

The Sunken Garden is announced by a pair of lions and four eight-foot marble urns. Massive stairways, gleaming white, lead down to a French

seventeenth-century fountain, and then to a short, stone-edged "lagoon," which joins Lake Carasaljo under a handsome bridge. While rather grand, this garden offers a secluded and quiet retreat, providing benches that are copies of those in the Vatican.

It's almost bizarre to then step into the contrasting sensibility of the Japanese Garden. An early example (1909–1910) of an Asian garden in the United States, it was a gift from George Gould to his wife, Edith, and was laid out by Takeo Shiota (1881–1943), later the designer of the well-known Japanese Garden at the Brooklyn Botanical Garden (1915). Rather depleted now, it is found on a one-acre space west of the main alley, surrounded by a pedestrian deer fence, and with a building looming on one side.

In 1924 George Gould's eldest son, Kingdom, sold the estate to what became Georgian University, which has carefully sited its own buildings beyond the Italian garden. The arboretum covers the entire 155 acres of the campus, 75 acres of which are landscaped. Tons of fine loam brought in by the Goulds to enrich the nutrient-poor soil enabled it to become home to exotic species along with solid collections of natives. Conifers, hollies, lilacs, and oaks are its strengths. The arboretum was dedicated (1989) to Sister Mary Burns, professor of biology from 1927 to 1968, for her involvement with the identification, care, and planting of trees on the campus. A few hundred trees have large plaques; a few thousand also have aluminum tags with scientific name and accession numbers. Following the suggested route on the guide (see above) is the best way to note representative specimens found within the main campus and the formal gardens.

Six full-time gardeners look after the arboretum. Michael F. Gross, professor of biology and director of the arboretum, writes, "Because we are a national historic landmark and many trees are reaching the end of their lifespan, our focus will be to replant the historic gardens with offspring of the existing plants. We will also expand the representation of New Jersey pinelands plants in our arboretum as part of our efforts to garden sustainably."

89 COLONIAL PARK ARBORETUM

56 Mettlers Road, East Millstone
(Franklin Township), NJ 08873
TEL: (732) 873-2459
WEBSITE: *www.somersetcountyparks.org*
(PARKS AND FACILITIES)
SEE MAPS: pp. 209, 213 & 216

Hours: Grounds open daily, sunrise to sunset. Admission free
Location: 48 miles from New York City
Parking: For the perennial and shrub garden, parking lot F; for the rose garden and arboretum, parking Lot A
Public transportation: NJ Transit to Bound Brook, taxi 4-1/2 miles
Facilities: No refreshments; restrooms in arboretum and by Spooky Brook Pond; picnicking; rose garden and fragrance and sensory garden wheelchair accessible; special run for dogs, otherwise dogs on leash
Programming: Annual rose Day and Garden Party, occasional talks
Nearby eateries: Manville, 3 miles; also Somerset, 6-1/2 miles, and Hillsborough, 5 miles
Also of interest: Direct connection from the arboretum to the towpath of the Delaware & Raritan Canal (1834)

The 685-acre Colonial Park was created from the former farm and garden of John Wyckoff Mettler (1878–1952), president and founder of the Interwoven Stocking Company. Acquired by Somerset County in 1965, it offers a host of recreational activities: golf, tennis, paddleboating, a putting course, softball, biking, walking, angling, two picnic areas for grilling, two playgrounds, a run for dogs, a nature trail, and more. Colonial Drive divides the eastern portion into northern and southern sections, while Mettlers Road, running north–south, acts as division between the more sporty offerings to the east and the horticultural interests to the west.

Most inviting is the 144-acre Arboretum, which harbors the Perennial and Shrub gardens, the Grass Garden and, separately, the Fragrance and Sensory Garden (1981) and the very well-known Rudolf W. van der Goot Rose Garden (1971).

Although there is no cohesive landscape design, the individual elements, in the care of Somerset County Park Commission, are of interest, and all are within walking distance of each other. The focal point of the four-acre Perennial Garden (a favorite wedding photo and ceremony location) is the 1986 conical roofed gazebo. Reached by a grass path, the circle of beds, with white entrance

arbors, have rich herbaceous and conifer displays with two good-looking Japanese lilac trees. This area is framed first by islands of attractive flowering shrubs with strong accents of golden Hinoki cypresses, and then woods. The Shrubbery Garden, just behind—suffering at the moment from rabbits and deer invasion—displays examples of, among others, Carolina allspice, the Japanese honeysuckle tree, lilacs, red buckeye, and Korean dogwoods.

The one-acre Rudolf W. van der Goot Rose Garden, further south, is named after Somerset County's first horticulturist, who drew on features of the Mettlers' formal garden in his designs. Closed since 2009, its reopening in 2011 is much anticipated. Formerly, it displayed over two hundred varieties of roses—hybrids, species, heritage, climbers and ramblers, etc., in beds and on trellises.

A walk to the Duck Pond (rather overgrown) goes through part of the tree collection, created by the Mettlers, which is in the process of being expanded. It has some noteworthy specimens (labeled): weeping beech, spruces, and other conifers, both native and from abroad. Visitors might conclude their tour with a game of bocce (bring your balls) or a walk along the Delaware & Raritan Canal.

90 CROSS ESTATE GARDENS

61C Jockey Hollow Road, Bernardsville, NJ 07924, or
Ledell Road, Mendham, NJ 07924 (OFF TEMPE WICK ROAD)
TEL: (973) 376-0348 or
(973) 539-2016 (NATIONAL PARK SERVICE)
WEBSITE: *www.crossestategardens.org*
SEE MAPS: pp. 209 & 212

Hours: Grounds open 8am–dusk. Admission free
Location: 43 miles from New York City
Public transportation: NJ Transit train to Bernardsville, taxi 3 miles
Facilities: A guide to twenty trees in and around the gardens and flyers at the
  entrance; no refreshments; no restrooms; picnicking; partially wheelchair accessible;
  dogs on leash
Programming: Occasional lectures, plant sales
Group garden tours: By appointment on Wednesday 9am–12pm, March through
  mid-November. Suggested contribution
Nearby eateries: Bernardsville, or on Route 202, south
Also of interest: Extensive trails to New Jersey Brigade Area, Morristown National
  Historical Park, can be accessed just before the entrance; Wick House kitchen
  garden, reminiscent of the eighteenth-century Revolutionary War period, Tempe
  Wick Road, usually open same hours as house, 9:30am–noon and 1pm–4:30pm

It is quiet now at Hardscabble House, the former 300-acre country estate of New York banker W. Redmond Cross and his wife, Julia Newbold Cross, who bought the property in 1929. The 1905 house—built for the previous owner, John A. Bensel, and substantially renovated after 1940—and grounds have a deserted, neglected look except for a small pocket now called the Cross Estate Gardens.

Approached through a shady kalmia grove surrounded by handsome mature trees, the (mostly) native garden and a charming walled, formal garden lie within a roughly rectangular half-acre. The former has gravel paths that loop around islands of lilac, dogwood, redbud, azaleas, and a fringe tree, with loose plantings of ferns, *Amsonia* and *Baptisia*, and self-seeded anemones, poppies, dame's rocket, and wild buttercups. It was formerly used by Mrs. Cross and her gardener for the lilac collection and as a holding area, in conjunction with the greenhouses, for her chrysanthemums and other horticultural interests.

The adjoining two-tiered garden, in contrast, presents the regularity and symmetry of straight brick paths crossing at right angles and brick-edged beds overflowing with perennials—peonies, irises, alliums, day lilies, columbines, etc.—and herbs, sedum, and self-seeded foxgloves in a very appealing English Country style. Two large clay pots form centerpieces at

the north end, and metal pyramids provide climbing support for clematis. A very wide and handsome 130-foot-long pergola links the two gardens, providing shade from well-established Asian wisteria and a newly planted American species.

This is what remains of Julia Newbold Cross's horticultural improvements around the house, carried out from 1930 with the help of landscape architect Clarence Fowler (1870–1935). A member of the Royal Horticultural Society, she was also president of the Horticultural Society of New York for ten years. After her death in 1972, the property went unsold until 1975, when the National Park Service acquired 162 acres, thus linking the Revolutionary War site of the New Jersey Brigade Unit to the Morristown National Historical Park.

The gardens fell into disrepair until a keen group of volunteers rescued one section of them in 1977. In 1987, in cooperation with the Park Service, they formed the New Jersey Historical Garden Foundation to officially preserve this area. On Wednesdays, volunteers from a core group of twenty-five to thirty meet for three hours to supplement the skills of the part-time gardener, who works three hundred hours annually. Over the years the long views to the west and north have been lost to unchecked tree growth, but the foundation has recently cleared the Norway Maple in front of the intriguing 1895 stone water tower (worked by wind until the 1920s) near the house and plans its external renovation. It also hopes to extend its gardening range around the house and to develop brochures for the Native Garden and the water tower.

DEEP CUT GARDENS

152 Red Hill Road, Middletown, NJ 07748
TEL: (732) 671-6050; (732) 842-4000
(PARK SYSTEM)
WEBSITE: *www.monmouthcountyparks.com*
SEE MAP: p. 209

Hours: Garden open daily, 8am–dusk. Admission free

Location: 46 miles from New York City

Public transportation: NJ Transit to Middletown, taxi or walk approximately 1-1/2 miles

Facilities: Brochure with map in the Horticultural Center (daily, 8am–dusk), with restrooms and the Elvin MacDonald Horticultural Library (Monday–Friday 9am–4pm; Saturday 10am–4pm); no refreshments; picnic tables; wheelchair accessible; no dogs

Programming: Horticultural, throughout the year

Group garden tours: By appointment

Nearby eateries: Café at 102 King's Highway, Middletown (1 mile), or selection on Route 35, north or south; Redbank (5-1/4 miles) on Broad and Front Streets

Nearby parks/arboretums: Tatum Park, across the road, 151 Red Hill Road, with walking trails. The David C. Shaw Arboretum at Holmdel Park (follow signs for Historic Longstreet Farm), 44 Longstreet Road, Holmdel, 4-1/4 miles

An unusual wall of peanut stone (a local, natural aggregate) enclosing the fifty-four-acre grounds on the road side heralds your arrival. The house (1928), purchased by crime boss Vito Genovese (1897–1969) in 1935 as a country retreat for his family, has gone, but other features of the grand landscaping designs by Theodore Stout remain: the impressive rockery of Italian volcanic stone with interesting shrubs and prostrate conifers on the steep hillside and its three pools; a miniature stone Vesuvius that used to emit smoke; the superb weeping hemlocks with their contorted trunks. The long axial view—encompassing the rose parterre and pavilion and ending at the swimming pool (but now filled in) with its adjacent sitting and entertainment area—is still striking.

Two years later Genovese had to quickly leave the country after being indicted for murder, and his pseudo-Italianate gardens, reminders of his Neapolitan childhood, and the surrounding English-style park were left unfinished, contractors unpaid. Soon after, the house mysteriously burned down. Onto this framework, later owners Karl and Marjorie Sperry Wihtol grafted new gardens at the top of the hill (between 1953 and 1977), close to their unpretentious house (now the Horticultural Center and library).

From the topiaried spruce dinosaur, the path leads up along herbaceous and annual borders, to a lawn on the left with excellent specimen conifer and deciduous trees (including two superb spreading *Acer palmatums*). Further on is a secluded garden room with a koi pond—in the area where the original house once stood. The Japanese garden

tucked in beside the greenhouse (which includes pots of cacti and orchids), a display of bonsai placed on tables, and a shade garden are unexpected discoveries.

At the death of Marjorie Wihtol in 1977, half of Deep Cut Farm (named for the narrow stream that flows through the steep valley) was donated to the Monmouth County Park System. Through New Jersey Green Acres the rest of the property was purchased, and new land was added. Underfunding seems to be a problem: the outer areas have been neglected and detailing in the rock garden has coarsened. Some expensive capital projects have been

undertaken: the rose parterre has been replanted and the pavilion rebuilt, but surrounding hedges and trees are still required to anchor the design successfully.

Along with historic preservation, Monmouth County Park has developed teaching gardens—All American Trial beds, a delightful ornamental vegetable, herb, and flower garden, and a composting demonstration area—to

further its mission of encouraging home gardening. A native plant garden is under development.

A deer fence enclosing the property protects the rich plant collections, and metal tags or signs help identify select plants and trees. A park superintendent oversees the two full-time gardeners and five seasonal employees. Free access and generous visiting hours insure Deep Cut's popularity—it received some 78,000 visitors in 2009, with seventy-two volunteers donating over 740 hours of time to various gardening and programming projects.

354 Stockton Road (Route 206), Princeton, NJ 08540
TEL: (609) 683-0057
WEBSITE: *www.drumthwacket.org*
SEE MAPS: pp. 209, 214 & 216

Hours: House and grounds open by reservation only, most Wednesdays and selected weekend dates. Closed August. Admission free but suggested donation
Location: 54 miles from New York City
Public transportation: Amtrak or NJ Transit to Princeton Junction, taxi 3-3/4 miles or local Dinky train to Princeton Borough, taxi 1-1/4 miles
Facilities: Thomas Ogden House (1759) for informative brochures and herb garden list, gift shop with booklet for sale *(Drumthwacket)*; no refreshments; restrooms; no picnicking; partially wheelchair accessible; no dogs
Group garden tours: Occasionally with Mercer County master gardeners
Nearby eateries: Downtown Princeton, 1-1/4 miles; Lawrenceville, 5 miles
Nearby park: Marquand Park, Lover's Lane, 1/4 mile
Also of interest: Historical Society of Princeton, 158 Nassau Street, Princeton, 1-1/4 miles

This Greek Revival mansion sits nicely back from the road. Its drive curves around a lawn—studded with fine shade trees (elms, beech, tulip poplar, sycamore, Norway spruce, linden, and maple)—to the Ionic-columned, porticoed front door, and then continues on to rejoin the road on the other side. The central core of the house (possibly designed by Charles Steadman) was built in 1835 for Charles Smith Olden (1799–1876), the outer wings in 1893 and 1901 by Raleigh C. Gildersleeve for Moses Taylor Pyne (1855–1921). All three private owners, the last of whom was Abram Spanel (from 1940 to 1966), played important civic roles in Princeton and beyond, the first two enormously influential in the expansion of the College of New Jersey, renamed Princeton University in 1896. In 1981, Drumthwacket became the official residence of the governor of New Jersey (replacing Morven), its first-floor rooms lending themselves to receptions and entertainment.

From the front door, the center hall leads directly into the Italianate formal garden, which is laid out on three descending terraces, with views of the woods beyond. Restored after years of neglect in 1992, the layout recalls the garden, designed after 1893 by Daniel W. Langton (1864–1909) for Moses Taylor Pyne. Equilibrium

characterizes the placement of statues, symmetry the patterns of the beds, and restraint the handling of water, which appears through a lip in the second terrace wall and is channeled down into the frog pool. The planting has been pared down for easy maintenance, an armillary sphere has replaced the main fountain, and river birches (an interesting solution) and peonies substitute for the lost balustrade. One senses, however, that the spirit of the garden remains.

Langton also designed the rest of the estate, eventually growing to 300 acres, in the eighteenth-century English landscape style. It incorporated a deer park, sheep meadows, lakes, a farm, extensive vegetable and flower cutting gardens, and large greenhouses. Since 1940 just twelve acres have remained from those Gilded Age days.

The state of New Jersey has owned Drumthwacket since 1966, and the nonprofit Drumthwacket Foundation, formed in 1982, runs tours of the house and garden for some 10,000 visitors a year (including schoolchildren). Proud that the garden was featured on the cover of the October 1905 issue of *American Homes and Gardens*, the foundation is committed to maintaining its historic character. Currently there are two outdoor staff members, helped by a dozen volunteer Mercer County master gardeners. Two foundation administrators are aided by forty volunteer tour guides.

93 DUKE FARMS

1112 Dukes Parkway West
(BETWEEN ROUTE 206 & ROYCEFIELD ROAD)
Hillsborough, NJ 08844
TEL: (908) 722-3700
WEBSITE: *www.dukefarms.org*
SEE MAPS: pp. 209, 213 & 216

Hours: For grounds, check website or call; house not open. Admission free
Location: 50 miles from New York City
Public transportation: NJ Transit to Somerville, taxi 3 miles
Facilities: New orientation center for trail guides, café, restrooms; sustainably powered tram to core of the property; wheelchair accessible; no dogs
Programming: Native seed propagation, organic gardening, orchid growing, and more
Nearby eateries: Hillsborough, along Route 206, and downtown Somerville, 3 miles

The goal of Duke Farms is nothing less than "to be a model of environmental stewardship in the 21st century and inspire visitors to become informed stewards of the land." With the transitional period of redefining its mission now complete, and the new orientation center opening in the fall of 2011, visitors will enjoy unrestricted access to 965 acres of the 2,700-acre grounds. Called by some "the ungardening of America," it seeks to restore and regenerate native habitats, including the reformation of wetlands, within what was once a highly landscaped or agrarian estate. Deer are excluded by a new, eight-foot-high fence, the problem of invasives is being tackled, and both Rutgers University and Princeton Hydro are conducting scientific studies and experiments on reducing the high levels of nutrients (and subsequently algae) in the lakes. New programs for the general public

include bird, butterfly, wildflower, and tree identification, and volunteer participation is encouraged.

The estate was initially (1893) the country home of James Buchanan Duke (1856–1925), the tobacco and hydropower magnate and philanthropist. As his interests in farming waned, he engaged the landscape architect James L. Greenleaf (1857–1933) to convert the flat acres of farmland into parkland with carriage drives, lakes, and fountains. Additional lakes, bridges, and other features were overseen by Horatio Buckenham between 1905 and 1911, and sophisticated technologies were used to pump and distribute the water from the Raritan River. This impressive designed landscape, along with the 1894 conservatory built by Lord & Burnham, were open to the public in 1899, but closed in 1915 due to vandalism. A grand new greenhouse complex (also by Lord & Burnham), completed by 1917, supplied the house and the park and was used commercially to grow orchids and flowers for the New York market.

Doris Duke (1912–1993)—just twelve years old when her father died—inherited an enormous fortune. Although living for long periods in Honolulu (Shangri La), and also at Rough Point, in Newport, RI (both now open to the public), she retained a special affection for her childhood home. Her particular contribution was to enlarge and convert the 1917 greenhouse/conservatories into highly manicured gardens representing the "styles" of nine countries (French, Chinese, English, Indo-Persian, etc.) and the settings of two locales—tropical rainforest and Mediterranean. These were open to the public for tightly controlled tours from 1964 until 2008—when the gardens were dismantled, her will having included no directives.

After four years of legal battles, the Doris Duke Charitable Foundation was established with new trustees, its main purpose being to support medical research and the performance arts. The Duke Farms Foundation (1998), under its control, interprets her environmental interests. From 2003 Duke Farms was open to the public for a short self-guided walk and a bus tour of part of the property. Now, a new and exciting period will begin. The smaller 1899 conservatory, converted to fulfill energy efficiency requirements, will also reopen, displaying native orchids and featuring a section devoted to the

southeast coastal plains of America (mainly those in Florida). In addition, the solar panel installation on two and a half acres near the orientation center will be on view.

94 THE FRELINGHUYSEN ARBORETUM

53 East Hanover Avenue, Whippany (MORRIS TOWNSHIP),
NJ 07962
TEL: (973) 326-7601
WEBSITE: *www.morrisparks.net; www.arboretumfriends.org*
SEE MAPS: pp. 209 & 212

Hours: Gardens and grounds open daily, 8am–dusk. Admission free. House is headquarters of the Morris County Park Commission

Location: 33 miles from New York City

Public transportation: NJ Transit train to Morristown, taxi 2 miles

Facilities: Haggerty Education Center, April through November, daily 9am–4:30pm; December through March, Monday–Friday 9am–4:30pm for brochures and maps, cell phone tours, vending machine refreshments, restrooms, and small shop; picnicking; the education center and a number of gardens are wheelchair accessible; no dogs

Programming: Many horticultural classes for all ages, events, outings; see Friends website

Garden tours: Part of program, and by appointment

Nearby eateries: Large selection in Morristown, 2 miles

Nearby garden: Acorn Hall (see p. 217), 1 mile

Also of interest: Morris Museum, 6 Normandy Heights Road, Morristown, 1 mile

---

The drive sweeps up toward the white Georgian-style house, well sited on the brow of the hill and offering long views of the Boonton Township hills to the northeast, and grassy valleys to the southwest, with scattered conifers and deciduous groves. Trees fringe the whole property (127 acres), and mature specimens grow on the expansive lawns near the house. Cherries, crabapples, dogwoods, and magnolias make a lovely spring showing.

The English landscape-style grounds and farmed areas were originally laid out by the Scottish landscape architect, James McPherson for the new house, called Whippany Farm,

designed in 1891 by Rotch & Tilden for the patent attorney George Griswold Frelinghuysen (1851–1936) and his wife, Sara Ballantine (1858–1940), granddaughter of the founder of the Ballantine Brewing Company. Produce from the farm was sent to them in New York when not in residence.

Approaching cars are directed toward the former service buildings and into an impressive parking lot that benefits from contemporary attitudes in dealing with these normally ugly spaces. A horticultural display starts right there, in the wide medians, with trees and shrubs well marked and lampposts used for climbers. Water runoff is collected in the adjoining Marsh Meadow Garden, where a white belvedere has been placed for viewing the native plants and bird activities.

Close to the Haggerty Education Center are the Home Demonstration Gardens: small designed spaces for rock, perennial, cottage, and shade gardens, which make appropriate use of walls, fences, pavers, and pools. From espaliered fruit trees and ornamental vegetables to a color-themed garden and a raised garden for wheelchair observation—there is much to linger over before peeking through the fence at Branching Out, the gardens tended by children.

A walk to the house by the lower drive brings the visitor to the Shade Garden and then the Fern Garden, before proceeding on to the 1920 formal gardens designed to complement the south side of the house. From a viewpoint gazebo, a red brick path leads to enclosed garden rooms: a knot garden, a perennial and fountain garden, and the patterned beds of the rose gardens. A summerhouse suggests relaxation, while the views over the wall call for explorations to the farther reaches of the estate.

The house and grounds were inherited by the couple's daughter, Matilda E. Frelinghuysen (1887–1969). She participated in the plans to turn the estate into an arboretum before bequeathing it to Morris County in 1969. About 500,000 visitors appear annually, and it is tended by seven full-time and three part-time gardeners, a group of about twenty-five regular

volunteers, and many others who participate either as individuals or through corporate volunteer days. The very active Friends of Frelinghuysen, founded in 1972, organizes programming and

fundraising in cooperation with the Morris County Park Commission, and contributes some $200,000 annually. A tented facility for weddings and corporate functions was erected in 2010, and a former cottage is to be transformed into a café. Replacement of dead trees and further deerproofing will help enrich the grounds. Traffic noise from I-287 is unfortunate, but one learns to block it out.

95 GREENWOOD GARDENS

274 Old Short Hills Road, Short Hills, NJ 07078
TEL: (973) 258-4026
WEBSITE: *http://greenwoodgardens.org*
SEE MAPS: pp. 209 & 210

Hours: Grounds open by appointment for tour, usually May through October,
  Thursdays at 2pm and first Saturday of the month at 10am. Admission fee
Location: 24 miles from New York City
Public transportation: NJ Transit to Millburn, walk 1-3/4 miles, or taxi
Facilities: Only restrooms; partial wheelchair access, golf cart available; no dogs
Programming: Workshops, outings, walks—to be expanded
Nearby eateries: Millburn, 1 3/4 miles
Also of interest: For picnics and walks, South Mountain Reservation (2,000 acres),
  accessed from the parking lot; Old Short Hills Park, opposite side of the
  entrance road

The $5 million phase 1 restoration of Greenwood Gardens, scheduled for completion in 2012, is under way. But even now—before the crumbling and mossy balustrades, walls, pools, staircases, and grottoes are renovated, and the fountains and the cascade flow again—visitors will find tours of the property intriguing.

Greenwood Gardens (originally called Pleasant Days) was in its prime in the 1920s and 1930s, when it was owned by Joseph P. Day (1874–1944), a leading New York real estate auctioneer, and his wife, Pauline, who bought the property in 1906. After the existing house burned down in 1911, they commissioned the architect William Whetten Renwick (1864–1933), a partner in the firm of his uncle, James Renwick Jr., to design a new house, with related gardens (1912). These, with some overlays from the lawyer Peter P. Blanchard (1912–2000) and his wife, Adelaide, who acquired the property in 1949, are the focus of the visit.

Although the Blanchards replaced the Day's large Italianate edifice with the current more modest Georgian-style home (1950) by D. Wentworth Wright (d. 1955), the terrace gardens are still strongly orientated toward the original two axes running down the hill from the center of the south front and the west side. The architectural elements are indeed dominant and the design Italianate, but an American touch is equally visible: in the green lushness of the lawns, the groundcovers, the clipped yew and box hedges, and the deciduous

trees and shrubs within the formal framework. Additional flower planting in beds and borders on two terraces, inspired by the Day-era gardens, are planned. The restoration is giving major consideration to the special Arts and Crafts features: the pavilions with their roughly hewn stone, the Rookwood Pottery tiles in the grottoes, the decoration in the alcoves, and the masks of the cascade.

With the advice of the Garden Conservancy, Greenwood Gardens became a nonprofit entity in 2003 through the generosity of Peter P. Blanchard III and his wife, Sofia. In addition to the house and formal gardens, the twenty-eight-acre property includes meadows, ponds, greenhouses, and domestic animals (goats, chickens, geese). Previously, forty-eight acres had been given to the town of Millburn to establish Old Short Hills Park. Note the good views of the park's landscaping from the entrance road, along with the long grove of plane trees on the left of Greenwood's drive (contrasting with the hemlocks on the right), originally planted as a screen but now a striking feature in itself. Some 3,000 visitors currently take the tour of the gardens, which are cared for by four full-time gardeners and thirty-five volunteers. Phases 2 and 3 will follow as funds allow.

Robert Wood Johnson University Hospital,
1 Hamilton Health Place, Hamilton, NJ 08690
TEL: (609) 584-6581 (RWJ UNIVERSITY HOSPITAL HAMILTON FOUNDATION);
(609) 584-6678 (PR)
WEBSITE: *www.rwjuhhfoundation.org*
SEE MAPS: pp. 209, 214 & 216

Hours: Grounds open dawn to dusk. Admission free
Location: 63 miles from New York City
Public transportation: NJ Transit to Hamilton, taxi 4-1/2 miles
Facilities: Roma Bank Garden Café, main building, ground floor; restrooms;
wheelchair accessible; no dogs
Nearby eateries: Hamilton Township; Grounds for Sculpture, 4-1/2 miles
(see p. 246)

The four Grounds For Healing gardens at the Robert Wood Johnson University Hospital reflect the hospital's commitment to "complement its clinical expertise by providing serene, contemplative outdoor spaces designed for healing" and will be of particular interest to landscape designers and garden theorists alike. All can be visited, except the earliest one, the Bruce W. Bux Grounds For Healing Garden (2001), a secluded space within the Cancer Institute of New Jersey for patients receiving lengthy treatment. They can view the garden from behind large windows or choose a spot outside in the sun or shade, beside either water, raised flower and shrub beds, or a miniforest of bamboos.

The second, situated in the angle between the emergency and maternity departments, is an outdoor room with curved brick walls, seating, and raised

planting, perhaps used particularly by staff. In the center of an inner area, a sculpture by J. Seward Johnson Jr. of a mother sitting on the ground reading to her child (*No Mommy, That One*) elicits a smile. Shaped hedges give additional form, with grasses and bamboo toward the edges.

Entering the Women and Infants Pavilion and following the signs to the Roma Bank Garden Café, one approaches the Christy Stephenson Grounds For Healing Garden (2008). It is on a much larger scale and is first seen to great advantage from above. Through the two-story glass wall of the café, medical staff and visitors view the clean lines of a synthetic cubist design—intercepting geometric shapes of pavers, pebbles, groundcover, and water, with rows of trees, clipped evergreens, and a berm supplying a little height. Although perhaps more sensed than consciously examined by most, it offers another example of "the restorative powers made possible through the combination of art and nature."

The exit at the far end of the Stephenson garden (where the planting patterns have been weakened by the addition of azaleas) leads past foundation and median planting to the Maurice T. Perilli garden (2005)— on the left (north) side of the main entrance. Here, a small area provides seclusion within a loose planting of shrubs and trees. The ideas embraced by Grounds For Healing would seem to carry over even to the large car parks, where, to the north, a series of irregularly shaped flowing berms help to mitigate their impact.

The Robert Wood Johnson University Hospital Hamilton Foundation has brought into being the four gardens, working in partnership with the nearby Grounds For Sculpture (see p. 246), which has loaned and placed the sculptures, and whose project architect, Brian Carey, has designed them all.

97 GROUNDS FOR SCULPTURE

18 Fairgrounds Road, or 126 Sculptor's Way,
Hamilton, NJ 08619
TEL: (609) 586-0616
WEBSITE: *www.groundsforsculpture.org*
SEE MAPS: pp. 209, 214 & 216

Hours: Grounds and exhibition galleries open Tuesday–Sunday 10am–6pm
(except for Thanksgiving, Christmas, and New Year's Day). Closed Mondays,
except for Memorial Day and Labor Day. Admission fee

Location: 61 miles from New York City

Public transportation: NJ Transit to Hamilton, taxi 1-3/4 miles, or Trenton,
taxi 2-1/2 miles

Facilities: Visitor center for introductory video, sculpture, and tree brochures;
restrooms in visitor center, exhibition buildings, and gazebo; refreshments in
Peacock Café with exterior maple grove courtyard (Tuesday–Thursday 10am–4pm,
Friday–Sunday 11am–5pm), the gazebo for snacks in the summer, and Rat's restaurant
(reservations, (609) 584-7800); book and gift shop in the Domestic Arts Building
(by café) and artisan crafts in Toad Hall Shop by Rat's restaurant; no picnicking
(except for school groups); emphasis on wheelchair accessibility, and special vehicle
tour by appointment; no dogs

Programming: Full schedule of exhibition openings, lectures, dance, music events

Grounds and sculpture tour: By appointment, fee

Nearby eateries: Not many; in-house offerings recommended

Also of interest: State Capitol Complex, 172 West State Street, Trenton,
for modern plaza and fountains

Perhaps no other designed landscape
in this book is as idiosyncratic as
Grounds For Sculpture, where the
planting is unusual, the palette rich,
and the partnership between nature
and art provocative. Often gloriously
successful in setting off the sculpture,
the planted elements in themselves
compete for our attention.

In 1987 the sculptor J. Seward
Johnson chose this site—originally
part of the New Jersey Fairgrounds—
for a landscaped park featuring
contemporary sculpture, and he
launched plans to transform the long-
neglected remaining buildings from
the 1920s and 1940s into exhibition
galleries. Brian Carey of AC/BC
Associates was selected in 1989 as the
landscape architect, and he and Bruce
Daniels, facilities and project manager,
have masterminded the evolving
development ever since.

The previously flat land with seven
trees now has contoured berms and
hillocks, a lookout from a tall gazebo,
a mound with a salvaged hopper, and
thousands of new trees and shrubs.

Water features abound: two lakes, misting devices, calm reflecting pools, and bubbling fountains. Hedges define spaces, trees form shady allées, and everywhere an appreciation of strong forms and bold statements is evident: fastigiate, weeping, clipped, and prostrate conifers; an orchard of cherry trees arranged geometrically by blossom color; and swathes of tall, ornamental grasses, offset occasionally by colored ribbons of perennials.

The contemporary sculpture collection—some 255 pieces (and growing) in a broad range of styles—by internationally known and emerging artists—shares this thirty-five-acre site. Many sculptures, however large, are moved around; others are linked more closely to their locations—in the middle of a pool (Bruce Beasley, *Dorion*, 1986), perched on a mound (Walter Dusenbery, *Tempio Bretton*, 1981), or backed by a wall (G. Frederick Morante, *Relative*, 2003). Abstract or figurative, surreal or political, monumental or delicate, all have considered environments, while in unexpected places J. Seward Johnson's humorous three-dimensional riffs on Monet (*Terrace at Sainte-Adresse*), Manet (*Déjeuner sur l'herbe*), and Matisse (*La Danse*) and others appear. A feeling of engagement reigns, extending even to children, who are encouraged to run around, climb up stairs, and try out spaces.

New areas are still being developed. Carey and Daniels have a penchant for buying up oddly shaped specimens that others avoid, sports (who else has a multistemmed ginkgo?), and leftovers from downsizing nurseries, and then devising new ways of displaying them. Currently, great chunks of stone from a quarry going out of business and discarded soil from a building site will lead to the creation of four acres of berms, planting, and sculpture placement.

In 2000, Grounds For Sculpture, Inc., was formed, a nonprofit organization that now manages the property. Immediate plans include expanding outreach programs to advance the appreciation of contemporary sculpture and redesigning the entrance to the sculpture garden and the circulation paths in order to clarify the layout. Labeling of plant material is not considered a priority here. Regardless, 120,000 people annually are drawn to the grounds, which are cared for by one full-time horticulturist, five master gardeners, and a contracted landscape

98 HEREFORD INLET LIGHTHOUSE GARDENS

111 N. Central Avenue, North Wildwood,
NJ 08260

TEL: (609) 522-4520
WEBSITE: *www.herefordlighthouse.org*
SEE MAPS: pp. 209, 215 & 339

Hours: Garden open dawn to dusk. Lighthouse open May 15 through October 29, daily, 9am–5pm. Garden free, lighthouse fee

Location: 155 miles from New York City

Parking: Street parking or small parking lot

Public transportation: None

Facilities: Gift shop in the lighthouse: nautical themed items, and *A Guide to the Hereford Inlet Lighthouse Gardens* by Steve Murray (2001); no refreshments; two portable toilets in garden; picnic tables; wheelchair accessible, gardens only; no dogs

Group garden tours: By appointment

Nearby eateries: Many in North Wildwood; inquire in lighthouse

Also of interest: Historic Cape May with Victorian houses, 12 miles

Built in 1874, the arresting residential lighthouse, designed by Paul J. Pelz (1842–1918) in the Victorian Carpenter Gothic style, was moved 100 feet inland in 1914 in response to the encroaching sea. It remained functional, sitting on sandy, barren ground until 1964, when it was boarded up. Rescued from its neglected state in 1982, it opened a year later, refurnished in the style of the 1874–1894 period, and offering informative displays on lighthouses. It became operational again in 1986.

Steve Murray, as superintendent of parks in North Wildwood, was then asked to supply a garden. In 1988 he devised a plan for the property of almost one acre. He planted a shelter belt of pines and native shrubs to lessen the effects of salt spray and wind, and then designed Victorian cottage-style flower gardens separated by hedges, a pergola, and shrubs to reflect the earlier period. Small shaped areas of lawn are bordered by a plethora of old-fashioned and new varieties of perennials and annuals, creating a happy mingling of color and range of heights; planted close together, they achieve maximum effect.

Easily accessible and visible from its sidewalk picket fence, the cheerful front garden has an impact on the neighborhood far beyond its size. Since the gardens offer access to the boardwalk and the coastal walk, many people delight in them throughout the seasons, some sitting quietly on the seats or under the trellised arbor in

the back garden. Here one also finds an ornamental herb garden within high box hedges, as well as a secluded garden room, which may well have a display of unusual coleuses—a special feature of the garden.

The property is owned by the state of New Jersey but leased to the Friends of the Hereford Inlet Lighthouse, who raise the operational funds. The booklet on the garden (see above) provides a list of the plants, and some of the herbs are labeled. The garden is cared for personally by Steve Murray, who is also chairman of the Friends. In 2009 he said, "I'll continue to experiment with new plant varieties and color combinations, and to improve the gardens' conditions as a back yard wildlife habitat. I'm retiring from the parks department, but I'm not leaving the Lighthouse." He strongly advocates chemical-free practices and encourages others to take up coastal gardening.

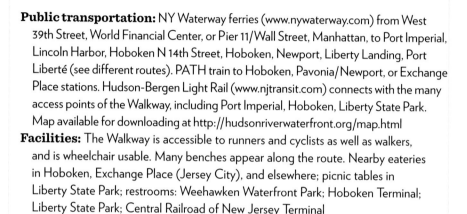

99 HUDSON RIVER WATERFRONT WALKWAY

From Bayonne Bridge, Bayonne, to George Washington Bridge, Fort Lee, NJ (and beyond)

TEL: None

WEBSITES: *www.hudsonriverwaterfront.org*
(HUDSON RIVER WATERFRONT CONSERVANCY); *www.betterwaterfront.com* (FUND FOR A BETTER WATERFRONT, INC.); *www.njparksandforests.org* (LIBERTY STATE PARK)

SEE MAPS: pp. 209 & 210

Public transportation: NY Waterway ferries (www.nywaterway.com) from West 39th Street, World Financial Center, or Pier 11/Wall Street, Manhattan, to Port Imperial, Lincoln Harbor, Hoboken N 14th Street, Hoboken, Newport, Liberty Landing, Port Liberté (see different routes). PATH train to Hoboken, Pavonia/Newport, or Exchange Place stations. Hudson-Bergen Light Rail (www.njtransit.com) connects with the many access points of the Walkway, including Port Imperial, Hoboken, Liberty State Park. Map available for downloading at http://hudsonriverwaterfront.org/map.html

Facilities: The Walkway is accessible to runners and cyclists as well as walkers, and is wheelchair usable. Many benches appear along the route. Nearby eateries in Hoboken, Exchange Place (Jersey City), and elsewhere; picnic tables in Liberty State Park; restrooms: Weehawken Waterfront Park; Hoboken Terminal; Liberty State Park; Central Railroad of New Jersey Terminal

The vision and persistence of dedicated and insightful nonprofit groups, and the financial commitment and cooperation among municipal, state, and national agencies have created the concept of a continuous, public waterfront park along the Hudson River—from Bayonne to Fort Lee. Many sections of this eighteen-and-a-half mile walk have been completed, transforming a 1970s coastline of abandoned factories and rotting piers—with no public access—into New Jersey's "gold coast." The Walkway along the shore—with stunning views of Manhattan, Ellis Island, the Statue of Liberty, and the Verrazano Bridge—comprises stretches of esplanades, small parks on both piers and land, and boardwalks and bridges across wetlands. In addition, a three-mile section goes through Liberty State Park, passing a marina, large open areas of grassland, a grove of plane trees for picnics, and numerous fishing spots. Sporting facilities, children's playgrounds, dog runs, and other facilities for all ages are integrated into the designs, connecting communities with their new waterfront.

Some developers within the townships have worked within the state guidelines (1984) and standards (1988), producing stunning results with excellent planting and detailing; others have been less generous and imaginative. Each township has a recognizable style for railings, benches, lighting, garbage containers, planters, and walking surfaces that defines each area within the unfurling variety of spaces. In more urban areas, trees tend to be planted in blocks or patterns of the same species, sometimes offset by shrubberies. Sites of historical, industrial, and cultural significance are sometimes referenced through design, artifacts, sculpture, and notice boards. Almost entirely free from noise and traffic, the Walkway is an extraordinary achievement and offers a striking alternative to Manhattan's parallel project on the east side of the Hudson. The missing links in the continuum are mainly southward from Port Liberté to Bayonne and northward from Roc Harbor (North Bergen Township). Signs indicating mileage to transportation terminals would be most helpful.

Suggested Route: (1) Take the NY Waterway ferry from West 39th Street, NYC, to Hoboken 14th Street and walk south to Exchange Place (PATH station), stopping in Hoboken for a meal and a visit to the 1907 Hoboken (train) Terminal with its tiled stained glass by Louis Comfort Tiffany. (2) Take the Liberty Landing Ferry from the World Financial Center Terminal, NYC, to Liberty State Park (www.libertylandingferry.com) and walk south around the Park, passing the historic 1889 Central Railroad of New Jersey Terminal (basic snacks, restrooms, tickets to Ellis Island and Statue of Liberty) and on to the end of the park (total 2½ miles). (The Liberty Park Café Diner at 14 Burma Road is just outside the park on the right.) Continue on the Walkway below Liberty National (golf club) to Port Liberté (no cafés or shops, but Le Pointe Restaurant) to end at the NY Waterway ferry terminal, 1 mile. Either return by ferry (weekdays only) or reverse the walk.

100 LAURELWOOD ARBORETUM

725 Pines Lake Drive West, Wayne, NJ 07470
TEL: (973) 202-9579
WEBSITE: *www.laurelwoodarboretum.org*
SEE MAPS: pp. 209 & 211

Hours: Grounds open year-round, dawn to dusk. Admission free

Location: 27 miles from New York City

Public transportation: PATH to Hoboken, then NJ Transit to Wayne/Route 23 Transit Center, taxi, 6 miles. NJ Transit Bus #194 to Pompton Lakes Wanaque Ave./ Ringwood Ave. stop, taxi, 3 miles

Facilities: Map of site, tree tour, and native plant tour flyers from notice board at entrance; no refreshments; portable toilet April through October; no picnicking; wheelchair accessible and motorized open air vehicle available by reservation; dogs on leash

Programming/events: Horticultural programs and two annual plant sales

Group garden tours: By appointment

Nearby eateries: Many on nearby Hamburg Turnpike–Wayne County Road 504; also Route 202, Oakland Business District, and Wanaque Ave; and Pompton Lakes Business District—all within 3 miles.

Nearby Parks: Ramapo Mountain State Forest, Wanaque (4,268 acres, trails, views), 7 miles

Also of interest: Van Riper-Hopper House, 533 Berdan Avenue, Wayne, 4-1/4 miles

A passion for rhododendrons and azaleas becomes a nursery business. A business becomes a private garden being prepared for public ownership. A town–volunteer partnership ensures the continuance of the horticultural eye and skills of Dorothy Knippenberg (1910–2006). She and her husband, John Knippenberg (1900–1995), who owned Country Club Ice Cream, bought thirty acres of land opposite their home in the 1930s. Over the years they drained and cleared areas, channeled the stream, created Laurel Pond with its two spray fountains, and

greatly enriched the valley and the slopes of native hemlock, white oak, and laurels.

By the 1940s, the wholesale nursery, Laurelwood Gardens, had been formed from their skill with rhododendron propagation and hybridization. Today, the grassed-over semicircles, which once held rows of plants—until 1995 when the business petered out—are the foreground to the series of surprising and multilayered gardens created by Mrs. Knippenberg.

Throughout the seasons, a succession of swathes of one color—the pink of

Ragged Robins or dianthus, the blue of forget-me-nots or *Ceratostigma*, the white of Shasta daisies, or the green of hostas—interlock with other shapes of groundcovers and ericas, prostrate junipers, hemlocks, and pines, which give way to an intermediate layer of flowering shrubs and trees (especially pendulant evergreens), and then a backing of taller trees. Often these loose shapes at ground level are integrated with tightly clipped box in the most inventive ways. The self-seeding of white foxgloves, poppies, and asters is welcomed and managed.

Naturally, azaleas and rhododendrons play a significant role in this combination planting, as do a great collection of ornamental shrubs (including tree hydrangeas) and many trees, now fifty to sixty years old, such as the Japanese umbrella pine and an early arrival of a Dawn Redwood. The gray gravel roads (too wide, but left over from the nursery days) provide the main "trails." Summer displays of annuals are not necessary in this sophisticated horticultural achievement, visually appealing year-round.

The Friends of Laurelwood Arboretum, created in 2003 to help Mrs. Knippenberg, formed a partnership in 2006 with the Wayne Township Parks and Recreation Department. It was a brave undertaking, as the arboretum had become run-down and the greenhouses dilapidated. They administer $100,000 provided by the town for the seasonal (March through November) salaries of a horticultural manager and two gardeners, and raise funds themselves for publicity (attracting some 5,000 visitors annually), programs, supplies, and capital improvements.

Two hundred volunteer gardeners contributed 8,800 hours in 2009, and many are trained in pruning techniques and, recently, propagation for replacement planting of rhododendrons. The Friends financed a gazebo on the pond's edge in 2010, dedicated to Dorothy Knippenberg. Working with the NJ Lions clubs of Wayne and West Milford and the Township of Wayne, a new Sensory Garden opens in 2011 that will provide educational, therapeutic, and volunteer experiences for the blind and those with physical and cognitive challenges. A 2010 Master Plan includes recommendations for a visitor center, to be completed in 2014.

101 LEAMING'S RUN GARDENS

1845 Route 9 North, Cape May Courthouse,
NJ 08210

TEL: (609) 465-5871
WEBSITE: *www.leamingsrun.com*
SEE MAPS: pp. 209, 215 & 339

Hours: Gardens open mid-May through early October, daily, 9:30am–5pm.
Admission fee

Location: 145 miles from New York City

Public transportation: None

Facilities: The Cooperage in former barn with gifts, home-produced dried flowers,
books by Jack Aprill, and *Leaming's Run Gardens: How It All Began* by Emily Heath
Aprill; two portable toilets; no refreshments; picnic tables; wheelchair accessible;
no dogs

Events include: Screamings Run Haunted Walk in October

Group garden tours: By appointment, small charge

Nearby eateries: Info in gift shop; basic ones a few miles north or south on Route 9

Nearby places of interest: Cape May County Park and Zoo, 707 Route 9 North,
Cape May Court House, 3-3/4 miles; Cape May and its historic Victorian houses, 18
miles; Wetlands Institute, 1075 Stone Harbor Boulevard, Stone Harbor, 7 miles

In 1957 Jack and Emily Aprill bought a 1706 house with fifty acres behind it. As Emily developed the gift store in the old barn, Jack opened up paths through twenty acres of the woods, created two ponds from the stream, and cleared the trees for a series of gardens spaces. Visitors follow the path under a canopy of oaks, hickories, and gums with an understory of holly, coming across instructions to slow down, to look back, and to notice this and that. They find themselves wending their way past twenty-five small themed gardens arranged along a path that crisscrosses the stream (Leaming's Run) and winds around so that selected views—of a gazebo, a bridge, special splashes of color—are multiplied.

The many bright bedding-out annuals, supplemented by dahlias, semitropicals, and ornamental shrubs, are arranged to create color motifs: the Blue and White Garden, the Sweetheart Garden (red), the Orange Garden. Some are more successful than others. Especially featured are flowers that attract butterflies and, in August, hummingbirds.

About halfway along is the Colonial-style homestead, built of logs from the property (and some modern cement),

reflecting Jack Aprill's interest in the early settlers and the original owner of his house, Thomas Leaming. The little produce gardens, the fruit trees, the farmyard birds and animals, and the cluster of other farmyard buildings suggest the multiple activities required for self-sufficiency, along with making this garden walk particularly suited to families. An additional touch is a collection of chickens representing the variety brought by various groups of immigrants.

First opened to the public in 1978, Leaming's Run Gardens are maintained privately by Jack and Emily Aprill and their son Gregg, who have plans to renovate the colonial farm and expand the livestock.

MACCULLOCH HALL HISTORICAL MUSEUM & GARDENS

45 Macculloch Avenue, Morristown, NJ 07960
TEL: (973) 998-5655 x10
WEBSITE: *www.macullochhall.org*
SEE MAPS: pp. 209 & 212

Hours: Garden open dawn to dusk. House open Wednesday, Thursday, and Sunday, by tour, 1pm–4pm. Admission to gardens free; fee for house

Location: 36 miles from New York City

Parking: In street

Public transportation: NJ Transit to Morristown, walk 3/4 mile, or taxi

Facilities: Brochure and gift shop open during house hours; no refreshments; restrooms only with house tours; no picnic tables but groups of under six may use garden; wheelchair accessible for view of garden; dogs on leash

Programming: Usually in connection with the house and its collections

Group garden tours: By appointment, fee

Nearby eateries: good selection in Morristown

Also of interest: Stickley Museum at Craftsman Farms, 2352 Route 10 West (at Manor Lane), Morris Plains, 5 miles

The main attraction at Macculloch Hall is the stately house itself and its collections. Sited on a quiet residential street, the red brick federal home was built for George Perott Macculloch (1775–1858), known later as the father of the Morris Canal, between 1810 and 1819, with a portico added in 1850 that unifies the front facade. Tours expand on the 150 years of the Macculloch-Miller families and their involvement in civic and national affairs, and on the philanthropist W. Parsons Todd (1877–1976), who bought the empty house in 1949. Although he never lived there, he restored it as a repository for his noteworthy collections of eighteenth- and early nineteenth-century American and English fine and decorative art, and formed a foundation to safeguard them.

The original twenty-six acres of gentleman's property—garden, orchards (for cider), and farmland—had been reduced to three acres by 1949. These were restored as much as possible to demonstrate their nineteenth-century heritage. Stretching in a roughly rectangular shape behind the house, they comprise a large lawn with shady trees and a walking area for the ladies; a pre-1876 sundial; a long perennial border that drops down on the southeast side toward the lovely rose garden with its tunnel arbor for climbing varieties; and a

shaded area within a strip of woods. Many of the sixty-five varieties of roses are heirlooms (pre-1920s) and the display refers to an account book entry recording roses bought in 1810. Two bushes of what is now called the Old Macculloch Hall Rose (yellow) may possibly have originated from this early planting. The wisteria growing up the columns of the back porch provides another link with the past—a cutting was given to the family by Commodore Matthew Perry around 1857, whose own plant was brought back from Japan in 1855—a wonderful reminder of the attraction of new imports that subsequently became garden favorites.

This tranquil spot, open to the general public, forms a pleasant setting for the house and its outdoor events. It is cared for by two seasonal part-time gardeners, supplemented by four volunteer gardeners, with spring and fall cleanup help from the Garden Club of Morristown. Labeling is minimal, but notice boards draw attention to the historic items. Carrie Fellows, executive director, mentions a new initiative: "Working with the gardeners, we are attempting to propagate several unknown species of table and *vinifera* grapes believed to be survivors of the vines planted by original resident, George P. Macculloch, in the early nineteenth century—as recorded in his account book/garden journal."

103 MORVEN MUSEUM & GARDEN

55 Stockton Street, Princeton, NJ 08540
TEL: (609) 924-8144
WEBSITE: *www.morven.org*
SEE MAPS: pp. 209, 214 & 216

Hours: Garden and house open Wednesday, Thursday, and Friday 11am–3pm, and Saturday and Sunday noon–4pm; house visit by tour. Admission to grounds free; charge for house and exhibitions
Location: 54 miles from New York City
Public transportation: Amtrak or NJ Transit to Princeton Junction (taxi 4 miles) or local Dinky to Princeton Borough, walk or taxi 3/4 mile
Facilities: Information in gift shop; *Morven: Memory, Myth & Reality* by Constance M. Greiff and Wanda S. Gunning (2004) for sale; no refreshments; restrooms; picnic tables; house wheelchair accessible, grounds partially; dogs on leash
Group garden tours: By appointment
Nearby eateries: Downtown Princeton, 1/2 mile

The colorful Stocktons—lawyers, politicians, military and business men, with their often forceful and well-educated wives—owned the land since 1701. The house dates back to the 1750s, and until 1945, when the family sold Morven, the history was one of expansions and restyling of home and garden, and ultimately of changed lifestyles, diminished fortunes, and a reduction of land to the current five acres. Recent exacting scholarship led to the decision in 2000 to restore the land in front of the house to the mid-nineteenth-century style (which incorporated mature trees from earlier generations) and a part of the back area to the Colonial Revival style, first introduced around 1925 by Helen Hamilton Stockton.

Trees were invariably mentioned by visitors to Morven, and today catalpas (first planted between 1766 and 1771) grow parallel to the road, elms on the east side of the horseshoe-shaped drive, and sycamores to the west. The beautiful white house—a central block with wisteria covered porch and lower wings on either side—is first viewed across a front lawn with scattered plantings of tulip poplar, redbud, and maple. Off to the east, a short allée of chestnuts recalls the once longer avenue planted in the late-eighteenth century by "the Duke." Records going back to the eighteenth century also describe small flower gardens to the rear of the house, along with kitchen gardens (now taken over by a nondescript car

park), the orchards, and the necessary outbuildings. The Colonial Revival Garden sits a little awkwardly in its space but has a nice display of perennials (with a good showing of peonies) edged by box. Its main axis leads around a *Chamaecyparis*, past a sundial, and then under a white wooden arch to a swimming pool and modern pavilion (1939–1941), both in need of restoration. These were built for Robert Wood Johnson (1893–1968) when he rented Morven from 1928 to 1944.

The last owner, Walter E. Edge (1873–1956), governor of New Jersey, deeded Morven to the state of New Jersey in 1954, to be used either by his successors or as a museum dedicated to the history of the house and the state. Governors occupied it until the grander and more spacious Drumthwacket was purchased in 1981.

Historic Morven, Inc., founded in 1987, spearheaded the comprehensive restorations of house and gardens, and administers Morven in cooperation with the New Jersey Department of State. It attracts some 5,000 visitors annually. One part-time and eight paid interns (for six weeks) look after the garden, along with five to ten volunteer gardeners. Four notice boards within the grounds explain its features, and some form of labeling may be introduced. Pamela Ruch, the Morven horticulturist, writes, "We anticipate having an Interpretive Center for visitors within three years, and the next phase of garden planning is under way. In the years ahead, visitors will see the results: a family garden space for events and strolling, a rose and cutting garden, and more."

NEW JERSEY STATE BOTANICAL GARDEN AT SKYLANDS

2 Morris Road (OFF SLOATSBURG ROAD), Ringwood, NJ 07456
TEL: (973) 962-9534 (SKYLANDS ASSOCIATION);
(973) 962-7031 (RINGWOOD STATE PARK)
WEBSITE: *www.njbg.org*
SEE MAPS: pp. 209 & 211

Hours: Grounds open spring, summer, and fall, 8am–8pm; winter, 8am–6pm.
House used for receptions, open on selected Sundays. Admission free, parking
charge on weekends from Memorial Day to Labor Day
Location: 40 miles from New York City
Public transportation: None
Facilities: Specialized brochures and map from kiosk in parking lot, or from
Carriage House visitor center and gift shop (open 10am–2pm weekends);
separate restrooms in Carriage House and beverage vending machine (no café);
no picnicking; limited wheelchair access but good views; no dogs
Group garden tours: By appointment
Programming: Walks, summer concert series
Nearby eateries: Limited—deli at 1 Cupsaw Drive, Ringwood (3 miles); Sloatsburg,
NY, 6 miles; list from visitor center
Also of interest: Shepherd Lake Recreation Area, turn left before the entrance
for picnicking, swimming, and trails

Arrival at the New Jersey State Botanical Garden—situated within the 4,044-acre Ringwood Sate Park and reached by a slowly ascending one-and-a-half-mile lane off a little-traveled country road—always elicits a sense of excitement. The mature trees, the formal gardens, the specialized collections, and the decorative sculpture are set within landscaped grounds opening on to long views of the tree-covered Ramapo Mountains.

Two private owners, both with strong horticultural interests, left their mark. New York lawyer and railroad director Francis Stetson (1846–1920) began assembling some 1,100 acres in 1891 for his farm and country estate, and he commissioned the landscape architect Samuel Parsons (1844–1923) to lay out and plant the grounds. Some of the specimen trees date from this period (the weeping beech, the Japanese umbrella pine by the house) and also the graded lawns, which seamlessly merge with the woods without revealing the sunken access road.

After Skylands was sold in 1922 to investment banker Clarence McKenzie Lewis (1877–1959), the older house was torn down and the current Tudor-Gothic mansion (1924), designed by John Russell Pope, was built on the site. The charming Pump House and Carriage House (c. 1906) remain from the earlier period. The landscape architecture firm of Vitale & Geiffert created the west terrace and a new formal garden centered on one wing of the house. It encompasses a series of garden spaces—a magnolia walk, an azalea garden with a central canal, and a rose garden (now the Summer Garden)—arranged along a central axis, and it descends by different levels to the Peony Garden. Mr. Lewis also enlarged the Lilac Garden, added many more conifers to create the impressive Winter Garden (by the house),and, over thirty years, enriched the horticultural collections with varieties from abroad and within the United States.

Gardens from Mr. Lewis's time are also found across the avenue (of maples), where a large Annual Garden with seasonal displays is laid out around a sixteenth-century wellhead and a circle of dogwoods. An attractive Perennial Garden—formerly a large

and surrounded by a deer fence, are the Hosta and Rhododendron Garden, and the Morraine Garden, where among rocks, stone, and gravel a microclimate for alpines, dwarf conifers, heather, sedums, and gentians has been formed. Further explorations along streams and over little bridges in the woods of the Wildflower Garden are especially enjoyable in spring.

New Jersey purchased Skylands and 1,117 acres from Shelton College (a gift from Mr. Lewis in 1953) in 1966 under the Green Acres program. In 1984, the core ninety-six aces were designated the state's official botanical garden. Eight full-time and four seasonal workers look after the gardens and the greenhouses, with some fifteen seasonal volunteers. Currently Skylands seems underfunded (the west terrace is crumbling, the Swan Lake is overgrown, etc.) but future plans include renovating the Carriage

cutting garden—is next, with three small decorative garden sculptures. The famous half-mile crabapple avenue, ending in a semicircle with sculptures of the four continents, is a strangely isolated design statement in an expanse of grass (formerly Lewis's orchards). Beyond, within the wood

House to create a first-class gift shop, office, and visitor center, and improving the labeling and signage throughout the gardens. The NJBG/Skylands Association, founded in 1976, assists with the preservation and restoration of the gardens, which are visited by some 140,000 people annually.

105 PEONY'S ENVY

34 Autumn Hill Drive, Bernardsville, NJ 07924
TEL: (908) 578-3032
WEBSITE: *www.peonysenvy.com*
SEE MAP: p. 213

Hours: Nursery and display garden open daily May 1 through June 15, 11am–5pm. No admission fee, but suggested donation
Location: 44 miles from New York City
Public transportation: NJ Transit to Bernardsville and pleasant 1-1/4 mile walk, or taxi
Facilities: Nursery center; no refreshments; restroom; wheelchair accessible for general view
Nearby eateries: Bernardsville, 1-1/4 miles

Up a quiet lane, a white clapboard house sits among tulip poplars, a clearing in the trees providing the setting for the peonies. One first sees a wave of green speckled with concentrations of color, then realizes the flowers have been planted in rows, with irises imparting a blue note amid the reds, pinks, and whites of the flamboyant yet delicate peony blooms. The flowers are all tagged, and paths lead around the garden with seats here and there for viewing and enjoying.

This is a fairly new venture for Kathleen Gagan, who after twenty years abroad, working as a corporate

language teacher, settled with her husband and children in Bernardsville in 1996, and began thinking of uses for the newly acquired seven and a half acres of mostly woodland. After a couple of false starts, she experimented with the first peony crop in 2002. Fluent in Mandarin Chinese, Gagan benefited from a stay in China, where the famous peony center of Heze offered her initial horticultural knowledge and contacts for importation.

Now the compact nursery has some 30,000 peony plants, with 150 different varieties of herbaceous peonies and 100 of tree peonies. Kathleen Gagan, who uses organic methods of growing, delights in these cold-hardy perennials because of their low maintenance, deer resistance, drought tolerance, and beautiful flowering. Along with her online and nursery business, she exhibits widely at flower shows and lectures on peonies.

106 PRESBY MEMORIAL IRIS GARDENS

474 Upper Mountain Avenue, Upper Montclair, NJ 07043
TEL: (973) 783-5974
WEBSITE: *www.presbyirisgardens.org*
SEE MAPS: pp. 209 & 210

Hours: Park open daily, but the blooming season for the irises is usually from mid-May through early June, when the gardens are officially open 10am–8pm. Admission free, but donation requested during blooming period

Location: 17 miles from New York City

Parking: Along Upper Mountain Avenue, or along Highland Avenue above the garden

Public transportation: PATH/NJ Transit to Mountain Avenue, Upper Montclair, walk 1/5 mile; DeCamp bus #66 to Valley Road and Laurel Road, Upper Montclair, cross tracks, turn right, and walk 1/5 mile

Facilities: Visitor center, open during the season, 10am–8pm; self-guided walking tour brochure at entrance; gift shop in the Bloom Room; no refreshments; portable toilets, handicap accessible; no picnicking in the iris section of the park; garden wheelchair accessible; dogs on leash

Group garden tours: By appointment, fee

Nearby eateries: Bellevue Avenue and Valley Road, Upper Montclair

Nearby gardens of interest: Avis Campbell Gardens at the United Way Building, 60 South Fullerton Avenue, Montclair, 3-1/4 miles, looked after by the Garden Club of Montclair

Also of interest: Montclair Art Museum, 3 South Mountain Avenue, Montclair, 2-1/2 miles

Within the seven-and-a-half-acre Mountainside Park, the Presby Memorial Iris Gardens have a splendid display for about three weeks—from mid-May to early June—when they attract some 6,000 iris aficionados, photographers, and appreciative visitors. The irises are arranged, at the bottom of a sloping, grassy sward, in thirty-five narrow beds (100' x 6'), forming a delicate rainbow of glorious color.

Bearded irises predominate. Arranged by period, they include Heirloom Historic Tall Bearded Irises (1500–early 1900s); Heirloom European Tall Bearded Irises (1900s–1930s); and Modern Tall Bearded Irises (1980s–1990s). Along a dry-bed stream are the nonbearded Siberian and Japanese irises. Each of the approximately 3,000 varieties in the garden is labeled by species, name, year of introduction, and hybridizer.

The history of the gardens reflects, as is so often the case, the passion and dedication of a few individuals and garden groups. Established in 1927 by the Citizens Committee of the town of Montclair, the layout was designed by John Wister (1887–1982, first president of the American Iris Society). The name honored Frank H. Presby, noted local horticulturist and a founding member of the American Iris Society, who died in 1924. Barbara Walther, whose house was adjacent to the newly formed Mountainside Park and iris gardens, was the president of the committee, and for the next fifty years, as a volunteer, she was the primary instigator behind the growth and cataloguing of the collection.

Her house became the base of operations for the Citizen's Committee after she died in 1977. Sold in 2009 for $1.1 million to Essex County to resolve a severe financial crisis, it was leased—

for $1 a year—back to the group, which will continue to manage the gardens. Organic methods of fertilization and pest control have been introduced, and partnership with Pittsgrove Farms nursery will provide support. The nursery will assist in the propagation of irises through the division of rhizomes and in the sale of peonies and lilies, in addition to irises, during the bloom season.

Nine seasonal full-time gardeners and ten volunteer gardeners look after this specialized garden, along with three administrators. Additional volunteers take turns manning the information table during the season. The Presby Memorial Iris Gardens of Essex County plans to continue its museum-standard garden, acquiring new introductions of irises, including those of historic value.

107 PRINCETON UNIVERSITY CAMPUS & PROSPECT HOUSE GARDEN

Main campus entered by foot from Nassau Street (AT WITHERSPOON STREET), Princeton, NJ 08542

Prospect House Garden (WITHIN THE MAIN CAMPUS, REACHED ON FOOT FROM NASSAU STREET, WASHINGTON ROAD, UNIVERSITY PLACE, ETC.)

Graduate College, 88 College Road West

TEL: (609) 258-3000

WEBSITE: *www.princeton.edu* (DOWNLOAD MAP BEFORE ARRIVAL)

SEE MAPS: pp. 209, 214 & 216

Hours: Grounds open 24 hours a day. Admission free

Location: 53 miles from New York City

Parking: Metered in surrounding streets

Public transportation: NJ Transit or Amtrak to Princeton Junction, the local Dinky to Princeton borough, then short walk

Facilities: Restrooms at the Woolworth Music Center or Frist Campus Center; wheelchair accessible; dogs on leash

Nearby eateries: Good choices on Nassau Street and nearby; Frist Campus Center

Also of interest: Princeton University Art Museum, south of Nassau Hall on the main campus (pedestrian entrance); Marquand Park, Lover's Lane (17 acres of good specimen trees and lawns of former private house), 1 mile; The Lawrenceville School, 2500 Main Street (Route 206 N), Lawrenceville, 5-1/2 miles, campus designed by Frederick Law Olmsted in 1883

A print of 1764 shows the newly built Nassau Hall (1756)—an enormous building for its time, containing the entire College of New Jersey—fronted by a neat, flat rectangle of grass divided by an entrance path. Six small, clipped conifers edge the lines of the surrounding fence. Today the main campus of Princeton University (renamed in 1896) is renowned for its quiet quadrangles of large shade trees set in green lawns traversed by pedestrian paths.

Beatrix Farrand's (1872–1959) first Princeton commission (1912) was for the grounds of the new Graduate College designed by Ralph Adams Cram in the Collegiate Gothic style reminiscent of Oxford and Cambridge colleges. Here she developed many of her planting ideas (still to be seen), and as the university's landscape consultant until 1943, she later extended these to the main campus, visiting several times a year. Restraint was key, and espaliering or pinning shrubs, trees, and vines to the walls and keeping their shapes well defined through clipping and pruning became a method of greening the architecture and

courtyards without blocking views and light. She also created seasonal color—often placing spring flowering trees and shrubs in the corners of buildings and giving attention to fall and winter colors, forms, and berries, using native deciduous and evergreen trees frequently.

Today, with a campus of over 500 acres and more than 180 buildings, the policy is to respect the classic Beatrix Farrand style in the areas where she advised while introducing new styles elsewhere. Green roofs, rain gardens, reconstructed woodlands, the use of tall grasses on embankments to reduce mowing, and cisterns for water retention, along with the elimination of synthetic chemicals, reflect the new priorities. Michael Van Valkenburgh Associates, Inc., has been retained to design and implement these initiatives. With three arborists on staff, and with its own greenhouses, the grounds and maintenance department plays a central role. The latter also collaborated with Quennell Rothschild & Partners on the memorial garden (2003). It honors the thirteen Princetonians killed on September 11, 2001 and is found on the west side of East Pyne with a bronze bell by Toshiro Takaezu at the entrance.

The garden of the Italianate villa **Prospect House** (1850) is not to be missed. Previously the residence of college presidents (1879–1968), it was designed by Woodrow Wilson's wife during his presidency at Princeton (1902–1910). Frequented by students and locals, it offers beautifully maintained wedge-shaped beds, with lawns in the interstices, arranged in a semicircle around a fountain pool and backed by tall hemlocks and magnolias. A few dark-green accents from columnar cypresses, rounded hollies, and short stretches of box hedges offset in summer the hibiscus, castor oil plants, cannas, grasses, caladiums, and many other perennials and annuals, with seasonal additions in spring and fall.

Throughout the campus, a small collection of sculpture, belonging to the university's art museum, is sited—sometimes prominently, as with Henry Moore's *Oval with Points* (1969–1970) at a busy pedestrian intersection, or Tony Smith's *Moses* (1969) on the north lawns of Prospect House amid the magnificent American beech, tulip poplar, ginkgos, and magnolia— or situated within the smaller quadrangles. The sculptures, unlike the trees, are often labeled. The two sycamores planted to commemorate the 1776 repeal of the Stamp Act (see Union County College, p. 278) are at the original president's house, 73 Nassau Street (Maclean House).

108 REEVES-REED ARBORETUM

165 Hobart Avenue, Summit, NJ 07901
TEL: (908) 272-8787
WEBSITE: *www.reeves-reedarborerum.org*
SEE MAPS: pp. 209 & 210

Hours: Garden open dawn to dusk. Admission free.

Location: 25 miles from New York City

Public transportation: NJ Transit to Summit, walk 3/4 mile along residential Franklin Place to Hobart Ave, or taxi

Facilities: Wisner House, open Monday–Friday 9am–5pm, first floor, serves as a visitor center with maps and pamphlets on the different areas; garden map also in doorway, from wooden kiosk at car park, and from website; cell phone information points in garden; download podcast from website; notice boards with historical photos and wayside signage; garden gallery in basement for exhibitions by local artists; no refreshments; restrooms; picnic tables; partially wheelchair accessible; no dogs

Programming: Ongoing horticultural and environmental programs for adults and children

Group garden tours: By appointment

Nearby eateries: Summit; see www.summitdowntown.org

Also of interest: Cora Hartshorn Arboretum, 324 Forest Drive South, Short Hills; Visual Arts Center of New Jersey, 68 Elm Street, Summit

The Reeves-Reed house, The Clearing, stands on a rise looking south over a "kettle," a large hollow with an irregular-shaped rim, which was scooped out during the ice-age period. Originally used for grazing by the family horses or goats, this area now has a display of thousands of daffodils in the spring, while during the summer it is left as a wild meadow. Woods of tulip poplar, oak, and other native trees largely screen out neighboring houses.

Owned by three consecutive families, The Clearing was built on about ten acres in 1889, as a family home for John Wisner, who was in the Chinese import-export business in New York, and his wife, Isabella. The New York firm of Babb, Cook & Willard designed the shingle-sided-and-roofed colonial-style house we see today.

The development of the gardens is connected with some well-known landscape names. Calvert Vaux (1824–1895) was consulted on the layout of driveways, shrubberies, and kitchen gardens in 1889. Although only partially implemented, his designs, which are in the archives, remain a fascinating period testament.

In 1916 the Wisners moved back to New York, selling The Clearing to another commuter, Richard Early Reeves. His wife, Susie Graham Reeves (d. 1968), a keen gardener herself, hired the well-known Ellen Biddle Shipman (1869–1950) in 1924, but her design lost out to Carl F. Pilat's (1876–1933) plan from the same year. Working closely with Mrs. Reeves, he adjusted Shipman's design, eliminating the swimming pool, and developed the flower garden. A rose garden was also

owners, Charles L. Reed Jr. and Ann Reeves Reed (the niece of the previous owners), and is now looked after by the Summit Garden Club.

The Clearing is owned by the city of Summit but managed and funded by the Reeves-Reed Arboretum, Inc. The story of how it was secured for the public in 1974 is one of commitment and determination (see *The Clearing on the Hill: The Story of the Reeves-Reed Arboretum* by Betty McAndrews, 2005). The mission to preserve the historic

laid out to the south and a fashionable rock garden and small pool constructed between the level of the house and the garden below.

These areas from the late 1920s are recognizable today—and are seen to great advantage from an enclosed porch on the east end of the house. The flower garden has been grassed over, but the surrounding borders and banks have been enriched with a strong collection of flowering trees and azaleas. The lovely rose garden has been enlarged, a perennial border planted along the front terrace, and an herb garden added (1960s) by the third

aspects and collections of the property is combined with a commitment to promoting good stewardship, giving rise to many programs dealing with environment concerns. New management of the woods is facilitated by the 1997 deer fence, which protects the thirteen and a half acres.

The arboretum is cared for by two full-time and several part-time and seasonal gardeners, along with fifteen volunteers. An estimated 40,000 visit each year.

109 RINGWOOD MANOR

1304 Sloatsburg Road, Ringwood, NJ 07456
TEL: (973) 962-7031 x0
WEBSITE: *www.ringwoodmanor.com*
SEE MAPS: pp. 209 & 211

Hours: Grounds open daily, dawn to dusk (except Christmas and New Year's Day). House open usually Wednesday–Sunday. Call ahead. Admission to grounds and house free, but admission fee for cars on weekends between Memorial Day and Labor Day

Location: 38 miles from New York City

Public transportation: None

Facilities: Visitor center in the park office at house; gift shop in the house; restrooms; no refreshments; picnic tables by parking lot; first floor of house wheelchair accessible and some areas of the gardens; dogs on leash

Programming: Revolutionary War and social history

Grounds tours: June through October, usually Sunday at 2pm and by appointment

Nearby eateries: Sloatsburg, NY, 5-1/2 miles; West Milford Township, 6-1/2 miles; list available from park office

Also of interest: Ringwood State Park, trails accessible from the parking lot; Long Pond Ironworks Historic District, Route 511, West Milford

The serenity of the grounds surrounding Ringwood Manor belies their industrial past. The small areas of formal gardens that remain and the strange collection of artifacts that they harbor take us into the world of a country house estate, long since gently abandoned.

As early as 1739 iron mining was established at Ringwood, and a blast furnace was added in 1742. After 1764 it became the center of the vast iron empire, the American Iron Company of Peter Hasenclever (1716–1793), its forges supplying ammunition and weapons to the revolutionary troops. During the Civil War—under the ownership of the inventor, industrialist, and philanthropist Peter Cooper (1791–1883), who increased the holdings to 100,000 acres—it supplied gun carriages, mortars, and gun-barrel iron. His daughter and her husband, Abram Stevens Hewitt (1822–1903), who was Cooper's business partner, developed Ringwood as a country estate, and two of their daughters, Sarah Cooper Hewitt and Eleanor Garnier Hewitt, eventually made it their home,

The house is well sited on a grassy bank above a stream—formerly used for industry and now channeled attractively through a series of descending pools to the lake. The view

from the south terrace of the house, where industrial iron artifacts sit like sculpture, is equally attractive, with the low hills of New Jersey Highlands in the distance. The Hewitts expanded the 1807 house of the previous owner, Martin J. Ryerson, several times—the 1870s Gothic revival home acquiring the neoclassical portico, front porch columns, and white stuccoed exterior in 1900.

No landscape architect is specifically connected with the development of the gardens (c. 1900), although Beatrix Farrand (1872–1959), a friend and guest at the Manor, possibly advised. A framework of long and transverse axes integrates outdoor rooms and rectangular groves—the most surreal being the Cedar Garden, where a double line of newel posts on plinths, from Colonnade Row (1833) in New York, are presented as sculptures with a double line of cedars. Ionic columns from the old New York Life Insurance Building are displayed in another grove, and sphinxes, gates, vases, and other decorative objects appear elsewhere, reminding us that the three

daughters of Abram S. Hewitt formed the museum collection in Cooper Union (founded by their grandfather), which is now the Cooper-Hewitt, National Design Museum. To the rear of the formal layout, the fine walls of a large former kitchen garden remain, as does the terracing with its southern exposure.

Ringwood Manor and its furnishing were donated to the state of New Jersey in 1936. One full-time and three part-time gardeners look after the 582 acres, with three volunteers. A project to restore the run-down grounds to the historical period of the Hewitt residency is under consideration, with a cultural landscape report due in the next few years. Sue Shutte, historic preservationist at Ringwood Manor, summarizes the goals: replanting the horticultural elements, dredging and maintaining the man-made ponds and shorelines, and restoring the historic statuary and other outdoor features.

THE JAMES ROSE CENTER
506 East Ridgewood Avenue,
Ridgewood, NJ 07450
TEL: (201) 446-6071
WEBSITE: *www.jamesrosecenter.org*
SEE MAPS: pp. 209 & 211

Hours: House and garden open probably mid-May through early September,
Tuesday–Sunday 10am–4pm; early September through October, Wednesday–
Sunday 10am–4pm. Check website for guided tours. Admission fee
Location: 22 miles from New York City
Public transportation: NJ Transit to Ridgewood, easy 3/4 mile walk or taxi
Facilities: No refreshments; restrooms; not wheelchair accessible; no dogs
Programming: Annual design exhibition, internships
Group tours: By appointment
Nearby eateries: Downtown Ridgewood
Also of interest: Right-of-way walk along old railway line just east of house
to Glen Rock for NJ Transit, 2 miles

The site of the James Rose Center appears at first as a block of trees. It demonstrates perfectly Rose's ideas on privacy and the spatial relationships he sought between inside and outside, as well as reflecting his disdain for the usual suburban house: a dominant driveway leading to the garage, the open space in front of the house unusable.

The testy and influential landscape architect and author James Rose (1913–1991), perhaps less well known than his fellow students at Harvard, Garrett Eckbo (1910–2000) and Dan Kiley (1912–2004), began his house in 1953 and tinkered with it for the next thirty years. Small internal or external courtyards relate to the three main sections—a studio/living area for himself, a central section for his mother, and a guest section for his sister—all having access to the garden on the east. Little pools of unusual shapes, raised and sunken, create an irregular geometry, and jets of water lessen the noise from the road outside. Layers of flat stone, upright rocks, or concrete pavers with small river stones in the interstices all have a hand-laid look, and this individuality is enhanced by Rose's bent-copper lanterns and sculpture.

Trees (honey locust and cherry) grow through the building, or rather the buildings have been designed around the existing trees, and others are very close, creating a shady canopy and dappled light. Within this quarter-acre property are also cherry, maples,

pines, hemlocks, spruce, willow, ginkgo, pine, and multitrunked lindens. At ground level, the emphasis is on green: ivy, hostas, ferns, small azaleas and rhododendrons (whose buds Rose evidently nipped off to avoid color), and small trimmed yews.

The roof garden, constructed in the early 1970s, is like a very sophisticated tree house, incorporating a boardwalk, built-in seats, and planters. The geometry of the exposed trusses is dazzling; sections covered by a translucent material turn the leaves of the trees extending through the "roof" into negative shapes. The small zendo room for meditation reminds us that James Rose visited Japan many times after 1960. His own aesthetic is a modernism tempered by the craftsmanship and mindfulness of Japanese gardens.

Although Rose briefly had a sizable practice designing gardens and atriums for corporations, most of his postwar work was for private clients who trusted his intuitive method of designing on the spot, where he incorporated rocks and trees from the site and built

his geometries of wood and gravel, water, paving, pebbles, and planting in relation to the spatial contours of the house.

Before his death he planned the establishment of a landscape research and design study center within his own house and created a foundation to fund it. The deterioration of the house and other problems have taken their toll, but James Rose's legacy quietly engages the visitor nevertheless.

111 RUTGERS GARDENS

112 Ryders Lane, New Brunswick, NJ 08901
TEL: (732) 932-8451
WEBSITE: *http://rutgersgardens.rutgers.edu*
SEE MAPS: pp. 209 & 213

Hours: Grounds open daily, 8am–dusk. Admission free

Location: 39 miles from New York City

Public transportation: NJ Transit or Amtrak to New Brunswick, taxi 4-1/2 miles

Facilities: No visitor center; download plan of garden before arriving; notice boards for map display and for some gardens; small gift shop during weekends from May through October; portable toilet during spring, summer, and fall; picnic tables; not wheelchair accessible; dogs on leash

Programming: Horticultural courses and lectures, plant sales

Group garden Tours: By appointment

Nearby eateries: Milltown, 2-1/2 miles; New Brunswick, 4-1/2 miles; or along Route 1

Also of interest: Jane Voorhees Zimmerli Art Museum, 71 Hamilton Street, New Brunswick, 4 miles

Containing notable collections as well as constituting a learning and research area for the Rutgers University School of Environmental and Biological Sciences at Cook Campus (across Ryders Lane), Rutgers Gardens has also assumed a strong community-orientated approach since the 1990s. Numerous courses for home gardeners and master gardeners are offered, and the slots for one hundred volunteers, who assist with greenhouse work, propagation, pruning, planting, and maintenance, are readily filled.

Some hints for the first-time visitor: the entrance is not clearly indicated; a long track leads onward, and neither where to park nor where to begin the visit are evident; the special bamboo grove near the entrance is easy to miss without a printed map; and noise from roads on two sides is to be expected. Nevertheless, it is worth persevering. Bear in mind that the site encompasses several plant-breeding programs and specialized projects, and that individual sections or wedges of land on both sides of Log Cabin Road are devoted to rich collections of a single horticultural aspect rather than to an involvement with landscape design. The renowned American Holly Collection (begun in the 1950s) occupies one area, the Shrub Collection another, while elsewhere dogwoods are tested for hardiness and antimalarial drug possibilities.

The Roy H. DeBoer Evergreen Garden (1958) is visually stunning and

also a scientific demonstration, with the trees (which include deciduous conifers) grouped by genus. The Rhododendron and Azalea Garden (and the flowering shrubs and trees within other collections) are a special attraction in the spring, while the smaller Tribute Gardens offer provocative new designs and horticultural ideas. For the annual garden, which tries out new displays each year, the best time to visit is late summer.

Under the leadership of director Bruce Crawford, a Master Plan is being developed which will include a new ecofriendly horticultural and visitor center, a conservatory, and numerous enhancements that coincide with the missions of various university departments, such as nutrition and sustainable energy. The garden sponsors a farmers' market near the entrance every Friday from May through October. In 2006 outreach to children began with after-school programs and a Community Youth Garden (vegetables).

Some 20,000 people visit Rutgers Gardens annually (a core of 50 acres within a total of 180) which are cared for by two full-time employees, twelve students in the summer, and five throughout the year. Labeling is in the process of being improved. The gardens, owned by Rutgers University, are financially self-sustaining, with the help of volunteers and fundraising events.

112 SAYEN BOTANICAL GARDENS

155 Hughes Drive, Hamilton, NJ 08690
TEL: (609) 890-3543
WEBSITE: *www.sayengardens.org*
SEE MAPS: pp. 209, 214 & 216

Hours: Grounds open daily, dawn to dusk. Admission free
Location: 64 miles from New York City
Public transportation: NJ Transit to Hamilton, taxi 3-1/2 miles
Facilities: Maps and brochures available from office by restrooms,
    Monday–Friday, 7:30am–4pm; no refreshments; picnicking (seats);
    wheelchair accessible; dogs on leash
Programming: Sporadic; Azalea Festival on Mother's Day
Group garden tours: By appointment
Nearby eateries: Hamilton Square, Route 33

The older garden is enclosed in its own world. It began when Frederick Sayen (1885–1981)—whose family owned the nearby Mercer Rubber Company—and his wife, Anne Mellon Sayen (1886–1977), planted a woodland garden around their 1912 bungalow. Filled with azaleas, rhododendrons, and flowering shrubs, it is a glorious sight in the spring.

From the entrance, paths run close together, separated by little hills with rich plantings of shrubs, striking conifers, and other specimen trees. Further along, the way opens up into spaces with pavilions and beds of peonies (Temple Garden) or a fountain area with annuals. One koi-filled pond is especially pretty with its white curved bridge, irises around the edges, and a spray fountain. There is a strange mixture of picture-ready gardens—the site is used for wedding photography—and "out of sight," less maintained areas.

In 1987 Hamilton Township purchased the property of twenty-eight and a half acres from a developer. The early spring display of bulbs has been developed, and a second area, LaBaw Pointe, was opened in 2003, different in character and intent. Reached from the opposite direction from the car park, it has open graded slopes of lawn—with islands of specimen trees, shrubs, and sometimes perennials—with serpentine paths suitable for wheelchairs. An older bandstand is incorporated and a nondescript new one sits above the man-made lake, which is plagued with the usual problems of algae. The white bridge provides a visual link with the older garden, and weeping willows thrive.

Future plans include improving the small frog pond, adding a waterfall, and developing additional paths and gardens to connect the older gardens with the new front area. Another current project is to label more of the rare and common species for the 15,000-20,000 people who visit the gardens each year. Horticulturist Harry Robinson, with five part-time gardeners, one seasonal, and about five volunteers care for the gardens. The Friends of Sayen House and Gardens, formed in 1994, assists.

113 UNION COUNTY COLLEGE'S HISTORIC TREE GROVE & ARBORETUM

1033 Springfield Avenue, Cranford, NJ 07016
TEL. (908) 709-7556; e-mail Dr. Tom Ombrello,
ombrello@ucc.edu
WEBSITE: *http://faculty.ucc.edu/biology-ombrello*
SEE MAPS: pp. 209 & 210

Hours: Grounds open daily, 7am–dusk. Admission free. Two greenhouses open by appointment
Location: 25 miles from New York City
Parking: In the visitors' parking lot, on the right entering from Springfield Avenue (on weekends park anywhere)
Public transportation: NJ Transit to Newark, Penn Station, change to Raritan Valley Line for Cranford, walk or taxi 1 mile to college. NJ Transit bus (#114) from Port Authority to Larchmont Road and change to the #66 to the campus
Facilities: Cafeteria in Campus Center building; restrooms available in all buildings on campus; picnicking; wheelchair accessible, viewing from nearby sidewalk; no dogs
Nearby eateries: Cranford, 1 mile; Westfield, 2-1/2 miles
Nearby parks: Nomahegan Park (118 acres) across the road from Union College on Springfield Avenue; Watchung Reservation and the Trailside Nature and Science Center (2,000 acres), 452 New Providence Road, Mountainside, 5-1/4 miles
Also of interest: Echo Lake Park, Park Drive, Mountainside/Westfield, with 9/11 World Trade Center memorial garden on the hill, to the north, 2 miles; Warinanco Park (landscaped city park), St. Georges Avenue, Roselle, 6-1/4 miles.

The quirkiest educational tool in New Jersey is surely the Historic Tree Grove of Union County College. It is a collection of some sixty small trees chosen not for shape, size, color, foliage, or any of the usual landscaping concerns, but because they are the progeny of trees that witnessed important events in American history. Planted according to no particular plan, in a roughly V-shaped swathe, they are to be found behind the Sperry Observatory and along the periphery of an existing wood. The excellent and helpful *Guide to Union County College's Historic Tree Grove Project* is available from a box in the grove or can be downloaded in advance from the website.

President Washington rested beneath a sycamore in Hope, NJ, on the morning of July 26, 1782, and tree #93 was grown from a seed of this 333-year-old lightening-struck but valiant survivor. Two sycamores were planted in 1776 in front of Maclean House in Princeton (see p. 267) to commemorate the repeal of the hated Stamp Act, and

#91 was collected as a seed from one of these old witnesses; the black locust #26 comes from the one located outside Independence Hall in Philadelphia that was there when the Declaration of Independence was unanimously adopted in 1776 and the United States Constitution written in 1797.

Dr. Tom Ombrello, senior professor of biology, who initiated the project in 1995—growing the trees from seed in a nursery on campus—has a penchant for American Revolutionary history, but the direct offspring of other trees also provide significant or moving testimonies to other events: the Cyrus Hall McCormick Catalpa (#61) from the tree that saw the invention of the Virginia Reaper; the Martin Luther King Jr. Sycamore (#52) from Selma, AL, witness to the stirring speeches of the Civil Rights movement; the Water Oak (#37) from Helen Keller's childhood home in Tuscumbia, AL.

The trees in the historic grove are used by the Union College history department as an evocative tool, while Dr. Ombrello's students deal with pruning, care, diseases and matters related to plant science. The respect for trees and their place in our historical consciousness are spread beyond this campus by gifts of duplicate seedlings to schools, municipalities, and other organizations throughout New Jersey.

The arboretum encompasses the forty-five-acre campus, which has very large parking areas. Dr. Ombrello, working with the grounds department, has increased the diversity and enriched the plantings in the remaining areas around the buildings and the lake. These trees are also used in the college-credit plant science/horticulture courses offered through Union College's Biology Department. Tree identification is naturally part of the courses. From the fifty or so species identified by the students in 1976, the count has grown to 164. The most representative example is marked with a white engraved plastic label (as opposed to the red engraved labels in the Historic Grove). Dr. Ombrello intends to add more tree species to the campus arboretum, and additional offspring of famous trees to the Historic Tree Grove.

114 VAN VLECK HOUSE & GARDENS

21 Van Vleck Street, Montclair, NJ 07042
TEL: (973) 744-4752
WEBSITE: *www.vanvleck.org*
SEE MAPS: pp. 209 & 210

Hours: Grounds open daily, 9am–5pm. House only open for classes and events. Admission free

Location: 16 miles from New York City

Parking: Through the gates and turn right

Public transportation: DeCamp bus #33 from NYC to North Mountain Avenue, walk 1/3 mile. NJ Transit to Bay Street, Montclair, taxi 1-3/4 miles or to Upper Montclair, taxi 1-1/2 miles

Facilities: By house, boxes with brochure and map; no refreshments; no restrooms; picnicking; partial wheelchair access; no dogs

Programming: Horticultural for children and adults, plant sale, concerts

Nearby eateries: Montclair

Also of interest: Brookdale Park, Watchung Avenue and Circuit Drive, Montclair and Bloomfield (within the 121-acre Olmsted Brothers-designed park (1928–1937), the 1959 rose garden has been looked after by the master gardeners of Essex County since 1997); Montclair Art Museum, 3 South Mountain Avenue, 1/2 mile

When the railway arrived in Montclair in 1872, making commuting to New York convenient, Joseph Van Vleck (1830–1903) acquired 5.8 acres for a large family home and garden. That house, built in the Tudor style, was demolished in the 1960s and the restrained classical Italian villa (1916), designed on the grounds by his son Joseph Van Vleck Jr. (1875–1948) became the focal point of the garden, still seen today. Composed of roughly three long rectangles side by side, it is surrounded by an attractive cast-iron fence.

The azaleas and rhododendrons are two of the garden's great delights,

making a splendid showing in the spring, as do the Korean dogwoods, magnolias, and many other flowering trees. The architect Howard Van Vleck, of the next generation, who lived with his family in the 1916 house from 1939 to the early 1990s, was a noted horticulturist, hybridizing rhododendrons to create a yellow-flowering variety and further developing the garden. He also planted the two wisterias around 1939, a special feature on the garden side of the house where two short projecting wings create a courtyard with a fountain and a row of Doric columns along the open end. The wisteria grows profusely up these

columns, spreading along the second-floor balconies. The view from the courtyard—a straight lawn leading to a great cedar of Lebanon, bordered by trees, shrubs (including rhodies and azaleas), and perennials—produces a richly tiered effect. A path to the left leads to the Aazalea Walk with its islands of looser plantings.

On slightly higher levels, are two further garden areas. The first, on the former tennis court site, contains the new parterre (2008), still filling out, and a fountain. In the second, mature spruces, hemlocks, *Cryptomeria*, Hinoki cypresses, and rhododendrons give distinction to the flowing shapes of a lawn, with two tall junipers standing as sentinels. This lovely space would have originally related (though with different planting) to the Tudor-style house. The pergola, providing a view point to the south, will eventually be covered in vines or climbing shrubs, and thus look less isolated.

In 1993, the heirs of Howard Van Vleck donated the house and grounds to the community-based Montclair Foundation. After a freak storm damaged the northeast corner of the garden, a Master Plan was commissioned in 2007 from Rodney Robinson Landscape Architects, and a campaign begun to raise approximately $2.2 million for the comprehensive restoration of the gardens. This included improved pedestrian access and the introduction of a winter garden and a perennial garden to extend seasonal interest. In addition, a new classroom and outdoor learning center will supplement the current greenhouse activities at the far end of the garden. Some 2,500 visitors attend events and classes, and many more use the gardens, which are cared for by two full-time gardeners and twelve volunteers. Labeling is sparse but there is a plant list on the website. The house serves as a center for nonprofit organizations.

WELL-SWEEP HERB FARM

205 Mount Bethel Road, Port Murray, NJ 07865
TEL: (908) 852-5390
WEBSITE: *www.wellsweep.com*
SEE MAP: p. 209

Toothache
Plant

Hours: Open Monday–Saturday 9am–5pm. Admission free
Location: 61 miles from New York City
Public transportation: NJ Transit to Hackettstown, taxi 6 miles
Facilities: Nursery and catalogue; gift shop; composting toilets, no refreshments;
  picnicking; partially wheelchair accessible; no dogs
Programming: Lectures and classes on growing, cooking, drying, decorating
  with herbs
Nearby eateries: Hackettstown, 6 miles; Washington, 7 miles

Betel Lea

A visit to Well-Sweep Herb Farm is a total surrender to the excitement of plants—especially if you can follow proprietor Cyrus Hyde (b. 1930) around the half-acre ornamental herb garden, begun in 1971. Steeped in the history and lore of plants, he—like any serious plant collector—can't forego the pleasure of growing, smelling, examining, touching, and nurturing many different varieties from all over the world. His wife, Louise, coproprietor, uses many of them for cooking, flavoring, or scenting, while both treat their medicinal values with great interest but some caution. Red brick paths define the layout, with beds arranged in a pattern around an armillary sphere and in borders along the sides. A knot garden of interwoven lines of clipped germander, box, lavender, and crimson pigmy barberry is a special feature, as is a charming, white pavilion, which turns out to be the privy.

The property, purchased by the Hydes in 1969, is situated along a quiet road among rolling low hills covered with trees. They gradually built up the nursery's enormous collection of herbs, ornamental perennials, and, recently, willows. If the well-known sweet basil (*Ocimum basilicum*) attracts you, then have a look at the Thai, Cuban, or African variety. If you thought there was only one kind of rosemary, then you might consider the other sixty-two cultivars and hybrids that Well-Sweep carries. If you would like a change from the more common varieties of French marigold, try the Minted Scented Marigold, and use its leaves like tarragon during the winter. Plants for sale, all carefully labeled, are often small in size, as keen gardeners take the longer view.

Well-Sweep is also a home, a place where three children were brought up and pets wander about. Close to the house are sheds and barns, the greenhouses, and the vegetable and fruit garden—as well as the family pool. A large cutting garden supplies the enticing selection of dried flowers that Mrs. Hyde produces for the gift shop, where books on herbs are also found, along with herbal soaps, oils, teas, potpourris, and more. The sound of cocks crowing comes from Japanese onagadoris with eight-foot-long tails or from other exotic fowl (another of Mr. Hyde's interests). A large root cellar in the side of a mound stores produce for the winter months as well as tender plants.

Mrs. Hyde has also planted a garden of healing plants and a rock garden (near the casual grass parking area), and she maintains a long perennial border that runs parallel to the wall by the road. Some six out of the 120 acres are in use around the house, and, in the next few years, she plans to create a woodland garden within a copse of trees.

Well-Sweep is a way of life as well as a family-run business that is shared by one of the Hyde's sons, his girlfriend, and one other helper. About 2,000 potential clients visit each year, complementing the mail order business.

116 WILLOWWOOD ARBORETUM

300 Longview Road, Far Hills (CHESTER TOWNSHIP)
NJ 07930
TEL: (973) 326-7601
WEBSITE: *www.morrisparks.net*
SEE MAPS: pp. 209 & 212

Hours: Grounds open daily, 8am–dusk. Admission free
Location: 49 miles from New York City
Public transportation: NJ Transit to Gladstone, taxi 2-1/2 miles
Facilities: Brochure and trail maps from the directory in the parking lot; no
   facilities other than restrooms (open at 9am); picnic tables—bring a blanket; limited
   wheelchair access; no dogs
Programming: Occasionally
Group garden tours: By appointment
Nearby eateries: Chester, 4-3/4 miles
Also of interest: A one-mile path leads to Bamboo Brook (see p. 219)

Willowwood—a very special garden and arboretum—reflects the horticultural skill and long devotion of the brothers Henry (1878–1958) and Robert (1882–1942) Tubbs. The current undesigned entranceway, although initially less appealing than the former drive with white pines, sugar maples, and eastern redbud, almost immediately reveals glorious pastures fringed with well-shaped woods on the rolling Hacklebarney Hills. The route leads past a few willows with the enticing lilac, cherry, and Amur honeysuckle arboretum glimpsed to the left, followed by a cluster of good-looking stone farm buildings. Mature trees—honey locusts, pecans, magnolias, an enormous dawn redwood (which arrived as a seed from China in 1947), and katsuras—delight.

The comfortable-looking olive-green wooden 1790s farmhouse, expanded over the years, sits on a slight rise, with a small conservatory to one side. Fronted by boxwoods, it looks across the drive to the wrought-iron gate of the cottage garden, whose axis is aligned with its front door. This delightful little garden—the layout is formal but asymmetrical, with good detailing—overflows with perennials, roses, and small trees, with a few dark-green accents of trimmed columnar boxwood and yew hedging. Beyond is one of the meadows, some areas left unmown to attract butterflies and birds. The path continues across the stream, up to the shelter belt of Norway spruce, looping back across the former drive to the catalpa avenue and further pastures. Although the Tubbs brothers purposely created a flowing, natural look, some of the collections are in danger of becoming overgrown or depleted unless older

specimens are replaced within a designed framework.

At the back of the house, a large porch overlooks Pan's Garden, a long rectangular space, calm in its greens. Information boards supply helpful details, especially the photograph of the Rosarie in the former vegetable garden (undergoing restoration in 2010). On the other side of the house, the Japanese maples around the Cypress Pool herald a concentration of interesting Asian shrubs and trees, some very mature. Paths wend deeper into the woodland, revealing tulip poplars, bald cypresses, persimmons, magnolias, azaleas, and viburnums, among other shrubs. Primulas and ferns grow beside the burbling stream.

Robert and Henry Tubbs bought Paradise Farm and its 130 acres, which they renamed Willowwood, in 1908 as a weekend retreat from their New York jobs. Until their deaths in 1942 and 1958, they developed the collections with the help of their friend and executor, Dr. Benjamin C. Blackburn (1908–1987), professor of botany at Drew University, who lived at Willowwood from 1946 and eventually inherited the estate. Willowwood became an arboretum in 1950. Since 1980 the Morris County Park Commission has managed the garden with the assistance of the Henry Tubbs Trust and the Willowwood Foundation. Currently five full-time gardeners look after Willowwood and Bamboo Brook (see p. 219). Future plans include opening up a new trail to honor the plant collector Ernest (Chinese) Wilson (1876–1930), which will supplement the special plant material received earlier through Wilson and the Arnold Arboretum.

PENNSYLVANIA

117 Ambler Arboretum of Temple University, Ambler
118 Andalusia, Andalusia
119 Awbury Arboretum (at the Francis Cope House), Philadelphia
120 Arboretum at the Barnes Foundation, Merion Station
121 Bartram's Garden, Philadelphia
122 Chanticleer, Wayne
123 Fairmount Park, Philadelphia
124 Haverford College Arboretum, Haverford
125 Highlands Mansion & Gardens, Fort Washington
126 Hortulus Farm Garden & Nursery, Wrightstown
127 Jenkins Arboretum, Devon
128 Laurel Hill Cemetery, Philadelphia
129 Longwood Gardens, Kennett Square
130 Meadowbrook Farm, Meadowbrook
131 Morris Arboretum of the University of Pennsylvania, Philadelphia
132 Pennsbury Manor, Morrisville
133 Scott Arboretum of Swarthmore College, Swarthmore
134 Shofuso: Japanese House & Garden, Philadelphia
135 St. Mary Medical Center Healing Gardens, Langhorne
136 Tyler Arboretum, Media
137 Tyler Formal Gardens at Bucks County Community College, Newtown
138 West Laurel Hill Cemetery, Bala Cynwyd
139 Wyck, Philadelphia

85 Lewis W. Barton Arboretum & Nature Preserve at Medford Leas, Medford, NJ
140 Eleutherian Mills at Hagley Museum & Library, Wilmington, DE
141 Gibraltar, Wilmington, DE
142 Goodstay Gardens, Wilmington, DE
143 Mt. Cuba Center, Hockessin, DE
144 Nemours Mansion & Gardens, Wilmington, DE
146 Rockwood Mansion & Gardens, Wilmington, DE
148 Winterthur, Winterthur, DE

See Greater Philadelphia Gardens: ***www.greaterphiladelphiagardens.org***

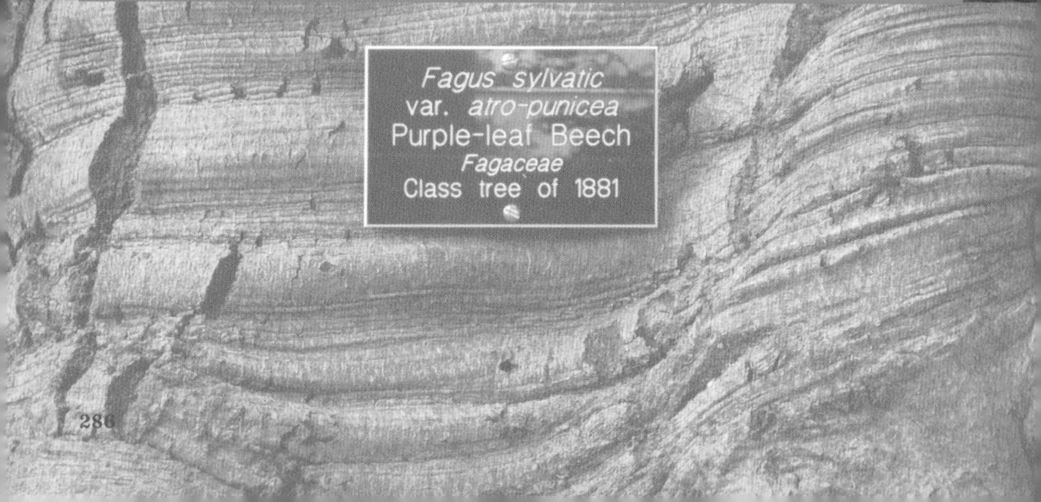

Fagus sylvatic
var. *atro-punicea*
Purple-leaf Beech
Fagaceae
Class tree of 1881

PENNSYLVANIA
(Greater Philadelphia)

PENNSYLVANIA

202

476

Wrightstown ● 126

Morrisville ●
95

Newtown ● 137
1
Ambler ● 117
276   Langhorne ● 135   132
125   Fort Washington ● 130   276
131   Meadowbrook
76   PA Turnpike   76   119   Andalusia ● 118
Schuylkill River   1

127   Bala Cynwyd
Devon   128
122   138   139
Wayne   Haverford   120
476   124   123
Merion
Station   134   123 Philadelphia
202   133 ● Swarthmore
136   Media   121
129   1
Kennett   202   85
Square   95
148 DELAWARE   Delaware River   NEW   NJ Turnpike
143 144   JERSEY   73
140
142 141   146
Wilmington ●

PHILADELPHIA AREA & MAIN LINE

119 Awbury Arboretum (at the Francis Cope House), Philadelphia, PA

120 Arboretum at the Barnes Foundation, Merion Station, PA

121 Bartram's Garden, Philadelphia, PA

123 Fairmount Park, Philadelphia, PA (several locations)

124 Haverford College Arboretum, Haverford, PA

128 Laurel Hill Cemetery, Philadelphia, PA

131 Morris Arboretum of the University of Pennsylvania, Philadelphia, PA

134 Shofuso: Japanese House & Garden, Philadelphia , PA

138 West Laurel Hill Cemetery, Bala Cynwyd, PA

139 Wyck, Philadelphia, PA

ARROWS TO:

129 Longwood Gardens, Kennett Square

133 Scott Arboretum of Swarthmore College, Swarthmore

BUCKS COUNTY & NORTHEAST PENNSYLVANIA

118 Andalusia, Andalusia, PA

126 Hortulus Farm Garden & Nursery, Wrightstown, PA

130 Meadowbrook Farm, Meadowbrook, PA

132 Pennsbury Manor, Morrisville, PA

135 St. Mary Medical Center Healing Gardens, Langhorne, PA

137 Tyler Formal Gardens at Bucks County Community College, Newtown, PA

AMBLER ARBORETUM OF TEMPLE UNIVERSITY

580 Meetinghouse Road, Ambler, PA 19002
TEL: (267) 468-8400
WEBSITE: *www.ambler.temple.edu/arboretum*
SEE MAP: p. 287

Hours: Grounds open daily, dawn to dusk. Admission free

Location: 97 miles from New York City

Parking: Visitor car park on opposite side of road, then enter through main pedestrian entrance with white pergolas

Public transportation: Amtrak to Philadelphia, SEPTA (Lansdale/Doylestown line) to Ambler, free shuttle bus service during fall and spring semesters, or taxi 2-1/4 miles

Facilities: Brochure with map in boxes at entrances and in Dixon Hall; university café during the semester; restrooms in Dixon Hall and elsewhere; picnicking; partially wheelchair accessible; dogs on leash

Programming: Credit and noncredit courses

Group garden tours: By appointment

Additional eateries: Ambler, 2-1/4 miles

Important particularly for its history as the site in 1910 of the founding of the Pennsylvania School of Horticulture for Women, Ambler Arboretum provides fourteen learning gardens around the campus developed (or let go) according to the current interests and requirements of the Department of Landscape and Horticulture. Its three areas of focus are "sustainability, the health benefits of gardens, and the history of women in horticulture, agriculture, and design." The sedum roof (2008) on the athletics building, the Wetland Garden, the emphasis on teaching sustainable practices, and the partnership with other agencies to "reforest" areas in the Philadelphia Zoo with 2,000 native trees propagated on campus, all stem from the school's commitment to the environment.

The Ernesta Ballard Healing Garden, a little labyrinth with a gravel pathway set between plantings of thyme and surrounded by a sitting wall, honors a woman who was a pioneer in ecological responsibility and who brought the Philadelphia Flower Show to national prominence. The herb garden and the dwarf evergreen and Japanese maple garden acknowledge the importance of other women. The legacy of Beatrix Farrand (1872–1959), who designed the formal gardens (1931) in front of what is now Dixon Hall, lends further interest. Here, steps lead down to a central lawn flanked by borders with a strong, updated planting of perennials and grasses, and a second pair of borders runs parallel to the enclosing hedges. In the lower garden, two charming open pavilions with Doric columns on a raised stone platform provide viewing points, with woodland in the background. The side gardens now contain a winter and a native plant garden.

The arboretum's gardens are cared for by three gardeners, plus student workers and volunteers. The most recent addition within the 187 acres of the campus is the Colibraro Conifer Garden (2009), which is being formed close to the Healing Garden.

Hours: House and grounds open by appointment for groups only, Monday–Saturday. See website for details. Admission fee

Location: 88 miles from New York City

Public transportation: Amtrak to Cornwells Heights or to Philadelphia, and SEPTA to Cornwells Heights, walk 1 mile

Facilities: Small visitor center, film on Andalusia; brochure and garden map; material on Andalusia and related history; no refreshments; restrooms; picnicking; not wheelchair accessible; no dogs

Nearby eateries: Street Road, Bensalem Township, 3-1/2 miles

Also of interest: Bristol, 8-3/4 miles north

Andalusia has been the country house of the Biddles since 1814, when Nicholas Biddle (1786–1844) bought his wife's family house and grounds after the death of his mother-in-law, Mrs. John Craig. Its position on the Delaware River and its views, unmarred by industrial development, are nothing short of spectacular. Even more remarkable is that the house, along with eighty acres and a number of estate buildings—unlike many of the neighboring mansions—has been preserved. The wharf has gone, but one can imagine the steamboat journeys to and from Philadelphia.

The Regency house, built around 1797 and enlarged by Benjamin Latrobe for the Craigs from 1806 to 1808, was used as a summer house by Nicholas Biddle, his wife, and family. It was greatly expanded between 1834 and 1836 and given the imposing Greek Revival extension on the river side, with its Doric-columned portico/piazza. The architect, Thomas U. Walter (1804–1887)—creator of the capitol dome in Washington—is also the presumed designer of the delightful guesthouse (1838, expanded 1852) in a contrasting Gothic Revival style, with furniture to match. The interiors of the Big House—with portraits and photographs of the family, their furniture, artifacts, and mementoes—immerse the visitor in the occupancy of the various generations.

The lawns running gently down to the river with scattered trees (tulip poplar, hemlock, beech, and willow oak) evoke the original planting. Along the River Walk, three small buildings expand one's sense of social history. The curious temple structure (1835–1836) perched rather awkwardly on its earlier base (1815) was a male retreat for billiards and card playing, cigars and drinks. Years later in 1913, Letitia Biddle met here with friends to plan the Garden Club of America, while just up river, the Grotto (1834–1836), constructed of roughly hewn stone in the Gothic Revival style and resembling an old chapel, provided a cool retreat for Jane Biddle and her female friends.

A short walk leads to the former pump house that conveyed water to the Graperies (late 1830s), two of whose high walls remain, along with a partially reconstructed greenhouse and the heating apparatus. Nicholas Biddle, the powerful President of the Second Bank of America (before its collapse in 1841 and his financial ruin), had the gentleman farmer's taste for experiment and tried—eventually succeeding—to grow table grapes here. Other passions included orchards of mulberry trees for silk worms (a failure), thoroughbred horse breeding, and Guernsey cattle.

Now a walled garden, the Graperies contains the rose garden, with old-fashioned and hybrid tea varieties, ilex hedge compartments, lawns, and flowering trees. Wisteria grows on parts of the wall and also serves as a backdrop to the Pool Pavilion Garden (1960s) outside. Other twentieth-century enrichments, fitted in on parallel axes, include the Green Walk (with an interesting collection of conifers, Japanese maples, and ferns

on one side, perennials on the other), and a peony walk.

James Biddle (1929–2005) formed the Andalusia Foundation to preserve the family home in 1980; the Friends of Andalusia assist. Some 1,500–2,000 visitors annually tour the house and grounds, the latter managed by two full-time and three seasonal gardeners.

Hours: Grounds open daily, dawn to dusk. House open 9am–5pm. Admission free to both, but donations welcome

Location: 101 miles from New York City

Public transportation: Amtrak to Philadelphia, SEPTA to last stop (Chestnut Hill East), Washington Lane, entrance to Awbury opposite station. Or from downtown Philadelphia, take SEPTA buses #18 or #26 to Chew Avenue, walk up Awbury Road to the Francis Cope House. SEPTA XH bus stops on Washington Lane, walk south on Chew Avenue to Awbury Road

Facilities: Visitor center in the Francis Cope House for brochures, with books on the Cope family and Awbury for sale; restrooms; no refreshments; picnic tables behind house; wheelchair accessible; dogs on leash after 3pm

Group garden tours: By appointment

Nearby eateries: North, on Germantown Avenue in the Mt. Airy and Chestnut Hill neighborhoods; snacks at intersection of Chew and Washington

This property originated when Henry Cope, the Philadelphian ship owner, bought farmland in 1852 to build a summer house for his family. His son, Francis Cope, given his own acreage, added the 1860 stone house designed by Yarnall & Cooper, with generous porches on two sides, now the arboretum headquarters. Other family members also built near them, so that by the 1920s there were twenty-four houses, all owned by descendents of the Copes, in what is now the historic district of Awbury. The grounds of the Francis Cope home were laid out around 1860 by the botanist and landscape architect, William Saunders (1822–1900) in the English landscape style of the early nineteenth century— well-graded, rolling, open spaces of grass with islands of trees and shrubs, good specimen trees, and woods. The main view from the house still suggests this expertise, and the mature trees are a pleasure. One finds a nicely cared for small perennial, shrub, and fern garden at the back of the house, while the rest of the grounds—though minimally cared for—provide open space in this now built-up section of Philadelphia.

Awbury is an interesting example of the way a once well-tended estate garden and landscape have been adapted, because of budget restrictions and pressing contemporary needs, to new uses—engaging children and members of the diverse neighborhood in environmental concerns, animal habitats, native plants, and urban agricultural initiatives. The nearby nonprofit organization. The thirty-three acres surrounding the Francis Cope House are cared for by two full-time gardeners. Two administrative and two educational staff members run the programs. Karen Anderson,

twenty-two-acre Awbury Agricultural Village sponsors community gardens, an organic farm, production greenhouses, and a teaching garden. An apprenticeship program in landscape maintenance and horticulture prepares some fourteen young adults annually for careers in the green industry, and providing other service-learning opportunities is also an important focus.

The Awbury Arboretum was established in 1916 as a public park by Francis Cope's descendents and, since 1986, has been managed and owned by the Awbury Arboretum Association, Inc., an independent

executive director, writes that future plans for the total fifty-five acres include "rebuilding an aging tree canopy and replacing dying, diseased, and invasive trees with more appropriate choices. We are also developing the Awbury Agricultural Village as a model of collaborative urban agriculture and food production."

120 ARBORETUM AT THE BARNES FOUNDATION

300 North Latch's Lane, Merion Station,
PA 19066
TEL: (610) 667-0290
WEBSITE: *www.barnesfoundation.org*
SEE MAPS: pp. 287 & 288

Hours: Grounds open by reservation with gallery ticket until the art galleries close, June 30, 2011. Check website for reopening

Location: 100 miles from New York City

Public transportation: Amtrak to Philadelphia, SEPTA R5 to Merion Station, walk 1 mile, or taxi from 34th Street, 5-3/4 miles; SEPTA bus #44 from downtown Philadelphia to Old Lancaster and North Latch's Lane

Facilities: No refreshments; restrooms; gallery shop; no picnicking; restricted wheelchair access; no dogs

Nearby eateries: Montgomery Avenue in Bala Cynwyd, 3/4 mile; Haverford Avenue, Narbeth, 1-1/2 miles

A visit to the extraordinary Barnes Foundation, with its Impressionist and Post-impressionist paintings by such artists as Renoir, Cezanne, Seurat, and Matisse, was previously supplemented by a walk around the twelve-acre arboretum. But when the art collection, scheduled to be taken from its home in June 2011, is relocated in Philadelphia (five and a half miles away), the arboretum will close temporarily. It will open sometime in 2012 and is expected to be more accessible to the general public, with the horticultural school expanded.

As Dr. Albert Barnes (1872–1951) added to his art collection, his wife, Laura L. Barnes (1875–1966), landscaped the grounds (acquired in 1922) and built up her collections of trees and shrubs. She sought out a wide variety within the same genus, often planting her Asian and European imports with natives and organizing parts of the garden for seasonal show and comparison. Many individual mature and unusual specimens accompany the excellent examples of conifers, lilacs, *Stewartias,* magnolias, and ferns. They grow on the lawns, in shaped areas on the edge, and within the woods—also the site of a teahouse. Terraced gardens for perennials below the house on its far side and a rose garden add interest to the walk. As with her husband's collection, hers calls for close looking and a slow pace.

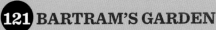

121 BARTRAM'S GARDEN

54th Street and Lindbergh Boulevard,
Philadelphia, PA 19143
TEL: (215) 729-5281
WEBSITE: *www.bartramsgarden.org*
SEE MAPS: pp. 287 & 288

Hours: Grounds open daily, 10am–5pm (except during city-observed holidays). House open April through October, Friday, Saturday, and Sunday for house and garden tours (see website). Admission free to grounds; fee for house and garden tours

Location: 103 miles from New York City

Public transportation: Amtrak to Philadelphia, transfer to SEPTA #36 subway-surface line to intersection of 54th and Lindbergh Boulevard. Ferry from Center City in the summer on some Sundays (see www.schuylkillbanks.org)

Facilities: Visitor center for walking tour brochure (also at kiosk outside); gift shop with Bartram material, basic snacks, coffee, tea, and cold drinks; restrooms; picnic tables in the Eastwick Pavilion and in the Bartram Meadow; partial wheelchair access; dogs on leash outside the historic garden area

Programming: Walks, lectures, kayaking, and more

Group garden tours: By appointment

Nearby eateries: University City, Philadelphia, 2-1/2 miles; Center City, Philadelphia, 4-1/2 miles

Also of interest: Woodlands Cemetery (formerly the estate of William Hamilton (1745–1813), a keen horticulturist, friend, and neighbor of John Bartram's sons), 4000 Woodland Avenue, Philadelphia, 1-1/2 miles. The grounds and significant house (1787)—now rather run-down—became part of the new rural Woodlands Cemetery in 1840. Heinz Wildlife Refuge, 8601 Lindbergh Boulevard, Philadelphia, 3-1/2 miles

A miracle of survival, this thrilling garden and house embody a story, not of superb garden design, but of plant collecting in the eighteenth and early nineteenth centuries—botanical explorations from the headwaters of the Schuylkill to the shores of Lake Ontario, and ultimately down to Florida. The garden was for growing, propagating, and observing native finds as well as imports sent by European botanists and horticulturists. Trees and shrubs were of special interest, but there were also beds of ornamental and medicinal plants along with those for vegetables. Beyond the garden were the orchard, grazing grounds for the cattle and sheep, and the agricultural fields.

Intellectuals came here to meet John Bartram (1699–1777), the famous self-taught naturalist and botanist, and from here seeds collected on travels were sorted into packages of a hundred different species and sent over to Britain (and later through Benjamin Franklin to France), where estate owners and nurserymen eagerly experimented with the new American finds. Correspondence from Carolus Linnaeus and the greatest botanists of the period found its way to this botanical garden.

Bartram, a third-generation Pennsylvania Quaker, bought the original 102 acres on the western banks of the Schyulkill River for a farm in 1728. He built the stone house himself, enlarging it between 1740 and 1770. The river facade has a distinctive, recessed porch and partly engaged columns with Ionic capitals—odd features for an otherwise plain home. Three generations of Bartrams lived here until 1850. Two sons, John Jr. and William, expanded the botanical garden, developing a thriving commercial nursery. William, who had accompanied his father on many of his seed collecting explorations, became a great explorer in his own right, and an author and botanical illustrator as well.

The garden stretches down the hill on three terraces, with long asphalt paths (unfortunate surface) and shorter horizontal ones dividing the plantings. Dappled shade and open areas provide varying habitats, which are being enriched through an exciting plan to reintroduce many of the 222 native trees and shrubs listed by the Bartram brothers in their 1783 nursery catalogue.

The first of its kind, and a priceless record, this catalogue was printed in English and French editions to attract sales from abroad after the war, as well as from Americans (George Washington and Thomas Jefferson were among the subscribers). Included were many American favorites: dogwoods, azaleas, tulip trees, and the lovely white-flowered *Franklinia alatamaha* tree—now so famous (and extinct in the wild since 1803) that it can hardly be mentioned without a reference to John Bartram, who noted it in Florida in 1765, and his son William, who returned to collect seeds and propagate it in 1777. These grow in the garden now, besides such other noteworthy specimens as a 1785 gingko, a toothache tree (*Zanthoxylum americanum*), and a spreading bottlebrush buckeye.

Sold in 1850, the Bartram property was bought and preserved by railway magnate Andrew Eastwick (1810–1879), and then became part of the city's public park system in 1891. Periods of neglect and difficulties followed, and industrial and housing developments encroached.

The John Bartram Association, in partnership with the Philadelphia's Department of Parks and Recreation, manage the house, the eight-acre garden (with one full-time and two part-time gardeners, assisted by a seasonal gardener and six regular volunteers), and the new tidal wetlands and extended grounds (37 acres). Some 35,000 visitors arrive annually. The director, Louise Turan, notes, "Improvements include the Schuylkill River Trail through the Bartram meadow, improved orientation and signage, and Board-approved plans for the restoration and preservation of the living and historic collections."

122 CHANTICLEER

786 Church Road, Wayne, PA 19087
TEL: (610) 687-4163
WEBSITE: *www.chanticleergarden.org*
SEE MAP: p. 287

Hours: Garden open April through October, Wednesday–Sunday 10am–5pm;
May through Labor Day, Friday nights until 8pm. Admission fee. House open
by appointment only

Location: 107 miles from New York City

Parking: Limited; first-come basis

Public transportation: Amtrak to Philadelphia, SEPTA train (Thorndale line)
to Wayne (café in mornings), walk 1-1/2 miles or taxi

Facilities: Visitor pavilion with map; guides and books on Chanticleer for sale;
no refreshments; restrooms; picnicking on Friday evenings in summer; wheelchair
accessible; no dogs

Programming: Workshops, photography, training of interns, Chanticleer Fellowships

Garden tours: By appointment

Nearby eateries: Lancaster or North Wayne Avenues, Wayne, 1-1/2 miles;
list available from visitor pavilion and website

Energy, innovation, and horticultural expertise define Chanticleer. Mindful of the past, the garden looks toward the future. Since opening to the public in 1993, gardens have been both embellished and created, and the main vista transformed. The former setting of trees, grass, and an unadorned pond is now a more dynamic landscape. Thousands of daffodils on the slopes open the garden season in the spring.

Chanticleer, sitting above a valley, was the home of the Rosengartens from 1913, with three houses, built in 1912, 1925 (acquired in 1933), and 1935, used mainly during the summer. Their very successful chemical firm, manufacturing products such as quinine, morphine, and strychnine,

was centered in Philadelphia, a family enterprise until 1927 when it merged with Merck & Co. The last owner of the compound, Adolph Rosengarten Jr. (1905–1990), arranged for the preservation of the property in 1977, setting up a trust to generously fund the Chanticleer Foundation.

Describing itself as a "Pleasure Garden," Chanticleer is indeed that—not in the usual sense of offering entertainments such as boating, concerts, parading, and dining, but of delivering a feast to the senses. The small formal areas by the house, adapted from the initial designs of Thomas Sears (1920s), are filled with tropicals and subtropicals and unusual container displays. Attention to detail

is apparent everywhere. During the winter the horticulturalists work in metal, stone, or wood to produce individualized seating, planters, railing, information boxes, and other handmade features.

A path runs around the thirty-five acres, taking in the strong serpentine design of junipers (banded by, perhaps, mustard, tobacco, or sorghum), the Korean, Chinese, and Japanese plantings within Asian Woods, the lush perennials and shrubs around the two ponds, the seductive stream garden, leading to the Gravel Garden with its succulents, thyme, and lavenders. Then comes the Ruin. In a bold move, Christopher Woods (the director from 1990 to 2003) persuaded his board in 1999 to demolish the 1925 Minder house—unnecessary and badly placed within the garden. Riffing on the eighteenth-century inclination for crumbling Gothic buildings, he incorporated within this constructed ruin the "library" with stone carved books, the "dining-room," with a water table (a nod to Pliny the Younger and the Villa Lante), and the eerie "pool room" with its submerged faces (the sculpture by Marcia Donahue). Outside, oversized stone chairs create a "sitting-room" en plein air.

Further on, we return to the present with the Cut Flower and Vegetable Garden or the Tennis Court Garden, where, backed by a rose arbor for ramblers, four quadrants of fulsome planting surround a circle of strongly colored berberis. Here, a succession of bulbs and perennials and self-seeded annuals bring seasonal color from April onward. A grand staircase leads back to the house.

Ten full-time gardeners and groundskeepers with four part-time seasonal helpers look after the garden, visited by 38,000 annually. Bill Thomas, the current executive director, emphasizes the garden's commitment to innovation and exciting design and affirms that their aim is "to be one of the finest gardens in the world."

123 FAIRMOUNT PARK

Philadelphia
TEL: (215) 683-0200
WEBSITE: *ww.fairmountpark.org*
SEE MAPS: pp. 287 & 288

Hours: Open dawn to dusk (except for enclosed areas or buildings, see below)

Location: 99 miles from New York City

Public transportation: Amtrak to Philadelphia or NJ Transit to Trenton, then SEPTA to Philadelphia. Buses throughout the city

Information: Download park map from either www.fairmountpark.org or www.phila. gov/recreation. Trolley Works bus tour: www.phillytour.com (all of Philadelphia, but includes Fairmount Park stops)

Nearby eateries: Sparse in park, but a café and restaurant in the Philadelphia Museum of Art, a restaurant in the Water Works by the river (215-236-9000), and family fare in the zoo. Many eateries in downtown Philadelphia

Fairmount Park defies the expectations of those who think of city parks as landscaped and designed areas within a defined space. It is very large (9,204 acres, compared with the 843 acres of New York's Central Park), lies on both sides of the Schuylkill River, and is connected by bridges with a high density of noise and traffic. It comprises sixty-three regional and neighborhood parks, many non-adjoining (such as Pennypack Park, Rittenhouse Square, and the Benjamin Franklin Parkway); seven houses rich in cultural and architectural history (and open to the public); and many other significant buildings, not least the Philadelphia Museum of Art (2600 Benjamin Franklin Parkway). Until recently, management was split between the Fairmount Commission, set up in 1867, and the Department of Recreation (1951). *A Bridge to the*

Future: Fairmount Park Strategic Plan (2004) addressed the major problems relating to the park's deterioration, recommended the merger of the two departments (begun 2009), and provided a way forward.

In **East Fairmount Park** the Water Works (640 Water Works Drive, designed in 1812 by Frederick Graff) is of particular interest. Here water was pumped up to the reservoir on Faire Mount (site of the Philadelphia Museum of Art), and its five acres of land and gardens generated Fairmount Park, officially formed in 1855. Many more parcels of land, often of previous country house estates, were purchased upstream to protect the water from commercial contamination.

The latest addition to Fairmount Park, the handsome one-acre Sculpture Garden (2009) at Art Museum Drive

Valley Forge (22 miles), while the exciting, new Schuylkill River Park runs along the waterfront to the south as far as Locust Street (extension planned)— an example of what community groups and coalitions have achieved through advocacy, fundraising, and pressing for innovative changes. In 2008 the city's mayor, Michael Nutter, pledged to make Philadelphia the number-one green city in America; a tree planting is underway and a further 500 acres for public parks will be acquired by 2015 through the "Greenworks Philadelphia" initiative.

Within **West Fairmount Park** lies the Horticultural Center (1976) at North Horticultural Drive and Montgomery Avenue. Open daily, except holidays, 9am–3pm, and the grounds daily, except holidays, April 1 through October 31, 9am–6pm, and November 1 through March 31, 9am–5pm. It replaced the famous Horticultural Hall, developed for the great 1876 Centennial Exhibition and demolished in 1955. A modern exhibition space and greenhouse offer displays, with more gardens and mature trees outside. Shofuso: The Japanese House and Garden is close by, see p. 326. The large Beaux-Arts Memorial Building (1876; also nearby), now houses the Please Touch Museum for children. Further south, the Philadelphia Zoo, 3400 West Girard Avenue (open daily, except Thanksgiving, December 24, 25, and 31, and January 1) incorporates The Solitude, the architecturally important house built by William Penn's grandson

and Kelly Drive, open 24 hours, was designed for the Philadelphia Museum of Art by OLIN landscape architects, working with Atkin Olshin Schade Architects. Planted over the museum's parking garage, it covers the facility with dramatic formations of enormous boulders, which contrast with smooth grass berms for sculpture and the transparent glass of the entranceway. A dominant terrace offers vistas of the tranquil Azalea Park (1952), the Water Works, and the Schuylkill, as well as the pretty gazebo on the rock escarpments above the river. A grove of honey locusts, pockets of perennials and flowering shrubs, and specimen trees soften the park's hardscape.

Below, a scenic trail leads north through the park and continues to

(1784), who laid out its park, with views towards the Schuylkill River, in the up-to-date English landscape style.

Also of interest: Just across the Delaware River in New Jersey is the **Camden Children's Garden** (3 Riverside Drive, Camden, NJ 08103), open Friday, Saturday, and Sunday, 10am–4pm, and other days by appointment. Of particular interest to parents of young children, along with landscape designers and architects, it offers activities set in gardened spaces and a butterfly house that provides quiet moments of observation. Future plans include creating a CSA (Community Supported Agriculture) farmers market to serve families in Camden, where access to fresh produce is limited.

124 HAVERFORD COLLEGE ARBORETUM

370 Lancaster Avenue, Haverford, PA 19041
TEL: (610) 896-1101
WEBSITE: *www.haverford.edu/arboretum*
SEE MAPS: pp. 287 & 288

Hours: Grounds open dawn to dusk. Admission free
Location: 109 miles from New York City
Parking: In Orchard or South lots
Public transportation: Amtrak to Philadelphia, SEPTA train to Haverford and, following signs, walk three blocks to the college or taxi
Facilities: *Tree Tour* and *Pinetum Tour* brochures for self-guided walks (also supplementary material) available from Facilities Management Complex close to south parking lot, and from boxes at strategic points on grounds; COOP café (and restrooms) at the Whitehead Campus Center, which also has the general visitor center; wheelchair accessible; dogs on leash
Group garden tours: By appointment, modest fee
Nearby eateries: Haverford
Also of interest: Appleford, 770 Mount Moro Road, Villanova. The house, used for receptions and events, has a small Thomas Sears formal terraced garden (1930s) on two sides, and a nice stream and pond

The entire 200-acre campus of Haverford College is termed an arboretum, and although requirements over the years have produced a density of buildings around Founders Hall, its original center (1833), the grounds have remained an important asset and have grown in collections and historical interest.

The Welsh Quakers who founded the college hired British landscape architect William Carvill (1797–1887) in 1834 to landscape what was formerly agricultural land. Carvill, during the eleven years he was employed there, laid out rather formal avenues lined with trees, but also open lawns (he introduced cricket), a serpentine walk with shrubberies, and areas with single specimen trees and clusters in the pastoral landscape tradition. Several trees, such as the bur oak and the swamp white oak (*Quercus macrocarpa* and *Quercus bicolor*), remain from this time. An unusual design element, in the northeast, were the fifteen groups, each featuring one native species, planted in a circle of six, with one central tree—symbolizing the Quaker belief in community and the individual Friend. Several of these clustered plantings have been reintroduced. Large kitchen gardens and propagating greenhouses were part of the nineteenth-century layout, and today Carvill's Arch is a reminder of that legacy.

The *Tree Tour* brochure recommends a self-guided walk through the central core of the campus, taking in thirty-six special trees, including two State Champions and the much revered descendent of the American elm on the banks of the Delaware River where William Penn signed his treaty with the Native Americans in 1682. The *Pinetum Tour* brochure leads visitors to the eighteen-acre site near the southwest boundary, begun in 1928, which now has an important inventory of over three hundred mature conifer species (not cultivars), including sixteen State Champions. A 2¼-mile nature trail circles the campus, winding through trees and shrubs attractive to wildlife and passing by another State Champion (*Hemiptelea davidii*) and the three-acre Duck Pond, replanted in 2009 with native species along the perimeter to discourage Canada geese from causing erosion.

In addition to the trees, thickly planted beds and banks of shrubs, grasses, perennials, ferns, and hostas have been introduced around the college buildings, and a dining room looks out on to an Asian-influenced garden. This residential campus actively endeavors to connect its 1,169 students to its horticultural traditions. Incoming freshmen receive plants suitable for their rooms, dedicate a new tree, benefit from the labeling of 2,500 trees, and have opportunities to work on the grounds. One third of them join the Haverford College Arboretum Association, open to

students, faculty, alumni and friends of the college, which sponsors newsletters and occasional lectures, tours, and events, and provides a link for financial involvement later in their careers.

William Astifan, arboretum director, affirms his commitment to preserving historic trees, advancing diversity, and maintaining the principles of the original landscape plan as new buildings are added. The arboretum is cared for by three full-time horticulturalists, twelve volunteers, a director, and a curator. Its staff also maintains two greenhouses providing potted plants and flowers to ornament campus rooms and buildings for academic and special college events, including commencement.

125 HIGHLANDS MANSION & GARDENS

7001 Sheaff Lane, Fort Washington, PA 19034
TEL: (215) 641-2687
WEBSITE: *www.highlandshistorical.org*
SEE MAP: p. 287

Hours: Garden and grounds open dawn to dusk. House and gardens open for tours at 1:30 and 3pm each Monday–Friday. Admission free to grounds; fee for tour

Location: 96 miles from New York City

Public transportation: Amtrak, or NJ Transit and SEPTA, to Philadelphia; SEPTA train (Doylestown line) to Fort Washington, taxi 2-1/4 miles

Facilities: Flyer in parking lot and in house during office hours, Monday–Friday 10am–4pm; interpretative signage in garden; no refreshments; restrooms in house during office hours; limited picnicking by prior arrangement; limited wheelchair access; dogs on leash

Programming: Educational programs available for school, garden, and general interest groups

Group garden tours: By appointment

Nearby eateries: Ambler, 2-1/2 miles; Flourtown, 2-1/2 miles; list available from office

Also of interest: Peter Wentz Farmstead, 2100 Schultz Road, Worcester, 8 miles

In 1842 Andrew Jackson Downing, in *A Treatise on the Theory and Practice of Landscape Gardening*, praised the country seat of George Sheaff, Esq., which, with its "pleasure-grounds and plantations of fine evergreen and deciduous trees," blended profit and culture admirably. Today the livestock and the skilled agricultural elements have gone, but the house is surrounded by wooden fenced pasture and open grazing.

Sitting nicely on a low hill, up a short drive, the Georgian house was designed by Anthony Matlock in 1794 for the 300-acre country estate of the Philadelphian merchant, land speculator, and politician Anthony Morris (1776–1860). Funds were lavished on its elegant interiors and on the farm buildings (a handsome barn built around 1800 remains).

The family's enjoyment was brief, however, for by 1808 Morris was forced to sell the estate, and after an interim owner it became the property of the Sheaff family from 1813 until 1917. The Highlands—its grounds diminished to sixty acres—was then acquired by Caroline Sinkler (1860–1949), who also had houses in Philadelphia, Gloucester, MA, and South Carolina, and used The Highlands in spring and fall.

The gardens today reflect the varied interests of the owners. George Sheaf (1779–1851) shifted the emphasis from below the house (the area of the octagonal 1799–1800 springhouse), to a large two-acre rectangular pleasure ground east of the house. Extremely tall walls for growing grapes were added around 1844 and crenellated for decorative effect. The Gothic Revival tool shed, also from that period, adds a picturesque note, as does the gardener's cottage at the far northwest corner and an octagonal garden house (from the Morris period).

accomplished. Lines of newly planted box hedges suggest areas mapped out for future improvements. It remains to be seen whether Miss Sinkler's awkwardly designed exedra can ever be thought of as a successful element. Restoration of the kitchen garden, with heirloom varieties of vegetables, fruit trees, and some herbs—begun in 2010—will add dimension to the story of this country house estate.

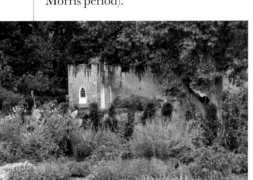

The details of the ornamental planting from this era are not known, and the restoration of Caroline Sinkler's Colonial Revival garden is based on the master plan prepared by Doell & Doell in 1999. This draws upon the extant 1918 plan of William Eyre (1858–1944), along with photographs and archival records.

One quadrant of small beds has been replanted as an ornamental scented and medicinal herb garden around the original armillary sphere, and new perennial beds, shrubs, and trees have appeared. The rebuilding of the tunnel arbor, the replacement of the sculpture by copies, and the initial restoration of the 1920s Lord & Burnham greenhouse have all been

In 1941, Caroline Sinkler sold The Highlands and its sixty acres to her niece Emily Sinkler Roosevelt and her husband Nicholas who, in turn, donated the property to the commonwealth of Pennsylvania in 1957. With the roof leaking and other obvious maintenance problems, an auction in 1971 emptied the house and garden of moveable contents. Since 1975 the house and its forty-four acres have been administered by The Highlands Historical Society. The formal garden is cared for by one full-time and two part-time seasonal gardeners and eight volunteers. To replicate the feeling of a private garden, no labeling is used.

126 HORTULUS FARM GARDEN & NURSERY

60 Thompson Mill Road, Wrightstown, PA 18940
TEL: (215) 598-0550
WEBSITE: *http://hortulusfarm.com*
SEE MAPS: pp. 287 & 289

Hours: Garden open May through October, Wednesday and Saturdays 10am–2pm. Admission fee. Nursery open Monday–Saturday 9am–4pm and Sunday 10am–3pm. Admission free

Location: 75 miles from New York City

Public transportation: Amtrak or NJ Transit to Trenton, taxi 17-1/2 miles; Hunterdon Valley bus to New Hope, taxi 8-1/4 miles

Facilities: Visitor center for map and gift shop; no refreshments (except bottled water); restrooms; picnicking in gazebo by entrance; not wheelchair accessible; no dogs

Nearby eateries: New Hope; Newtown; Doylestown

There's an exuberance about Hortulus Farm Garden—as though the world of horticulture is so rich and inviting, and the play with historical styles of planting such fun, that one is continually tempted to extend the boundaries to embrace and showcase new possibilities—often on a large scale.

In spring the woods surrounding the pond—with its white, sharply roofed gazebo (no seats)—are filled with thousands of bulbs, while in summer—after the long peony borders have had their turn—the herbaceous and shrub borders call out for attention. The visual punctuations—of a pool, a large pot, a gate—draw the visitor on within a geometric framework of grass paths and allées. It is the planting, though, that is most striking. For instance, there's the unusual combination of an

avenue of white pines and dogwoods and blowsy white hydrangeas that leads up to a semicurved metal bench backed by a gigantic eighteen-foot-tall vase filled with scrambling roses and framed by two fastigiate copper beeches. The sense of being deep in the Bucks County countryside is fortified by the next part of the trail: through natural meadows, with views over gently rolling hills.

A different style prevails to the side of the main farm house of 1723–1797 and the cluster of other structures (where ducks and geese are padding about): smaller, separated, gardens are filled with patterns of tightly formed Alberta spruce; topiary in bobbles, pyramids, and spirals; clipped box hedges; and standards. The ornamental vegetable garden

has tall fanciful iron tuteurs for a luxuriance of climbers within wooden boarded beds, which are laid out in sharp geometries.

Garden writer and author Jack Staub (see his books on herbs and vegetables) and events designer Renny Renolds (who trained as a landscape architect) bought the property in 1980 and, initially from their base in New York, started the garden, now covering thirty acres within the hundred acres of farmland. In 2000 they set up the

Hortulus Farm Foundation to insure that the garden "will continue to exist as a public place of tranquility and horticultural inspiration in perpetuity upon our demise." The large nursery, with nine greenhouses and five display houses, sells many of the plants viewed in the garden. Owned by the foundation, it supports the garden.

# 127 JENKINS ARBORETUM
631 Berwyn Baptist Road, Devon, PA 19333
TEL: (610) 647-8870
WEBSITE: *www.jenkinsarboretum.org*
SEE MAP: p. 287

Hours: Grounds open daily, 8am–sunset. Admission free

Location: 109 miles from New York City

Public transportation: Amtrak to Philadelphia, SEPTA to Devon,
walk 1 mile

Facilities: Education center (9am–4pm) for maps, brochures, shop, restrooms;
no refreshments; picnicking at entrance area; education center wheelchair accessible,
but grounds hilly; no dogs

Programming: Flower, tree, and bird identification, art and craft shows, seasonal
plant sale

Group garden tours: By appointment

Nearby eateries: Wayne; Lancaster Pike (US Route 30) in Devon and Berwyn,
all within 3 miles; list available from education center

The Jenkins Arboretum is a surprising find, a woodland garden on forty-six acres of hillside in a lightly residential area within Philadelphia's highly populated Main Line. Planted in a naturalistic but managed style, azaleas and rhododendrons make a wonderful display from April to June. Some 5,000 specimens—deciduous and evergreen, species and hybrids, Asian and native—grow beneath a canopy of mostly chestnut-leaved oaks, red oaks, and tulip poplars, interspersed with hollies and hemlocks. The hard-surface path loops through the arboretum and also descends to a very different, open habitat around the pond, where sun-loving perennial wildflowers have been planted and a cluster of bald cypresses flourishes in the bog garden.

A detour along the Elisabeth Walk brings the visitor to the rhododendron section, while individual specimen trees such as the pawpaw, persimmon, Carolina silverbell, and *Franklinia*, are found throughout the arboretum. Many woodland wildflowers and ferns are also nurtured, and *Enkianthus*, viburnum, and high-bush blueberry provide an additional intermediate layer of natives.

In 1965 H. Lawrence Jenkins (d. 1968) set up a foundation and donated twenty acres to form a public park, arboretum, and wildlife sanctuary as a living memorial to his wife, Elisabeth Phillippe Jenkins (d. 1965). Louisa P. Browning (d. 1971) donated a further twenty-six acres in 1971 (the houses of both are private and seen from afar)

and the arboretum was opened in 1976 and extensive planting (and labeling) of the azaleas and rhododendrons begun.

In response to current environmental concerns, the mission now focuses on land and watershed stewardship, native wildflower, shrub, and tree diversity, and accompanying wildlife activities. The 2009 John J. Willaman Education Center (gold LEED certification), with geothermal heating and cooling, rainwater collection, and solar roof panels (soon to be installed) aims to be a model of environmental responsibility. The arboretum is supported by the Elisabeth Phillippe Jenkins Foundation (minimal endowment initially), which also sponsors internships and fellowships.

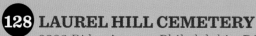

128 LAUREL HILL CEMETERY

3822 Ridge Avenue, Philadelphia, PA 19132
TEL: (215) 228-8200
WEBSITE: *www.thelaurelcemetery.org*
SEE MAPS: pp. 287 & 288

Hours: Grounds open Monday–Friday 8am–4:30pm; Saturday and Sunday 9:30am–4:30pm. Admission free

Location: 96 miles from New York City

Parking: In lot across the street from main entrance; visitors can also drive through the cemetery

Public transportation: Amtrak to Philadelphia, taxi 4-1/2 miles, or take SEPTA bus #61 (Ridge Avenue line) from any stop in Center City, on 9th Street between Walnut and Arch, and get off at Clearfield Street across from the gatehouse entrance. Alternatively, take any bus, subway, or El (blue) line that crosses Allegheny Avenue, and catch the #60 Allegheny bus that ends at Ridge Avenue—the cemetery gatehouse is one block south

Facilities: Brochures, newsletters, maps, cell phone tour maps in office at gatehouse entrance; small museum; small gift shop; walking tour guides for sale; no refreshments but list of eateries at office; restrooms; no tables but picnicking welcome; most areas wheelchair accessible; dogs on leash

Programming: Walks and events

Group tours: By appointment

Nearby eateries: Marketplace at East Falls down the street; village of East Falls, 1/4 mile north; village of Manayunk, 1 mile north

Also of interest: Fairmount Park (9,200 acres) (see p. 301) borders the cemetery

After Mount Auburn Cemetery outside Boston was created in 1831 by the Massachusetts Horticultural Society as a picturesque landscape with excellent planting, many nineteenth-century American cemeteries modeled themselves on this rural style, offering enjoyment to the living as well as, presumably, the dead. A serene place of "eternal rest," with beautiful views, provided an attractive venue for relatives and day-trippers alike before the advent of public parks. Laurel Hill Cemetery, the second major rural cemetery in America, continues this tradition today, still tranquil, despite some traffic noise on the road below and on the Schuylkill Expressway across the river.

Opened in 1836 on a former small estate outside Philadelphia—a city with unsanitary and unreliable burial conditions—the thirty-two-acre site was chosen by the remarkable John

Jay Smith (1798–1881) and his three partners for its accessibility by boat and, more specifically, its position on the slopes above the Schuylkill River. The Scottish-American architect-gardener John Notman (1810–1865) won the informal competition for the classical, Doric-columned Gatehouse and for the layout, which incorporated a few formal elements (terraces above the river, a patterned Shrubbery Section, and a loose grid for burial plots) within the natural landscape style of drives created in harmony with the land's contours. Hundreds of trees and shrubs were planted in picturesque arrangements under the supervision of Smith, who—besides being a librarian, aspiring businessman, and editor—was a knowledgeable horticulturist.

With additional land acquired in 1848 and 1861, it achieved its current size of seventy-eight acres. Extremely popular, the cemetery was visited by nearly 30,000 people in 1848, and 140,000 in 1861. Then, as now, people strolled, had picnics, and enjoyed the fresh air. Time has filled this nonsectarian cemetery with a wide variety of obelisks, tablets, gravestones, mausoleums, and sculpture, providing rich layers of aesthetic, social, and political history. The view from the higher slopes of the southern end takes in densities of trees in the valley, and elsewhere groves and single specimens of tulip poplar, ginkgo, horse chestnut, copper beech, London plane, holly, dogwood, purple-leafed maples, wild cherry, pines, spruces, locust, and cucumber magnolia among others. None of these are currently labeled.

In 1978, the Friends of Laurel Hill Cemetery was formed to assist the Laurel Hill Cemetery Company in the conservation of the monuments, archives and the historical character of the cemetery. *Old Mortality*, James Thom's sculpture (c. 1835) of Sir Walter Scott, his pony, and the eponymous character in his 1816 novel, was restored in 2010. In 2011 the 1844 Shrubbery Section (now called the Medallion Gardens) was replanted for the cemetery's 175th birthday celebrations. Specialized tours on Civil War generals, Philadelphia notables, and funerary architecture and sculpture are now supplemented by horticultural tours as well as birdwatching, concerts, moongazing, and Halloween events. Four full-time gardeners, along with two administrative and two educational staff members, work for the Friends, who are aided by a volunteer educational staff of fifteen. About 10,000 visitors explored the cemetery in 2009.

129 LONGWOOD GARDENS

1001 Longwood Road, Kennett Square,
PA 19348 (OFF ROUTE 1)
TEL: (610) 388-1000
WEBSITE: *www.longwoodgardens.org*
SEE MAPS: pp. 287, 288, 339 & 340

Hours: Gardens and house open daily at 9am with seasonal closing variations.
Summer usually Sunday–Wednesday 9am–6pm, Thursday–Saturday 9am–10pm.
Admission fee

Location: 131 miles from New York City

Public transportation: Amtrak to Wilmington, taxi 12-1/2 miles

Facilities: Visitor center for maps, brochures, cell phone tour information,
large gift shop, and plants; restrooms throughout the garden; restaurant and café;
picnicking adjacent to garden; wheelchair accessible, and wheelchairs and motorized
scooters available for a small fee; no dogs

Programming: Daily—pick up schedule on entry; also Festival of Fountains every
summer. Professional horticultural training

Group garden tours: By appointment

Additional eateries: Along Route 1 within 1 mile; Chadds Ford, 5 miles

Also of interest: Brandywine River Museum, 1 Hoffman's Mill Road, Chadds Ford,
4-3/4 miles

Longwood Gardens bring new meaning to the word "display." Fond of comparing the garden to a large store, full of different departments, with seasonal specials, Pierre du Pont (1870–1954) saw his garden as a place for pleasing and entertaining, first his own guests, and then the general public. He and his successors have succeeded splendidly, and the expertise that produces the horticultural results is matched by the technology of the spectacular fountain shows, especially in the evening, when water, colored lighting, and music combine in a computerized whole, with fireworks topping things off six times a season.

Trained as an engineer at MIT and chairman of the family company and of General Motors, Pierre du Pont—who knew the European gardens well—was more than a little competitive as he developed an eclectic vision for his own garden, improving on existing technology and making it all work to perfection in America. The 1927 Italian Water Garden is an admirable interpretation of classical (particularly French) formal geometries, with fountains playing at scheduled times. The naturalistic lake is reminiscent of those in eighteenth-

century English parks, and the Open Air Theater (1913) reveals its roots in sixteenth- and seventeenth-century Italy. The Flower Garden Walk (1907) seems a marvelous Victorian extravaganza of spring, summer, and autumn colors, with thousands of bulbs and bedding-out grown in the greenhouses. Especially lovely in spring, Peirce's Woods, enriched with ephemerals and ferns, recalls the "wild garden" style of William Robinson (1838–1935).

New "departments" have been continuously added, both before and after du Pont's death (1954), resulting in a loose layout, with clusters of defined areas followed by more open ones. The modest house (1730 onward, with 1914 addition) is outclassed by the grand conservatory (1921, with later additions), the focal point of the western section. Sitting on a terrace above the sunken garden (1921–1931)—site of the main fountain displays—it served the du Ponts as a horticultural showcase and as a venue for large-scale entertainments (the Aeolian Organ has recently been restored). Visitors are drawn to exuberant seasonal displays of camellias, lilies, and marguerites, poinsettias at Christmas, and the Chrysanthemum Festival (where the thousand bloom chrysanthemum is featured). Equally impressive, within the (now) four acres under glass, are the East Conservatory, Mediterranean, Cascade, and Silver gardens, the Palm House, the Children's Garden, and many other specialized sections— orchids, roses, and ferns among them. Outside, the courtyard holds the Waterlily Display.

From the conservatory terrace, the zany topiary garden (1936 and 1959) beckons to the left and—in the distance to the right—the Chimes Tower (1931–1932) and Hillside Garden. Other attractions include areas for conifers, pawlonias, roses, and, not least, the Idea Garden. Walks on the periphery through forest and meadow offer further investigations.

Pierre du Pont purchased the 202-acre property in 1906 primarily to save the arboretum (planted by the Peirce brothers from 1798). After 1921, when large numbers of visitors began coming to the gardens, he carefully prepared for its future, placing it in a well-endowed foundation in 1946. It is managed now by the nonprofit Longwood Gardens, Inc., which is committed to preserving his legacy of excellence, good management, and fiscal responsibility. Currently 1,077 acres (325 open to the public), Longwood, which has some 883,000 visitors annually, is cared for by seventy gardeners and more than 600 volunteers.

130 MEADOWBROOK FARM

1633 Washington Lane, Meadowbrook
(Abington Township), PA 19046
TEL: (215) 887-5900
WEBSITE: *www.meadowbrookfarm.org*
SEE MAPS: pp. 287 & 289

Hours: Garden and house open every Thursday, April through October, for a guided tour at 11am. House and garden also open for groups by appointment. The nursery is open year-round, Monday–Saturday 10am–5pm, and from late April to mid-June, Sunday 11am–4pm. Admission fee for tour. Admission free to nursery

Location: 90 miles from New York City

Public transportation: Amtrak to Philadelphia, SEPTA train to Meadowbrook station, walk 3/4 mile (no taxis)

Facilities: Nursery and gift shop; no refreshments; restrooms; picnicking for tours; nursery is wheelchair accessible, but not garden; dogs on leash

Programming: Workshops on propagating, terrariums, patio pots, cacti, succulents, etc.

Nearby eateries: Along Route 611

The gardens of Meadowbrook Farm reflect the instant charm, everything-in-its-place displays that J. Liddon Pennock Jr. (1913–2003) designed for many years at the Philadelphia International Flower Show—first as owner of Pennock's Florist in Philadelphia and later as proprietor of Meadowbrook Farm nursery. Some of his trademark pavilions found their way into his garden, along with a plethora of garden ornaments. He had an eye for dressing up a space—whether for a wedding at the White House or in a private garden, and apparently fresh floral arrangements and potted plants from the cutting garden and the greenhouses became a vital part of the carefully orchestrated interior décor.

Doors lead out to the terraces on the south side, wonderful entertaining spaces, arranged along two east–west axes, with a steep drop down to woods and a pond ahead. Two weeping hemlocks on either side of a vigorous lead eagle on the balustrade are the first instances of the shaped, espaliered, topiaried, and styled shrubs that are arranged with expertise in the walled or hedged spaces. Well-built stone stairs lead down to further rooms with a fountain or pool as focal points and a pavilion as the terminal point. Planters are also a distinctive feature, while mass seasonal bedding-out of pansies, begonias, or impatiens provide bold one-colored ribbons or circles within the formal areas, always viewed against the looser backdrop of trees. In spring

azaleas and flowering trees are a special feature

The house, built in 1936 on 150 acres as a wedding gift to Liddon Pennock and his wife, Alice Herkness (1915–1996), from her mother, was designed by Robert McGoodwin in an English Cotswold style. It is reached by a short drive, with good specimen evergreens in evidence and a cloud-pruned yew on the facade. Two full-time and two seasonal gardeners, with two volunteers, look after the gardens relating to the house—for the 1,000 annual visitors.

Off to the right of the drive is the nursery, opened in 1971 by Mr. Pennock, after he sold Pennock's Florist to his employees in 1966. The display houses of cacti, succulents, ferns, and orchids reflect John Story's propagating skills. The nursery sells a wide variety of perennials, annuals, trees, and shrubs, and specializes in forcing plants in preparation for the annual March Philadelphia International Flower Show—for its own display as well as for nearly forty other groups and garden club exhibitors.

Mr. Pennock left the house, garden, nursery (7 acres in all), and woods (18 acres) to the Pennsylvania Horticultural Society, with which he had been linked for many years. Meadowbrook Farm—now operating as a separate nonprofit organization under the guidance of the PHS Meadowbrook Committee—plans to preserve the integrity and structure of the Pennock garden. It will incorporate more "green" practices into the nursery business and summarizes its long term goals as increasing its educational program via workshops and lectures, establishing new theme gardens and expanding existing ones, supporting community outreach programs that further the mission of the PHS, and remaining the preeminent grower for the Philadelphia International Flower Show and other specialty shows.

131 MORRIS ARBORETUM OF THE UNIVERSITY OF PENNSYLVANIA

100 East Northwestern Avenue, Philadelphia, PA 19118
TEL: (215) 247-5777
WEBSITE: *www.morrisarboretum.org*
SEE MAPS: pp. 287 & 288

Hours: Grounds open weekdays 10am–4pm; extended hours on Thursdays from June through August, 10am–8:30pm; weekends: April through October, 10am–5pm, November through March, 10am–4pm. Admission fee

Location: 99 miles from New York City

Public transportation: Amtrak to Philadelphia, then SEPTA train (Chestnut Hill West line) to Chestnut Hill, walk 1-1/2 miles, or L bus (Plymouth Meeting) to Northwestern Ave, walk 1/2 mile

Facilities: Visitor center in former carriage house for brochures and maps, restrooms (and in garden April through October), gift and book shop, Bruno's Café (May through Labor Day, and autumn weekends, usually 11am–2:30pm, extended hours summer Thursdays), and vending machines; picnicking in café area; core route wheelchair accessible, and golf cart by appointment; no dogs

Programming: Continuing education courses, classes, trips, yoga, concerts

Garden tours: Usually Saturday and Sunday at 2pm and by appointment

Nearby eateries: Chestnut Hill area of Philadelphia, 1-1/2 miles, see www.chestnuthillpa.com

Also of interest: Woodmere Art Museum, 9201 Germantown Avenue, 1 mile

The arrival itself is a perfect prelude to visiting the Morris Arboretum: generous greenswards on both sides of the drive—which curves up the hill, with some Cor-ten grazing sheep by Charles Layland (1980), to the left. Trees are already a feature, and walking around one pays homage to their diversity, coming across them as gatherings of conifers, as individuals standing finely in their own space, or as splendidly layered compositions of varying heights, colors, and textures, joined by myriad shrubs and set off by groundcover and grass. The hilly terrain creates composed views that draw the visitor on to features: whether a horticultural display, a structure, or a seasonal sculpture.

Compton was the country house of the brother and sister John (1847–1915) and Lydia (1849–1932) Morris, who purchased the farmland in 1887 for their country home after John Morris had retired early from the family business of I. P. Morris & Co. Iron Works in Philadelphia. Pursuing their interests in horticulture, they met

University of Pennsylvania, and it was opened to the public in 1933.

With the passing of time, the formal gardens were neglected, the hardscape crumbled, and the arboretum was undermanaged. Since 1977, however, major ongoing restoration of the planting and waterworks has been under way. The challenge has been to incorporate some of the formal areas, which had been designed in relation to the house (demolished in 1968), and remained as isolated elements. Other features, in the eclectic Victorian style of the Morrises, remained as nonworking elements within the park contrasting with the naturalistic lake and little temple (c. 1896). An enormous amount has been accomplished: highlights among many include the very beautiful little 1899 Fernery (reopened in 1994); the Pennock Flower Walk, designed by Andropogon, with exuberant herbaceous and tropical planting;

Ernest (Chinese) Wilson (1876–1930) of the Arnold Arboretum and became the recipients of the many newly discovered trees and plants (Dawn Redwood, Dove Trees) collected on his explorations. Supplementing these, they created their estate, conservatories, and greenhouses, which they intended as a public garden and teaching collection. At the death of Lydia Morris, the property was willed to the

and all the new areas within the Rose Garden, where perennials and shrubs in beds of one dominant color harmonize with the roses.

Under the directorship of Paul Meyer since 1991, the arboretum has developed a multidimensional approach. The horticultural research and development continues through expeditions abroad, propagation, plant introductions, collection enrichment, publications, advice on urban horticulture to outside communities, the training of interns, and more. In addition, features to make the arboretum "a place of destination" have been very consciously introduced: great splashes of color and a miniature train (from 1997) in the summer (with thematic presentations such as Great American Light Houses and Houses of the Presidents), concerts and picnics on the lawns, and an annual sculpture space. In addition, in 2009, Out on a Limb, an arboreal jungle gym delighting adults and children, was opened in 2009.

Phase I of the new $60 million Horticulture Center (across the road) opens in 2010, with Phase II—which allows for onsite conferences—to follow. (LEED Platinum certification is being sought for this building). A future goal is to reopen the gate on Germantown Avenue, enabling visitors to enter the arboretum from the bus stop, and so serving the Arboretum's commitment to sustainability. Thirty-five full-time gardeners, assisted by fifty volunteers, care for the grounds: ninety-two acres of public gardens, visited by 110,000 people annually, and sixty-seven acres for research. More than 13,000 plants of over 2,500 types are labeled.

132 PENNSBURY MANOR

400 Pennsbury Memorial Road,
Morrisville, PA 19067
TEL: (215) 946-0400
WEBSITE: *www.pennsburymanor.org*
SEE MAPS: pp. 287 & 289

Hours: Grounds and house open Tuesday–Saturday 9am–5pm and Sunday noon–5pm. Closed Mondays and holidays (except Memorial Day, July 4, and Labor Day). Check website for tour times for the house. Admission fee

Location: 79 miles from New York City

Public transportation: NJ Transit or Amtrak to Trenton, SEPTA train to Levittown Station, Tullytown, taxi 3-1/2 miles

Facilities: Visitor center and introductory film; soda vending machine, no food; restrooms; picnicking pavilion; wheelchair accessible, except for upper floor of the manor house; no dogs

Programming: Colonial history, demonstrations, workshops

Nearby eateries: On Route 13 or Route 1

This alluring site beside the Delaware River immediately steeps visitors in early colonial history and immerses them in William Penn's (1644–1718) aspirations to be the proprietor of an American country estate. The small garden areas are placed within the larger context of manorial activities: animal husbandry, fruit and vegetable growing, baking, brewing, cooking, blacksmithing, and fence making. Costumed docents bring the period to life, though much is conjecture. The garden is based on a few written references and the assumption that Penn and his gardeners would have transposed contemporary British style and customs.

Since the main approach was by water, the regular, brick Georgian house of 1683–1684 faced the river.

The garden is part of the orchestrated entry to the main door: a short allée of trees leads to steps up to the gate in the white picket fence of the Front Court. Divided into sections by gravel paths, the garden features clipped pyramids of eastern cedar, bobbles of inkberry holly, and privet standards, planted in the corners of the symmetrical grass plats, with narrow borders of mixed flowers at the sides. The garden is elegant and very simple, as Penn, despite his ambitions for Pennsbury Manor, was beset by political and financial difficulties, and resided in America only from 1682 to 1684 (when the house was begun) and again from 1699 to 1701. Otherwise he lived in Britain, dying there in 1715. Only 40 of his 8,400 acres, it seems, were cleared during Penn's lifetime.

The Kitchen Garden and Orchard, a large rectangular space divided by straight paths crossing at right angles in the traditional way, is wonderfully ambitious, and during years of good maintenance—and when the rabbits are under control—provides cut flowers and produce similar to those grown in colonial times. Instructions by Penn in 1684 to his gardener read, "Set out the garden by the house; plant sweet herbs, asparagus, carrots, parsnips, artichokes, salatin, and all flowers and kitchen herbs there." Fruit trees and plants were sent over from Britain or supplied from Philadelphia.

After Penn's death, the house deteriorated quickly. Its location—five hours by river from Philadelphia—was inconvenient, and the property, inadequately supervised, became a drain on resources. By 1792 his descendents had sold the property.

In 1938 the Pennsylvania Historical Commission rebuilt the manor house, designed by R. Brognard Okie (1875–1945). On the reduced site of forty-three acres, fifteen other outbuildings were reconstructed, animals were installed, and the well-known Thomas Sears (1880–1966) was commissioned to create the gardens (1942). From this period also dates an area enclosed by an inkberry holly hedge behind the house, with two white garden seats in a style appropriate to a smart British garden in Penn's time, a sundial in the center, and additional period shrubs and flowers. One gardener and ten volunteers care for the ornamental and productive gardens. The nonprofit Pennsbury Society provides additional support for this historical site—just off the industrial sprawl.

133 SCOTT ARBORETUM OF SWARTHMORE COLLEGE

500 College Avenue, Swarthmore, PA 19081
TEL: (610) 328-8025
WEBSITE: *www.scottarboretum.org*
SEE MAPS: pp. 287 & 288

Fagus sylvatic
var. atro-punicea
Purple-leaf Beech
Fagaceae
Class tree of 1881

Hours: Grounds open year-round, dawn to dusk. Admission free

Location: 116 miles from New York City

Parking: Benjamin West car park, visitor section, off Route 320/Chester Road, south of College Avenue main entrance. Walk up hill into campus, turn right on College Avenue, and the Scott Arboretum offices are on the right

Public transportation: Amtrak to Philadelphia, SEPTA to Swarthmore Station, walk up hill via oak alley (Magill Walk), turn right in front of Parrish Hall (large 1869 building) at top of hill and find the Scott Arboretum offices past McCabe library, on right.

Facilities: Visitor center in Scott Arboretum office, open Monday–Friday 8:30am–4:30pm, for brochures, self-guided tour map—also from website; cell phone audio tours, call (408) 794-2850 and follow the prompts; refreshments at Kohlberg Hall, Science Center, and Sharples Dining Hall during the semester; restrooms available in all campus buildings; tables, benches, and seating throughout the grounds; mainly wheelchair accessible (not Crum Woods); dogs on leash

Programming: Ongoing workshops, arboretum tours, classes

Group garden tours: By appointment

Nearby eateries: Swarthmore town center, within walking distance; Springfield, 3 miles

---

In 1929 the whole of Swarthmore College campus (now three-hundred thirty acres) became an arboretum, established and endowed in memory of alumnus Arthur Hoyt Scott (1875–1927), the second president of the successful Scott Paper Company. The mission statement for the endowment, set up by his family, reflected his innovative view that "it is not the primary purpose of the Scott Arboretum merely to beautify the college campus," but rather to "acquire, cultivate, and propagate the better kinds of living trees, shrubs and herbaceous plants which are hardy in the climate of eastern Pennsylvania and which are suitable for planting by the average gardener."

This has ensured that the arboretum has balanced the interests of the college and the surrounding community, and through its director for the first fifty years, the renowned plant breeder and horticulturalist John Caspar Wister (1887–1982), the college has become linked to a network of major botanical experts. The arboretum today continues this legacy by hosting conferences, building up the specialized collections, using modern tools to inventory and map its holdings of over 3,000 distinct woody taxa (representing ninety-six plant families and 9,607 woody plants), and organizing an ongoing program of classes, lectures, events, and guided tours.

Swarthmore was founded in 1864 by the Religious Society of Friends (Quakers) as one of the first coeducational colleges in America. Its foundational building, Parrish Hall, is still central to the campus, and a walk around the main campus, which lies on a hill, leads to four large "sacred" spaces of lawn, never to be built on; a long, historic oak alley; mature trees, including huge, majestic elms from 1875; and grouped collections of, for instance, lilacs, cherries, tree peonies, hydrangeas, roses, magnolias, and conifers.

Around or extending from buildings and in courtyards are intensive areas of plantings—variously designed gardens that use specific microclimates to showcase new combinations: perennials, climbers, sun-loving cacti, rock plants, fragrance flowers, and others. Brochures at several gardens provide background information for each site along with a list of the main plants. At least seventy-five planters suggest ideas for the home gardener, with a concentration of pots of bold tropicals outside the arboretum offices.

An unforgettable outdoor auditorium, dedicated in 1942 and attributed to Thomas Sears and John Casper Wister, accommodates itself to straight-trunked tulip poplars forming a dappled canopy. A walk in Crum Woods (200 acres) passes through the rhododendron and azalea section and to woods left to themselves, other than being cleared of invasives. A path along the river leads to the famous holly collection, begun in 1974 and now containing some 350 different species, and emerges eventually at the pinetum, part of the core campus.

Under the directorship of Claire Sawyer, the $3.8 million LEED-certified Wister Education Center and Greenhouse opened in 2009, with rain gardens to follow. A joint project is planned with the American Conifer Society, and the twenty-five Arboretum staff, assisted by one-hundred twenty volunteers, hope to play a significant role in the college's becoming a model for green, sustainable campus management.

134 SHOFUSO: JAPANESE HOUSE & GARDEN

Lansdowne and Horticultural Drives,
within West Fairmount Park, Philadelphia, PA 19131
TEL: (215) 878-5097
WEBSITE: *www.shofuso.com*
SEE MAPS: pp. 287 & 288

Hours: Garden and house open May through October, Wednesday–Friday 10am–4pm, Saturday and Sunday 11am–5pm. Admission fee

Location: 102 miles from New York City

Parking: Within Fairmount Park

Public transportation: Amtrak to Philadelphia, taxi 3-1/2 miles, or SEPTA bus #38 from Center City or the Wissahickon Transfer Station to the intersection of Belmont Avenue and Montgomery Drive. Shofuso is a five-minute walk down Montgomery from the bus stop, through the iron gates and over the hill to the right. City Tourist Transportation: Philly Phlash Shuttle from a Center City or West Philadelphia pickup point to stop #16 at the Please Touch Museum.

Facilities: Brochures at the ticket booth; gift shop; restrooms; no refreshments; not wheelchair accessible; picnicking outside in West Fairmount Park; no dogs

Group garden tours: By appointment

Nearby eateries: List available for those in nearby Bala Cynwyd and West Fairmount Park

Also of interest: West Fairmount Park (see p. 302)

To step through the traditional Japanese wooden doorway between white walls topped by clay roof tiles is to become immersed in a cultural aesthetic so distinctive that the open style of West Fairmount Park in which it nestles seems bland by comparison. The clean lines and simple elegance of the house, based upon the early seventeenth-century Shoin style, are extended to the verandas, which look over the carefully shaped pond, compact little hills and valleys, and closely clipped mounds of azaleas, Japanese cedars, and box.

One shape is played off against another, heights are carefully controlled, pine trees show off their contorted and venerable branches, and a red-leafed Japanese maple provides an important emphasis in the distance. The strong accents of a small stone pagoda, a few lanterns, and the rocks contrast with the delicacy of the peony blooms and the flowering plums or cherries, while a little cascading stream falls into the pond, adding a sparkle to that end of the garden. Everything is on a small scale in this two-acre garden, which is obviously appreciated by the

11,000 visitors who, especially at the height of the flowering season in May, edge past each other on the narrow stepping stone paths, taking photos and gazing at the koi in the pond.

Shofuso (Pine Breeze Villa) has an interesting history: it was a gift from the American-Japan Society of Tokyo to the Museum of Modern Art in New York as a token of friendship following World War II. Designed by Junzo Yoshimura in 1953, it was made in Japan, sent over by ship, and constructed by a team of Japanese craftsmen in the garden of MoMA. Displayed in the summers of 1954 and 1955 as the third (after Marcel Breuer and Gregory Ain) in the series of *The House in the Museum Garden,* it caused quite a sensation, attracting 223,124 visitors.

The Japanese House was then moved to Fairmount Park and rebuilt in an area that, appropriately, had been used for Japanese exhibits during the 1876 centennial and, from 1906 until it burned down in 1955, for a three-hundred-year-old Japanese temple gate. The garden designed at MoMA by Tansai Sano was redesigned and greatly enlarged for the new location. Renamed, the house, teahouse, and garden opened to acclaim in 1958. As the years went by, vandalism and natural deterioration took their toll, and a massive restoration was necessary before the Bicentennial in 1976, and another in 2000.

Shofuso, owned by the city of Philadelphia, is administered by the Friends of the Japanese House and Garden (formed in 1982). They plan to engage a new Japanese garden consultant (for about ten days per season) to ensure the high standard of horticulture. The garden is cared for by one full-time site manager, one part-time and three full-time seasonal workers, and twenty garden volunteers. Labeling isn't considered appropriate, but garden tours, tea ceremonies, bonsai exhibits, workshops, a summer camp for children, moon viewing, and other Japanese cultural events are available.

ST. MARY MEDICAL CENTER HEALING GARDENS

1201 Newtown-Langhorne Road (US 413),
Langhorne, PA 19047
TEL: (215) 862-2967
WEBSITE: *To come*
SEE MAPS: pp. 287 & 289

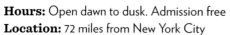

Hours: Open dawn to dusk. Admission free
Location: 72 miles from New York City
Parking: Follow signs for main entrance of main hospital
Public transportation: Amtrak to Philadelphia, SEPTA to Langhorne, then
  SEPTA bus #130 to gardens, 3 miles
Facilities: Hospital café; restrooms; wheelchair accessible; no dogs
Nearby eateries: Newtown, 2-1/2 miles north

Within the stressful environment of a hospital, the administration of St. Mary Medical Center has been responsive to the Friends of Healing Gardens, now the Community League of St. Mary Medical Center, accepting their ideas (along with financial aid) for creating tranquil gardens for patients and staff and replacing gray, boring surfaces with vibrant, living designs. Three gardens—initiated by two friends, Carter van Dyck and Susan Wert, whose mothers had been treated there for cancer—have so far been realized. All were designed by van Dyck's firm and can be seen by the public.

The Cloister Healing Garden (2000) incorporates a Japanese aesthetic into a large courtyard garden, which can be viewed from the corridor or appreciated from the cafeteria, as well as being enjoyed from within the main building. Attractive and rich plantings of the main building Japanese cedar, magnolias, weeping cherries, cypresses, Japanese maples, bamboo, azaleas, and groundcovers are found within an intimate area—and then around the larger space of an open, slightly mounded lawn with a pond on one side. Rocks, sometimes with a little fringe of lilyturf, appear at the edges of the path and in little coves. A variety of benches sit in sunny or shady spots, and the blandness of the broad (wheelchair) width of one path is attractively mitigated by an insert of pebbles flowing like a river. Problems with leaking have disturbed some of the careful detailing around the pond and the entrance fountain, but they are being resolved.

The Cancer Center Garden (2007), also in the main hospital, northwest of the Cloister Healing Garden, features dramatic white triangular sails that provide shade in summer and privacy from above. As a rain garden, it has a different palette and its own theme:

inner strength, like these plants, may shrivel during dry, stressful times, but has the possibility of becoming rejuvenated. A door, eventually to be installed, will give patients direct access to the garden.

Another initiative arose from the hospital's need to renew a roof, providing a fortuitous opportunity to transform its gravel surface into a rooftop garden. Planted in 2007, wavy colored bands of sedum create strong patterns that incorporate the air conditioner units and animate the view from the surrounding rooms and corridor. Five more roof gardens are being planned as part of the current $100 million extension, and signage will be furnished for the healing gardens in the future. To access the rooftop garden from the main hospital, turn right just passed café entrance, take elevator to third or fourth floor, exit to the left, and view the garden through the windows straight ahead.

TYLER ARBORETUM

515 Painter Road, Media, PA 19063
TEL: (610) 566-9134
WEBSITE: *www.tylerarboretum.org*
SEE MAPS: pp. 287 & 339

Hours: Grounds open daily, 9am until between 4pm and 8pm, depending on the season. Closed Thanksgiving and Christmas Day. House open first Sunday of each month for tours. Admission fee

Location: 119 miles from New York City

Public transportation: None

Facilities: Visitor center for map and three self-guided brochures and gift shop with horticultural, natural history material, and basic snacks and beverages; restrooms in education center in the barn; seven picnic tables; partially wheelchair accessible; no dogs

Programming: Ongoing for schools and adults

Group tours: By appointment

Nearby eateries: Media; list from visitor center

Also of interest: Ridley Creek State Park (2,606 acres) and Mansion, 1023 Sycamore Mills Road, Media, 4 miles. Hunting Hill (now the park office and a wedding/reception location), designed by Wilson Eyre in 1914 for the Jeffords family, has the remains of an atmospheric formal, terraced garden, with minimal but attractive planting. Also, Taylor Arboretum, 10 Ridley Drive, Wallingford—lovely walks within thirty acres, largely reverted to their natural state (plus invasives), but with collections of dogwoods, magnolias, and hollies

The Tyler Arboretum delicately balances the preservation of its heritage collections and the new environmental concerns that engage younger generations. Its horticultural history is impressive, its trees splendid. Some twenty that were either planted by the Painter brothers, Minshall (1801–1873) and Jacob (1814–1876), between 1825 and 1876 or are descendants from their arboretum (which once had over 1,000 varieties of trees and shrubs), continue to grow in the lovely valley below the portico of Latchford Hall and on both sides of the stream. (Pick up *A Guide to Historic Buildings and Plants* at the visitor center for a self-guided tour of the labeled trees.) A massive ginkgo survives, as well as five state champions: Yulan magnolia, cedar of Lebanon, giant sequoia, oriental spruce, and Corsican pine. The Quaker brothers, well-read Victorians with a great range of intellectual interests, planted their "study area" in rows (like the Peirce brothers, from 1800, at Longwood) and built the stone library beside the house to hold their natural science collections, herbarium, and equipment.

The second horticultural layer stems from John Casper Wister (see also Scott Arboretum, p. 324), appointed the first director of the Tyler Arboretum, formed and endowed by Laura Tyler at her death in 1944. She was the wife of the last of eight generations of the Minshall/Painter/Tyler family to have owned the property (descending twice through females) since it was acquired in 1681 from William Penn. Dr. Wister and his wife, Gertrude, introduced collections of lilacs, magnolias, cherries, crabapples, and especially rhododendrons. Until the fence was installed in 1999, surrounding the inner core of a hundred acres, these suffered from deer and invasives. The restoration of the important thirteen-acre rhododendron area, adjacent to Dr. Wister's pinetum, is now under way, access paths have been added, and the species and cultivars that once grew there are being propagated and replanted.

Also within the fenced area, a managed Native Woodland is used to demonstrate the advantages of ecological diversity and the importance of the stewardship of natural resources. Along with the Meadow Maze, Butterfly House, and Bird Garden, this section serves the expanding educational program in nature studies for children. Regular birdwatching and wildflower walks are also available

to adults and families, as well as a sensory garden, and themed summer exhibitions, such as tree houses or fairy dwellings, are used to attract the new audiences to the arboretum. Exploring the trails in the five-hundred and fifty acres beyond, which once were cleared for farming (grains and then cattle, dairy, and orchards) but have now reverted to a more "natural" state, are also encouraged.

Some 75,000 visitors use the Tyler Arboretum annually (with four hundred visiting the 1738 house). A full-time director of horticulture and four full-time and two part-time gardeners, backed up by some twenty volunteers, care for the grounds. Nine staff members and thirty-five educational volunteers run the much-emphasized educational programs.

TYLER FORMAL GARDENS AT BUCKS COUNTY COMMUNITY COLLEGE

275 Swamp Road, Newtown, PA 18940
TEL: (215) 968-8224; (215) 504-8500 x6007
WEBSITE: *www.bucks.edu/tylergardens*
SEE MAPS: pp. 287 & 289

Hours: Garden and grounds open dawn to dusk. Admission free. Tyler Hall, used as an administration office, can be entered; tours available by calling (215) 968-8224

Location: 74 miles from New York City

Parking: In the visitors' car park: from east gate (at traffic light) follow Linden Lane to parking on right; from west gate entrance, continue along drive and turn left. Walk down slope toward the Gateway Center (with flagpoles), and right to the Orangery and garden entrance

Public transportation: Amtrak (or NJ Transit to Trenton and SEPTA train) to Philadelphia, SEPTA to Langhorne and SEPTA bus #130 to the college

Facilities: Flyer with history, planting list, and plan in boxes in the garden and inside Tyler Hall; refreshments from college cafeteria in Charles E. Rollins Center; restrooms in Tyler Hall and elsewhere on campus; picnic tables; partially wheelchair accessible; no dogs

Programming: The science and art departments utilize the garden for laboratory purposes

Group garden tours: By appointment with Lyle Rosenberger, (215) 504-8500 x6007

Nearby eateries: Historic Newtown, 2-1/2 miles

Also of interest: Tyler State Park (1,711 acres), 101 Swamp Road, Newtown, 1 mile, originally part of the Tyler estate; Bowman's Hill Wildflower Preserve, 1635 River Road, New Hope, 11 miles; Henry Schmieder Arboretum (Delaware Valley College), 700 East Butler Avenue, Doylestown, 14 miles

In 1932 George Frederick Tyler (1884–1947) and his wife, Stella Elkins Tyler (1884–1963), moved from Philadelphia into their new Franco-Anglo manor house, designed by Willing, Sims & Talbutt. Indian Council Rock (called after the name of the rocky ledge on the bluff high above the Neshaminy Creek), now Tyler Hall, amid some 2,000 acres accumulated since the 1920s, became their home and country estate, reflecting their multiple interests in farming, forestry, riding, and the pleasures of entertaining.

The garden, designed by the same architects, extends from the side of the house and then descends downhill on three levels of formal terracing. In the manner of the popular Edwardian style in England, it drew upon Italian ideas but translated them into a comfortable mix of flower beds, trimmed hedges, fountains, and sculpture, with the modern addition of a swimming pool and tennis court.

Since 1999 a group of college enthusiasts have been devoted to the mammoth task of restoring these formal gardens, drawing upon 1934 photographs and other archival material, such as the original landscaping designs. College sponsorship, grants, and fundraisers have aided in this astounding transformation. The planting has been greatly simplified for maintenance reasons, the adjoining orangery has become a classroom, and the greenhouses—once supplying a large number of varied and colorful potted plants for the top three terraces—are gone, but the architectural framework remains, and the fountains, staircases, and two charming bath houses convey the spirit of the former garden. The key plants and trees are discreetly labeled, the names of donors less so, except on the brick pathway.

To be noted is the reinstatement of six of the many bronze sculptures by Stella Elkins Tyler that formerly adorned the terraces. Tyler worked within a conservative academic style and, like her older peer Gertrude Vanderbilt Whitney, had to combine her social duties and philanthropy with her dedication to the studio (now the Faculty Center). Her story (see *Stella Elkins Tyler: A Legacy Born of Bronze* [2004] by Roberta Mayer) and her work personalizes the garden, which is a tranquil and secluded spot, destined

to become even more representative of its period in the future.

Owned by the Bucks County Community College and Bucks County Community College Authority, the formal garden of one and a quarter acres is looked after by four core volunteer members and some twenty-four others. College grounds staff lend a hand with the mowing. Lyle Rosenberger, president of the Garden Committee, summarizes the goals: "Within the next ten years an endowment will be established, a reflecting pool constructed and a period tennis court restored," adding that "Tyler Formal Gardens is indeed a gift for anyone interested in the elegance and beauty of the 1930s."

138 WEST LAUREL HILL CEMETERY

215 Belmont Avenue, Bala Cynwyd, PA 19004
TEL: (610) 664-1591
WEBSITE: *www.forever-care.com*
SEE MAPS: pp. 287 & 288

Hours: Gates open May 1 through October 31, 7am–6pm; November 1 through April 30, 7am–5pm. Office hours for information: Monday–Friday 8am–4:30pm, Saturday 9:30am–3:30pm. Admission free. Visitors can drive slowly through the cemetery, along the winding drives

Location: 110 miles from New York City

Public transportation: Amtrak to Philadelphia, taxi 5 miles (no good public transportation)

Facilities: Plan, flyer, brochure from Bringhurst Funeral Home lobby and the conservatory lobby, and also booklets, *The Arboretum at West Laurel Hill Cemetery: A Walking Tour* and *The Architecture at West Laurel Hill Cemetery: A Walking Tour*; and for sale in funeral home, *West Laurel Hill: A Visual Walk Through a Historic American Cemetery*; no refreshments, but list available from office and conservatory; restrooms during office hours; picnic tables behind the conservatory; wheelchair accessible; dogs on leash

Programming: 12 events per year

Group tours: By appointment

Nearby eateries: Manayunk, 2-1/4 miles and Narbeth, 2-1/2 miles; list from staff at Bringhurst

Also of interest: Eastern State Penitentiary, 2027 Fairmount Avenue, Philadelphia, 5-1/4 miles

West Laurel Hill Cemetery was created in 1869 by John Jay Smith (1798–1881) and his partners when the expansion of Laurel Hill Cemetery (see p. 312), three miles away on the east side of the river, was curtailed by the formation of Fairmount Park (see p. 301). Lying high above the Schuylkill, it was to be accessible by train rather than steamboat. The site of 150 acres—formerly three large farms—was chosen for its pastoral and landscape potential. Smith, it is thought, played an important role in its layout and planting, and crowds of visitors from the city were drawn to its parklike setting on weekends.

Today, as the Schuylkill Expressway blocks off former access roads on the east and woods obscure the views, it feels more enclosed and inward-directed than its sister cemetery with its expansive river views. Within the wilder area are the old Receiving Vault and hillside mausoleums, more prominent before the entrance was moved. In the future, the Cynwyd Trail will follow the course of the former railroad below.

Expanded now to 187 acres, West Laurel Hill has a well-maintained, manicured look, with broad central vistas across a valley and waves of funerary monuments set in closely cut grass amid mature trees—mostly deciduous, with yews and box here and there. A weeping Japanese pagoda tree (*Sophora japonica* 'pendula') is a state champion, while flowering cherries, dogwoods, and crabapples are a feature in the spring, and modern azaleas and rhododendrons introduce a rather colorful palette.

Operating fully as a burial place, with up-to-date audiovisual technology in its chapel, and the atrium and conservatory for receptions, the cemetery has also introduced "green" burials in an area of indigenous grasses, trees, and shrubs where biodegradable or environmentally friendly urns and caskets are used—an interesting example of burial customs adapting to environmental concerns. A Garden of Peace and a Garden of Memories near the crematory chapel enlist horticulture for reflective purposes, while a hummingbird garden behind the bell tower suggests a more active form of observation.

No less dedicated than Laurel Hill Cemetery to its landscape, history, and prominent buried citizens, the

West Laurel Hill Cemetery Company maintains the grounds with nine full-time and nine seasonal gardeners and one full-time arborist. Rachel Wolgemuth, the administrator, writes: "Our future plans include the introduction of a Visitors Center in 2011–2012 to welcome and educate visitors on the history of the cemetery and its status on the National Register of Historic Places. We will also continue to plant a diversity of trees and shrubs to maintain the integrity of the arboretum. Other plans include the continuation of tours and events that introduce visitors to West Laurel Hill; obtaining certification as an Audubon Cooperative Sanctuary; and the introduction of private gardens maintained by members of the community." Labeling of trees for the many visitors who use the cemetery for walks is under way. To maintain the rural ambiance, regulations in both Laurel Hill and West Laurel Hill cemeteries preclude the placing of trinkets and mementoes.

139 WYCK

6026 Germantown Avenue,
Philadelphia, PA 19144
TEL: (215) 848-1690
WEBSITE: *www.wyck.org*
SEE MAPS: pp. 287 & 288

Hours: Garden open weekdays and Saturdays 9am–5pm; house (by tour) open April 1 through December 15, Tuesday, Thursday, and Saturday 1pm–4pm. Admission fee

Location: 89 miles from New York City

Parking: Parking lot or street

Public transportation: Amtrak to Philadelphia, SEPTA train R8 to Tulpehocken station, walk 1/2 mile, or SEPTA bus, Route 23 from downtown Chestnut Street. Taxi from station or from downtown, approximately 8 miles

Facilities: Brochure with map, flyer from house; small gift shop; antique roses and ornamental plants; no refreshments; restrooms; picnic tables; wheelchair accessible; no dogs

Programming: Adult workshops on traditional horticultural techniques

Nearby eateries: Chestnut Hill; list available from house

The charming historical house and two and a half acres of Wyck embody a multilayered story of nine generations of Quakers who passed the property on to daughters, sons, nieces, and nephews, the name changing from Milan to Jansen to Wistar to Haines. Eventually the house was absorbed into the density of Germantown, which itself became a part of Philadelphia in 1854.

The site began in the 1690s as a farm of fifty acres with a log cabin and became a quietly elegant home, remodeled in 1824 by William Strickland for Reuben (1786–1832) and Jane (1790–1843) Haines. Honeysuckle, *Bignonia,* and virgin's bower clematis (now climbing roses) grew on the white stuccoed exterior. They kept the earlier kitchen garden and orchards and laid out a new ornamental garden on the south side of the house. The extensive archives—mined for the interpretation of the house and its occupants—have also provided invaluable references to the garden. In a letter of 1820, Jane Bowne Haines writes of an abundance of roses in the garden, and in another, written around 1821, she sketches the layout of her rose garden: a rectangle of two squares that have a central roundel surrounded by four shaped beds.

Glass doors lead out into the famous rose garden at the back of the house where, within bushy box hedges, some thirty older varieties grow in a profusion of different heights and colors within a layout that refers to Jane Bowne Haines's sketch. A small, white painted pavilion from the nineteenth

century and the grape arbor that runs parallel to the house provide viewing spots for the garden. Some varieties of rose are thought to be direct descendents from Jane's day; others are known from the lists that she and her husband kept. Later nineteenth- and early twentieth-century roses in the front of the house complete the collection, which is labeled for convenient identification.

Mature trees and shrubs—tulip poplar, horse chestnut, pine, magnolia, beech, locust, holly, spruce, bottlebrush, dogwood, and hornbeam—are scattered casually through the grassy areas, and a border of old-fashioned perennials runs parallel to the former ha-ha. The cold frame, greenhouse, and lower kitchen gardens now serve the educational purpose of growing vegetables, fruits, and flowers through traditional methods. They are sold at the Wyck Farmers' Market, held on Fridays from May through November.

The Wyck Charitable Trust, created in 1973 by Mary Troth Haines, established Wyck as a historic site, and it opened to the public in 1974 and has been managed by the nonprofit Wyck Association since 1978, with one full-time gardener and ten volunteers caring for the gardens. The house and garden (both ornamental and utilitarian), along with the smokehouse, coachhouse, and icehouse, all function to evoke aspects of colonial life, Quakerism, nineteenth-century middle-class culture, and the history of Philadelphia. As for the garden, Barbara Overholser, development coordinator, describes the goal as being recognized nationally "as one of the oldest intact domestic landscapes in the country, and one of the oldest rose gardens to contain large numbers of significant antique plants."

DELAWARE

See Greater Philadelphia Gardens: *www.greaterphiladelphiagardens.org*

DELAWARE

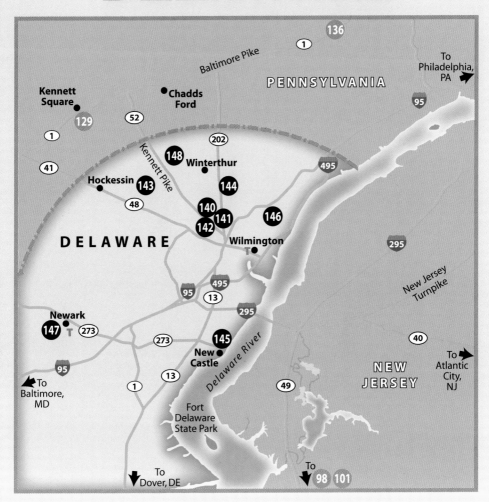

WILMINGTON AREA

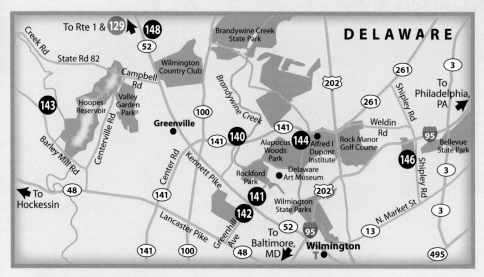

140 Eleutherian Mills at Hagley Museum & Library, Wilmington

141 Gibraltar, Wilmington

142 Goodstay Gardens, Wilmington

143 Mt. Cuba Center, Hockessin

144 Nemours Mansion & Gardens, Wilmington

146 Rockwood Mansion & Gardens, Wilmington

148 Winterthur, Winterthur

ARROW TO:

129 Longwood Gardens, Kennett Square, PA

140 ELEUTHERIAN MILLS AT HAGLEY MUSEUM & LIBRARY

200 Hagley Road, Wilmington, DE 19807
TEL: (302) 658-2400
WEBSITE: *www.hagley.org*
SEE MAPS: pp. 339 & 340

Hours: Grounds and house open daily, 9:30am–4:30pm; closed Thanksgiving and Christmas day. Admission fee. Shuttle buses

Location: 131 miles from New York City

Public transportation: Amtrak to Wilmington, taxi 4-1/2 miles

Facilities: Brochures and map from visitor center, with exhibition areas, gift and book shop, restrooms (and at various places); box in garden for additional information; Belin House Organic Café, 11am–3pm; wheelchair accessible; no dogs

Programming: Industrial history for schools

Garden group tours: By appointment

Nearby eateries: Greenville, 1-1/2 miles; list from visitor center

To visit the remains of the DuPont Company gunpowder factory is to return to the source of the French family's wealth—from which all the du Pont gardens now open to the public emerged. Somewhat at odds with our sense of this industrial enterprise is the tranquil walk along the Brandywine River, with its large shade trees and millstreams that now appear like ornamental canals, and ferns and ivy greening the walls of the stone powder yard buildings, evoking picturesque ruins. The demonstrations of some of the restored engineering refocuses our attention, however, as does the social history recounted on Blacksmith Hill.

Eleutherian Mills is a short bus ride away. It overlooks the river, with the first of the manufacturing works in full view—so close that it was continually damaged by explosions, and even vacated in 1890. The comfortable two-story house was built by Eleuthère Irénée du Pont (1771–1834) for his family between 1802 and 1803, when the first mills, barns, and the garden and orchards were being formed on the initial sixty-five aces.

Agricultural and horticultural interests prevailed here. Produce was required for the household, draft animals for the powder yards, and sheep for the planned woolen manufacturing enterprise. After du Pont implored his father and a friend in France to send seeds and plants, three large cases arrived in 1804 with almost two hundred fruit and nut trees, raspberries and grapevines, lavender

and tarragon, four varieties of roses, and vegetable and flower seeds. He laid out, to the south of the tree-lined drive, a one-acre flower, fruit, and vegetable garden in the age-old arrangement of four quadrants. The borders of espaliered dwarf fruit trees were a particularly French feature. Before long American plants were being incorporated. The large, regularly spaced orchard was to the south and west. By 1817 a little summerhouse covered with honeysuckle and a cold frame had appeared and, in 1822, a greenhouse used for bulbs, camellias, and ornamentals for the house, and for purposes of propagation.

The next generation (1834–1890) expanded the garden, adding more ornamental features, such as a rose garden, a tunnel arbor for grapes, and boxwood borders. Replanted in the early 1970s, it is currently in a transitional stage, suffering from deer problems, peach blight in the orchard, and spotty planting. However, some excellent examples of tall pear espaliers and fragments of the low, two-foot-high apple borders remain. The goal is to

restore it to its full nineteenth-century glory, with an emphasis on the early period.

One more generation did return to Eleutherian Mills. After the gunpowder mills closed in 1921, Henry Algernon du Pont (of Winterthur) bought it and fifty-two acres, for his daughter Louise (1877–1958). She and her husband, Francis Crowninshield (1869–1950), created the unusual garden (1920s) below the house on the river side, making use of the barrel-vaulted ruins and old saltpeter cauldrons and bringing in broken classical columns and fragments. Thickly planted with flowering shrubs, it also featured waterworks. As many structures are now in a precarious condition, plans are under way not to restore but to slow the deterioration and open up views from the piazzas of the house, and from the bus, to suggest its former industrial and garden life.

Louise Crowninshield donated Eleutherian Mills to Hagley Museum in 1952. Visited by some 50,000 people annually, the garden is looked after by one full-time and one part-time gardener. Some labels exist, especially on such great old trees as the osage orange near the house.

141 GIBRALTAR

1405 Greenhill Avenue,
Wilmington, DE 19806
TEL: (302) 651-9617
WEBSITE: *www.preservationde.org*
SEE MAPS: pp. 339 & 340

Hours: Garden open dawn to dusk. Admission free

Location: 128 miles from New York City

Parking: Limited; use streets

Public transportation: Amtrak or SEPTA to Wilmington, DART bus or taxi 2-3/4 miles

Facilities: No refreshments; no restrooms; no picnicking; partially wheelchair accessible; no dogs

Garden tours: By appointment

Nearby eateries: Greenville, 1 mile; Centerville, 5 miles; downtown Wilmington, 2-1/2 miles; and Wilmington Riverfront, 2-3/4 miles

Also of interest: Rockford Park (1889), 19th Street (close by); Delaware Art Museum, 2301 Kentmere Parkway, 1 mile

Note: Goodstay is across Pennsylvania Avenue (see p. 346)

In 1998 Preservation Delaware, Inc., courageously decided to restore Gibraltar's terraced, formal two-acre garden, designed by Marian Cruger Coffin (1876–1957), and found within the six-acre property. Entered today from the stable/garage courtyard, the lovely garden is experienced from the bottom to the top, where the house (not open) sits on its rocky plateau (hence the name), once providing views of downtown Delaware and the river.

The original house (1844), with over a hundred acres of farmland, was built by cotton merchant John Rodney Brinckle and lived in by members of the Brinckle family until 1909. It was then purchased by philanthropist, preservationist, and amateur

horticulturist Hugh Rodney Sharp (1880–1968) and his wife, Isabella Mathieu du Pont Sharp (1882–1946), who had close relatives at Longwood and Winterthur. They added wings on both sides of the house as well as the Marian Coffin gardens to the south in 1916 and 1923. These contrast nicely with the lawns and scattered mature trees around the entrance driveway.

The main axis on the lower level connects the rectangle of the flower garden to the narrower allée and ends at the teahouse belvedere. Incidents along the way—a fountain with planting in concentric circles, a wrought-iron gate, or symmetrical "rooms" at right angles to the main thrust, provide quiet breaks, as does

the sculpture placed symmetrically within boxwood alcoves or at defining angles. While the hardscape of this level and in the section with curving, marble staircases, is gently Italianate in character, the plantings on all levels reflect an English/American preference—tree peonies and roses, oak-leaved hydrangeas, six varieties of magnolia, mock orange, dogwoods, and many more. In spring (which was when the Sharps used Gibraltar) the allée—where the bald cypress hedge has grown into trees—is ablaze with orange and white azaleas, and the adjacent woodland has carpets of bluebells under the oaks.

By 1990 when the Sharp's son, H. Rodney Sharp Jr., died, the gardens had been sadly neglected. His heirs, wishing to dispose of what had become a white elephant, eventually accepted a much-reduced purchase price of the development rights by the Delaware Open Space Council and donated the property to Preservation Delaware. To offset the cost of restoring and maintaining the gardens, plans called for the house to become a fine restaurant or be converted to offices, but difficulties have ensued. Meanwhile, a campaign with a goal of $2.1 million was undertaken, and the firm of Rodney Robinson Landscape Architects, drawing upon the extant plants and planting lists of Marian Coffin, was able to restore the garden, with some modifications. Gibraltar was opened to the public in 1999. A further restoration project involves some forty garden ornaments—Venus, the seasons, children playing with a dolphin, eagles, vases, urns, etc.— which were carefully collected by the Sharps both in Europe and the United Sates. These were an integral part of the garden, and many of them were placed by Marian Coffin. Currently one gardener and about seven biweekly volunteers care for the garden.

142 GOODSTAY GARDENS

2600 Pennsylvania Avenue, Wilmington, DE 19806
(University of Delaware, Wilmington campus)
TEL: (302) 573-4450; (302) 573-4419
WEBSITE: None
SEE MAPS: pp. 339 & 340

Hours: Gardens open daily, dawn to dusk (except during university functions). Admission free

Location: 129 miles from New York City

Parking: By Arsht Hall on campus

Public transportation: Amtrak or SEPTA to Wilmington, DART bus or taxi 2-3/4 miles

Facilities: Brochures for self-guided tours at the unmanned Apple House visitor center near the entrance archway; no refreshments, restrooms, or picnicking; partially wheelchair accessible (gravel paths); no dogs

Garden tours: By appointment, and box lunches

Nearby eateries: Greenville, 1 mile; Centerville, 5 miles; downtown Wilmington 2-1/2 miles; and Wilmington Riverfront, 2-3/4 miles

Also of interest: Delaware Art Museum, 2301 Kentmere Parkway, 1 mile

Across Pennsylvania Avenue from Gibraltar is the charming one-acre garden of historic Goodstay Gardens. It relates to the south wing of Goodstay Center (1740, with additions), now used for receptions and meetings by the University of Delaware. The house, an 1807 barn, a root cellar (the Apple House), and the little garden are all that remain of Green Hill Farm. In 1861 the larger property was acquired by Margaretta E. du Pont, widow of Alfred Victor du Pont (and grandmother of the famous du Pont cousins—T. Coleman, Pierre S, and Alfred I, who, among other achievements, bought out the family's explosive business). The name was changed to Goodstay after the first du Pont home, Bon Séjour in Bergen Point, NJ.

Ellen Coleman du Pont received Goodstay as a wedding gift in 1923. The uncomplicated layout of the garden, divided into six sections with straight gravel paths, is thought to stem from the original nineteenth-century vegetable and flower garden edged with box hedges. The conception, however, is hers. With her husband, the landscape architect Richard Wheelwright, she enhanced the gardens, a source for her paintings, replacing vegetables with "rooms" for separate showings of roses (1923), irises (1955), a parterre garden of small beds around a sundial, and peonies (1923). The fifth section makes a feature of

large rocks where turkeys used to roost, and the sixth contained the greenhouse. "The Park," a small piece of woodland, running parallel with the garden, is particularly delightful in the spring, with the delicate color of native rhododendrons flowering under deciduous trees, and the groundcover full of bluebells.

Waist-high (or even higher) billowy box hedges define some sections, a lilac hedge another, and blowsy peonies, perennials, and annuals appear throughout the garden—except in the iris section that showcases both historic and modern varieties in stone-edged beds laid in lawn. A tamarisk tree with delicate fronds adds height, as do the tall ginkgos near the house. The main axis continues through a hedge to the magnolia allée—a larger scale 1938 addition—which leads to a reflecting pool.

The gardens (and house) were given to the University of Delaware at the death of Mrs. Ellen du Pont Meeds Wheelwright in 1968. The Friends of Goodstay, formed in 1993, assist the university in maintaining the gardens in the style of their previous owner. One full-time gardener (with other duties on the campus) and a summer intern care for the garden, which is used by 1,500–2,000 visitors annually. The iris collection of at least one hundred varieties is labeled, and some of the other plants and trees.

143 MT. CUBA CENTER

3120 Barley Mill Road, Hockessin, DE 19707
TEL: (302) 239-4244
WEBSITE: *www.mtcubacenter.org*
SEE MAPS: pp. 339 & 340

Hours: Open by reservation spring, summer, and fall. Two-hour docent-led tours. See website for times and days, which vary with the seasons. Admission fee

Location: 133 miles from New York City

Public transportation: Amtrak or SEPTA to Wilmington, taxi 7 miles

Facilities: Visitor center in the house; brochure and maps; books on Mt. Cuba and research collections; no refreshments; restrooms; no picnicking; limited wheelchair access; no dogs

Programming: On Piedmont native plants, naturalistic gardening, conservation, bird habitats, and more

Nearby eateries: Hockessin, 4-3/4 miles; or Greenville, 4-1/4 miles and shopping center at Centreville, 5-3/4 miles, both on Kennett Pike

Spring—when the trilliums, azaleas, flowering trees, and delicate ephemerals are blooming—is the most spectacular time to visit Mt. Cuba, but summer and fall have their strong attractions too. A country road approaches the special wrought-iron entrance gates, and then a slow drive up the hill—revealing open views of rolling pastures on the right, and the house on the brow of the hill on the left—leads to a car park circled by straight-trunked tulip poplars, hollies, dogwoods, and rhododendrons—a fitting introduction to this astounding woodland wildflower garden.

Mr. and Mrs. Lammot du Pont Copeland bought the property in 1935, built the Georgian-style house designed by Victorine and Samuel Homsey in 1936 on a worn-out corn field, and in 1937 commissioned Thomas

Sears (1880–1966) to design the forecourt and moderate-sized formal gardens extending from the south wing. Another well-known landscape designer, Marian Cruger Coffin (1876–1957), was engaged between 1951 and 1953. The tour moves through these spaces: the alley of sweet gums, the azalea bank, the lilac walk, and a pool garden with colorful seasonal displays. Most memorable and stimulating, however, are the woodlands themselves.

Mrs. Copeland became increasingly cwoncerned, from the 1960s, about the wildflowers, shrubs, and trees of Delaware and then extended her focus to the whole Piedmont Appalachian area (from the George Washington Bridge to Alabama). Advised by Seth Kelsey and then Richard W. Lighty, she began planting a woodland garden,

creating the four ponds, and collecting and studying species native to her chosen area. Here light filters through a canopy of tall trees to smaller trees to the shrubs and drifts of wildflowers and groundcover, creating different habitats in the woodland.

Meadow flowers flourish in more open areas, and other species thrive in wetter or dryer areas, so that over 1,800 taxa find a "natural" home here. Everything is rigorously planned and sited—the drifts of the same species, the companion planting, the layering, and the views around corners and across water. One leaves with a deep respect for Mt. Cuba Center's goal, which, as Rick J. Lewandowski, director since 1998, writes is "to continue to develop and promote a deeper appreciation for plants native to the eastern United States, to conserve valuable biodiversity, and engage the public in a greater awareness of the role native plants play in the improvement of our environment."

Mrs. Copeland, after the death of her husband, former president and chairman of the DuPont Company, in 1983, continued the woodland expansion, and she generously endowed Mt Cuba Center, Inc., which took over at her death in 2001. Ongoing research emphasizes the propagation and evaluation of native plants for the home garden; nine native cultivars, including trilliums and asters, have been introduced into the nursery trade. Other strengths are the native azaleas (gradually replacing the Asian variety) and *Hexastylis* (native wild ginger). Fifteen full-time gardeners and fifteen volunteers manage the 558 acres, with its twenty-five acres of gardens, which welcome 9,000 visitors a year.

144 NEMOURS MANSION & GARDENS

Alapocas Drive and Powder Mill Road (Route 141 South),
Wilmington, DE 19803 (or 850 Alapocas Drive)
TEL: (302) 651-6912; (800) 651-6912
WEBSITE: *www.nemoursmansion.org*
SEE MAPS: pp. 339 & 340

Hours: House and gardens open for scheduled tours (two hours for house and
gardens), May through December, Tuesday–Saturday at 9am, 12pm, and 3pm;
Sunday, 12pm and 3pm. Reservations recommended. Admission charge
Location: 131 miles from New York City
Public transportation: Amtrak or SEPTA to Wilmington, taxi 5 miles or DART
bus from Rodney Square, five blocks from the train station
Facilities: Meet at visitor center for guided tour, brochures, shuttle bus to mansion;
no refreshments; restrooms; no picnicking; wheelchair accessible; no dogs
Nearby eateries: Route 202; list available at visitor center
Also of interest: Delaware Museum of Art, 2301 Kentmere Parkway, 2-1/2 miles

There is a rather austere splendor
about the grounds of Nemours—a
garden of parade. It's a fascinating
example of a twentieth-century
interpretation of the seventeenth-
century French formal style. The main
gardens are an architectural extension
of the house, with a dominant main
axis extending for a third of a mile. The
house (1909–1910), a central block with
a recessed portico and a short wing on
either side, was designed by Carrère &
Hastings in the Beaux-Arts tradition
for Alfred I. du Pont (1864–1935) and
his first wife, Alicia—who, the story
goes, never much appreciated it nor its
3,000-acre farm. The tour covers many
of the principal and also downstairs
rooms and touches on the remarkable
career of Mr. du Pont, a partner in the
family gunpowder firm until 1916, an
inventor with some 200 patents, and
latterly a banker and real estate investor
in Florida and a philanthropist.

Hastings laid out the gardens,
although in 1926 Stewart & Donahue
added the colonnade that cuts across
the main vista and the sunken garden
was designed by Alfred I. du Pont's
son, Alfred Jr., a trained landscape
designer, and Gabriel Messéna (1928–
1932). The descent is by a graded
grass slope, defined by parallel lines
of large sculptured vases at the steps,
which are filled with flower displays in
summer. These are flanked by a row
of clipped, cone-shaped *Cryptomeria*
within *Stephanandra* hedged beds,
with an outer line of pink flowering
chestnuts. Beyond is a vast pool with
a circular spray fountain, and the
"maze" garden with a gleaming, gold-

leafed statue of Achievement (a nice tribute to Mr. du Pont's third wife, Jessie) by Henri Crenier (1873–1948). Past the colonnade appear additional waterworks and sculpture, the sunken garden—with patterned designs in box with bedding-out displays—and then, beyond the naturalistic ponds, the finale: an eighteenth-century-style Temple of Love with a 1790 cast of Diana the huntress by Jean-Antoine Houdon.

To the south of the house is the immaculately maintained French embroidery parterre—small box hedges defining the pattern with light or dark gravel filling the interstices. The house tour offers striking views of this garden, the turtle pool garden to the north, and the main vista—setting the formal gardens within the context of lawns, scattered trees (splendid copper beeches), and the woods beyond. Note the set of magnificent wrought-iron gates (one belonging to Catherine the Great in the eighteenth century) and two sculptures of sphinxes (originally at Jean-Baptiste Colbert's seventeenth-century Chateau de Sceaux). To the east, a long green carpet of grass with clipped hedges leads to a water tower, the defining feature of this outdoor room.

Following Alfred I. du Pont's wishes, after the death of his wife in 1970 Nemours became the property of the Nemours Foundation, opening to the public in 1977. Between 2005 and 2008 it underwent a $39 million restoration that included the waterworks, planting, statues, house interiors, paintings, furniture, and tapestries. Each year some 18,000 people visit the house and its garden—set within 222 acres and maintained by fourteen full-time gardeners. At the end of the tour, visitors may explore the formal garden area; a later shuttle bus brings them back along the oak alley to the visitor center.

145 READ HOUSE & GARDENS

42 The Strand, New Castle, DE 19720
TEL: (302) 322-8411
WEBSITE: *www.hsd.org*
SEE MAP: p. 339

Hours: House open April through December, Wednesday–Friday and Sunday 11am–4pm; Saturday 10am–4pm; January through March, group tours by appointment. Admission to gardens free, house fee

Location: 124 miles from New York City

Parking: On street

Public transportation: Amtrak or SEPTA to Wilmington, DART bus to New Castle (6th and Delaware Streets), walk 6 short blocks

Facilities: Small reception area, gift shop, and exhibit space in the house; photocopy of garden plan and plant list available upon request; no refreshments; restrooms in house; no picnicking but tables in nearby Battery Park; limited wheelchair access; no dogs

Group garden tours: By appointment

Nearby eateries: Within walking distance, Delaware and Market Streets; list available

Nearby places of interest: The historic town of New Castle on the Delaware River has many beautiful houses, a courthouse (1732), churches (1703 and 1707), a green, a library (1892), a town hall (1826), and Battery Park; Amstel House (1738) and Dutch House (1700), open to the public, both have small gardens with boxwood parterres. Also historic houses of Odessa, 18 miles

On a lovely street, with open views of the Delaware River, stands the elegant red brick Read House. It was constructed by master builder Peter Crowding for the lawyer George Read II (1765–1836) and his family between 1797 and 1804. No expense was spared on its interiors. When the house next door, inherited from his father (a signer of both the Declaration of Independence and Constitution), burned down in 1824, George Read added the cleared site to his own garden. The purchase in 1833 of the lot behind his father's house provided the grand Read House with an unusually large, triple-lot town garden. This rectangle extends back to 2nd Street and is surrounded by well-crafted brick walls.

Exactly how the gardens and productive areas were arranged at that point is not known, but a year or so after the China merchant William

Couper acquired the property in 1846, the front and middle sections were laid out as ornamental gardens, with the back reserved for the orchard and the vegetable and cutting garden, along with the outhouses. Photographs from the 1880s and a 1901 article suggest that the present layout of the first two gardens is substantially authentic. The front flower garden has a small central mound on the main axis, with a billowy pattern in box and two arbors with seats painted white. Box-lined beds and borders, filled with period perennials and annuals, and taller accents from a crape myrtle and hydrangea complete this charming design.

The middle garden, with a larger pattern of paths in ovals and semicircles, offers an interesting collection of shrubs and striking trees. The gravel paths were bricked after Philip and Lydia Laird acquired the property in 1920, and the higher back area—site of the previous kitchen garden and cutting gardens, orchard, and outhouses—was laid out in a broad grid as an extension of the ornamental garden, incorporating some of the fine older trees as well as new ones. A pergola and a swimming pool (now filled in) were also added.

At the death of Mrs. Laird in 1975, the house and garden were willed to the Delaware Historic Society along with an endowment that she had raised. Significant restorations of the interior and exterior of the house have recently taken place. Michele Anstine, Read House and Gardens director, indicates that a plan to commission a cultural landscape report on the area (over two acres) surrounding the house is under way: "The report will aid us in interpreting the landscape for visitors and neighbors, maintaining plantings and fixtures, and planning for the future of our unique urban landscape." The garden is cared for by twelve volunteers, with a landscape company mowing lawns and clearing debris. Two full-time administrators, with usually fifteen part-time paid guides, run the site, which is visited by about 18,000 people annually.

146 ROCKWOOD MANSION & GARDENS

610 Shipley Road, Wilmington, DE 19809
TEL. (302) 761-4340
WEBSITE: *www.friendsofrockwood.org;*
www.rockwood.org
SEE MAPS: pp. 339 & 340

Hours: Grounds open daily, dawn–dusk; house open Wednesday–Sunday, tours on the hour 10am–3pm. Admission free to grounds, fee for house tour
Location: 124 miles from New York City
Public transportation: Amtrak or SEPTA to Wilmington, taxi 6 miles
Facilities: Brochures and maps in the house with the Butler's Pantry café (Wednesday–Sunday 8am–3pm). Victorian gift shop and restrooms in house and Rockwood Center; picnicking; partially wheelchair accessible; dogs on leash
Programming: Holiday open house in December with many festivities
Nearby eateries: On nearby Concord Pike (Route 202)
Also of interest: Trails connect with those of the Northern Delaware Greenway

The restrained rural Gothic villa style of Rockwood was novel to Delaware when Joseph Shipley (1795–1867) built his retirement home there between 1851 and 1855. Born in Wilmington, he had worked in Anglo-American trade and merchant banking in Liverpool, England from 1819 to 1850. Rockwood, and its designed landscape, is almost a textbook example of the ideas of John Claudius Loudon (1783–1843), taken up in America by Andrew Jackson Downing (1815–1852). The site eventually consisted of eight parcels of farmland totaling 300 acres, and a few outcroppings of rock and cliffs lent the perfect touch of the picturesque and inspired its name. Shipley's gardener was brought over from Britain to work on the landscaping for the new house, designed by George Williams, architect of his previous home.

The arrangement of mature trees at Rockwood is very special, particularly those on the north lawn: a weeping beech, ginkgo, and blue Atlas cedar and, in keeping with the pointed gables of the house, a couple of eastern hemlocks and an eastern white pine. They are planted very effectively in the natural style as singles or in groups, with shrubs providing middle height and variety. A large spreading rhododendron grows in the middle distance, while the lawn flows around these groupings and the two featured rocky areas.

From the veranda, with its noteworthy painted wooden columns, the view is of open lawn, merging seamlessly with pasture across the ha-ha (a very British feature) with woods beyond. The loss of some mature specimen trees has caused gaps, but

354

a great copper beech, a weeping hemlock, and magnolias remain, and signs of recent planting are visible. A further delight at Rockwood is the 1852 cast-iron and wood conservatory (also designed by George Williams), with a little ornamental balustrade running around the top. Reached directly from the house or from the garden, where the glimpse of the plantings is immediately alluring, it is evidently the only one of its kind still standing in the United States. A house tour takes the visitor further into the life of Joseph Shipley and the later residents.

Notable changes: A new entrance bypasses the original arrival point, past the porter's lodge and along the flowing curves of the drive, and instead leads to a rather intrusive car park. The site's outer areas of the landscape have proved too much to manage, but trails connect with the Delaware Greenway. The flower beds, the greenhouses, and the orchards have gone, but the walled kitchen garden has been put to new use with ornamental gardens for visitors to the Rockwood Center (receptions and meetings).

Inherited by Joseph Shipley's three sisters and then other relatives, Rockwood was willed to a charitable organization in 1972, and the county of New Castle became the new owner of its seventy-eight acres. The Friends of Rockwood, formed in 1977, assist with preservation. They are currently fundraising for the $500,000 required to restore the conservatory.

UNIVERSITY OF DELAWARE BOTANIC GARDENS
531 South College Avenue, Newark, DE 19716
TEL: (302) 831-0153
WEBSITE: *http://ag.udel.edu/udbg*
SEE MAP: p. 339

Hours: Grounds open daily, sunrise to sunset. Admission free
Location: 135 miles from New York City
Parking: Weekends and after 4:30pm, anywhere; otherwise obtain permit for free parking from Townsend Hall, Room 113
Public transportation: Amtrak to Wilmington, SEPTA train to Newark, walk 1/4 mile
Facilities: Obtain map from Townsend Hall, Room 113, or download from website; restrooms in Townsend Hall during business hours; no refreshments; picnicking; partially wheelchair accessible; dogs on leash
Programming: University and extension courses
Group tours: By appointment
Nearby eateries: Newark, 1-1/2 miles

Visitors to the College of Agriculture and Natural Resources of the University of Delaware gain a sense of the way this 350-acre campus functions as a living laboratory. Course descriptions indicate the training being given to those who will manage our environments, shape policy, or produce significant research in the future. The departments of Natural Resource Management, Environmental Soil Science, Plant Science, Entomology, and Food and Agribusiness Management all draw upon the working farm, the thirty-five-acre woodlot, a habitat trail, greenhouse laboratories, and the botanical gardens. The effects of these studies on the home-gardener are far-ranging: from the plant breeding of ornamentals and natives to pest management, disease control, soil properties, and landscape design.

The visitor is encouraged to view the following: The Emily B. Clark Garden screens the road with unusual trees and shrubs (note the good view across the lawn from the front of Townsend Hall),

and the path running through allows for a closer look at the dwarf conifer collection; the Herbaceous Garden at the back of the large Townsend building showcases grasses as well as hardy flowers; the Lepidoptera Trail, with native plants designed to attract and support butterflies, provides ideas for creating more diverse landscapes; the large border of the Color Trial Garden, with the newest annual cultivars and a display of All-American Selections that have proved outstanding in national evaluations, is a useful reference. Finally, another composition of good-looking specimen trees (especially hollies) and shrubs, with a lower layer of perennials, is found by the Fischer Greenhouse Laboratory. Unfortunately labeling is sparse.

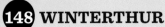

148 WINTERTHUR

5105 Kennett Pike, Winterthur, DE 19735
TEL: (800) 448-3883
WEBSITE: *www.winterthur.org*
SEE MAPS: pp. 339 & 340

Hours: Grounds, and house (by tour) open daily, 10am–5pm, Tuesday–Sunday. Admission fee

Location: 133 miles from New York City

Public transportation: Amtrak or SEPTA to Wilmington, taxi 6-1/2 miles

Facilities: Visitor center, cafeteria, restrooms, gift shop; also café, restrooms, and exhibition gallery, and gift and plant shop by house; picnic tables; wheelchair accessible; no dogs

Programming: Ongoing

Garden tours: Scheduled daily; private tours by appointment

Nearby eateries: Centerville, 1-1/2 miles; Greenville, 2 miles

Winterthur was carefully planned by its last owner, Henry Francis du Pont (1880–1969), to welcome large numbers of visitors. The new entrance drive (1960) is an exciting introduction: long views of meadows and woods regale visitors as they slowly descend to the car park, screened by pines. From the visitor center, they may choose either the tram that circulates or pedestrian paths that lead to the house or through Azalea Woods, the great attraction in spring.

Azalea Woods, ironically, owes its existence to the chestnut blight. Once the dead trees were cleared, spaces opened up to receive new plantings: the first Japanese karume azaleas in 1917, then flowering dogwoods and viburnums and a mass of early bulbs and spring ephemerals that carpet the

ground so delightfully both there and in the nearby March Bank.

H. F. du Pont—horticultural degree (1903) from Bussey Institution in hand—had a lifelong passion for planting. Although influenced by William Robinson's ideas in *The Wild Garden* (1870) of enriching woodlands with naturalized planting, he chose a more ornamental style as he developed blooming sequences and his own color harmonies for his large scale designs: thousands of daffodils in freeform blocks, and hundreds of azaleas in the woods. His use of eye-catching densities of brilliant red and pink azaleas at key points increased as he got older.

The du Pont presence here started even earlier: in 1810 Irénée du Pont (1771–1834) of Eleutherian Mills

began purchasing land (later greatly increased) for its farming potential. His daughter and husband built the house (1837) that would be enlarged by H. F. du Pont's father and ultimately by himself to hold his collection of American decorative arts (dating from 1640 to 1860)—a reason in itself for a visit to Winterthur.

The gardens around the house also evolved—particularly after H.F. inherited the property in 1927. Landscape designer and friend Marian Cruger Coffin (1876–1957) was commissioned to design the Reflecting Pool Garden (1929) relating to a new extension. The view from the terrace, shaded by tulip poplars, looks down on this exquisite formal garden, follows a central staircase down the slope, pausing at a semicircle, and continues through a wrought-iron gate to the pool (formerly for swimming), ending at a semicircular terrace with two delightful changing pavilions on either side. The planting includes flowering trees (Handkerchief, dogwoods, viburnums, and azaleas) and the green densities of boxwood, ivy, ferns, and groundcovers.

Mr. du Pont also added substantially to the pinetum that he and his father had originally planted (1918–1925), developed Magnolia Bend (both of great interest), and in 1955 asked Marian Coffin to design the Sundial Garden as an April attraction of flowering shrubs. Views were also orchestrated through the placement of little pavilions, and planting extended into the Sycamore Area. His last major addition was the Quarry Garden (1962) for a spring display of Japanese

primulas and other damp loving plants. The du Ponts used Winterthur in spring and fall, hence the initial emphasis on these seasons.

Winterthur Museum was opened to the public in 1951 as a nonprofit corporation. After Mr. du Pont's death in 1969, the house and its collections were the priority. Since 1988, however, there has been a growing commitment to restoring and maintaining the uniqueness of Henry Francis du Pont's intensively landscaped sixty acres in its rural setting (about 900 acres). The 100,000 visitors who arrive annually find additional pleasures in the expanded planting for summer and the Enchanted Woods (2001) for children. Sixteen full-time gardeners and five summer interns are assisted by some thirty-seven active volunteers.

PHOTO CREDITS

CONNECTICUT

Page 26: Bellamy-Ferriday House & Garden. Photograph courtesy of Connecticut Landmarks

Page 27: Bellamy-Ferriday House & Garden. Photographs of the parterre garden by Nick Lacy, courtesy of Connecticut Landmarks

Page 42: Cricket Hill Garden. Photographs courtesy of Cricket Hill Garden

Page 49: Beatrix Farrand Garden at Three Rivers Farm. Photograph by Jen Iannucci, courtesy of Promisek, Inc.

Page 70–71: George & Olive Lee Memorial Garden. Photographs by F.B. Kerchoff, courtesy of George & Olive Lee Memorial Garden

Page 78: Riverfront & Lincoln Financial Sculpture Walk. *Equality* by Del Geist, 2007. Photograph courtesy of the artist

NEW YORK

Page 113: Cedar Grove, Thomas Cole National Historic Site. *Thomas Cole's Cedar Grove* by Charles Herbert Moore, 1868, oil on canvas, 6 x 9¼". Courtesy of Thomas Cole National Historic Site, Catskill, NY

Page 133: Donald M. Kendall Sculpture Gardens at PepsiCo. *Kiosque l'evidé* by Jean Dubuffet. Photograph by Magda Salvesen, courtesy of PepsiCo Foundation

Page 134: Donald M. Kendall Sculpture Gardens at PepsiCo. *Double Oval* by Henry Moore. Photograph by Magda Salvesen, courtesy of PepsiCo Foundation

Page 136: Kykuit. *Triangular Surface in Space* by Max Bill, 1962 (top) and *Bather Putting up her Hair* by Aristide Maillol, 1930. Photographs by Magda Salvesen, courtesy of Historic Hudson Valley, www.hudsonvalley.org

Page 140: Locust Grove Estate. Photograph courtesy of Locust Grove

Page 141 (top): Locust Grove Estate. *The Morse Family and Friends on the Lawn*, c. 1870, courtesy of Locust Grove

Page 158: Philipsburg Manor. Image by Rob Schweitzer for Historic Hudson Valley, www.hudsonvalley.org

Page 159: Philipsburg Manor. Top right image by Bryan Haeffele for Historic Hudson Valley, www.hudsonvalley.org

Page 160: Springside Landscape Restoration. "Jet Vale Fountain" from *Vassar College and Its Founder* by Benson John Lossing & Matthew Vassar, 1867, wood engraving, courtesy of Springside Landscape Restoration

Page 169: Storm King Art Center. (Top) *Untitled* by Robert Grosvenor, 1970, weathering steel painted black, 10' x 212'5½" x 12' 6"; (bottom) *Mother Peace* by Mark di Suvero, 1969–70, steel painted orange, 41' x 49'5" x 44'3". Photographs by Jerry L. Thompson, courtesy of Storm King Art Center, Mountainville, NY

Page 170: Storm King Art Center. *Suspended* by Menashe Kadishman, 1977, weathering steel, 23' x 33' x 4'. Photograph by Jerry L. Thompson. Courtesy of Storm King Art Center, Mountainville, NY

Page 171: Storm King Art Center. *Storm King Wavefield* by Maya Lin, 2007–08, earth and grass, 240,000 square feet (11-acre site). Photograph by Jerry L. Thompson, courtesy of Storm King Art Center, Mountainville, NY

Page 176: Van Cortlandt Manor. Image by Bryan Haeffele for Historic Hudson Valley, www.hudsonvalley.org

Page 196: LongHouse Reserve. *Cobalt Reeds* by Dale Chihuly, 2000. Photograph by Magda Salvesen

Page 197: LongHouse Reserve. (Left photo) *Warriors* by Paolo Staccioli, 2007, photograph by Magda Salvesen, courtesy of Paolo Staccioli and Kiesendahl+Calhoun Fine Arts, Ltd. *Curved Benches* (overlooking Peter's Pond) by Howard Ben Tré, 2005, photograph by Magda Salvesen, courtesy of LongHouse Reserve, NY and with permission of Howard Ben Tré. (Right photo) *Reclining Figure* (in front of a Weeping Blue Atlas Cedar) by Willem de Kooning, 1969–82, photograph by Magda Salvesen, courtesy of LongHouse Reserve, East Hampton, NY, © 2011 The Willem de Kooning Foundation / Artists Rights Society (ARS), New York.

NEW JERSEY

Page 217: Acorn Hall. Photograph courtesy of Morris County Historical Society at Acorn Hall, Morristown, NJ

Page 218: Acorn Hall, the house in 1900. Photograph courtesy of Morris County Historical Society at Acorn Hall, Morristown, NJ

Page 245: Grounds For Healing. *No Mommy, That One* by Seward Johnson, 1995, bronze, 7/8, 47 x 60 x 22", © 1992 The Sculpture Foundation, Inc., courtesy of Robert Wood Johnson Foundation, Hamilton, NJ. Photograph by Magda Salvesen

Page 246: Grounds For Sculpture. *Tempio Bretton* by Walter Dusenbery, 1981, yellow travertine, 120 x 40 x 40", courtesy of The Sculpture Foundation, Inc. Photograph by Magda Salvesen, courtesy of the artist

Page 247: Grounds For Sculpture. (Top) *Resting Place* by Roy Wilson, 1990, painted steel, 316 x 312 x 96", courtesy of The Sculpture Foundation, Inc.; (bottom) *Sagg Portal* by Hans Van de Bovenkamp, 2004, courtesy of The Sculpture Foundation, Inc. Both photographs by Magda Salvesen, courtesy of the artists

PENNSYLVANIA

Page 299: Chanticleer. *Sleeping Giant* by Marcia Donahue, 1999. Photograph by Magda Salvesen, courtesy of the artist

Page 292–293: Andalusia. Photographs by Katharine H. Norris, courtesy of the Andalusia Foundation

Page 297: Bartram's Garden. © John Bartram Association, Bartram's Garden, Philadelphia

Page 303: Fairmount Park. (Top) *Dance* by Isamu Noguchi, American, 1904–1988, Manazuru stone, 82-1/2 x 23 x 19-5/8" (209.6 x 58.4 x 49.8 cm); base: 7 x 25-1/4 x 16-1/2" (17.8 x 64.1 x 41.9 cm). On extended loan to the Philadelphia Museum of Art for the Anne d'Harnoncourt Sculpture Garden. Photograph by James Jason Wierzbicki, courtesy of the Philadelphia Museum of Art. © 2011 The Isamu Noguchi Foundation and Garden Museum, New York / Artists Rights Society (ARS), New York

Page 304–305: Haverford College Arboretum. Photographs by Mike Startup, courtesy of Haverford College Arboretum

DELAWARE

Page 352: Read House & Gardens. Photograph courtesy of Delaware Historical Society

INDEX

NOTE: *Items in bold indicate the main garden entries in the book. Italicized page locators indicate photos.*

AC/BC Associates, 246
Acorn Hall, Morristown, NJ, 208, 212, *217*, **217–18**, *218*
Ahrens, Peter and Bonnie, 152
Ain, Gregory, 327
Aldrich, Abby, 136
Allom, Charles, 200
Ambler Arboretum of Temple University, Ambler, PA, 208, 286, *290*, **290–91**
American Chestnut Foundation, 153
American Conifer Garden Society, 325
American Iris Society, 264
American Iron Company, 270
American-Japan Society of Tokyo, 327
American Woman's Home, The (Stowe), 84, 85
Andalusia, Andalusia, PA, 208, 286, 289, *292*, **292–93**, *293*
Andalusia Foundation, Andalusia, PA, 293
Anderson, Karen, 295
Andropogon Associates, 320
Anstine, Michele, 353
Aprill, Gregg, 255
Aprill, Jack and Emily, 255
Arnold Arboretum, Boston, MA, 48, 191, 219, 285, 320
Astifan, William, 305
Atkin Olshin Schade Architects, 302
Atterbury, Grosvenor, 204
Audubon Cooperative Sanctuary, 335
Austin roses, David, 122, 203
Averill, Norman, 128
Awbury Agricultural Village, Philadelphia, PA, 295
Awbury Arboretum Association, Inc., Philadelphia, PA, 295
Awbury Arboretum (at the Francis Cope House), Philadelphia, PA, 286, 288, *294*, **294–95**, *295*

Babb, Cook & Willard, 268
Ballantine, Sara, 240
Ballantine Brewing Company, 240
Balmori, Diana, Associates, 179
Balsamel, James V., 218
Bamboo Brook Outdoor Education Center, Far Hills, NJ, 208, 212, *219*, **219–20**, *220*
Bard College: Landscape & Arboretum & Blithewood Garden, Red Hook, NY, 98, 104, *105*, **105–7**, *106*, *107*
Barnes, Dr. Albert and Laura L., 296
Barnes Foundation, Arboretum at, Merion Station, PA, 286, 288, **296**, *296*
Bartlett, Dr. Francis A., 24

Bartlett Arboretum Association, Stamford, CT, 24
Bartlett Arboretum & Gardens, Stamford, CT, 16, 18, *24*, **24–25**, *25*, 98
Barton, Clara, 139
Barton, Coralie Livingston, 150
Barton, Lewis W., Arboretum & Nature Preserve at Medford Leas, Medford, NJ, 208, *221*, **221–22**, *222*
Barton, Thomas, 150
Bartram, John, 297, 298
Bartram, John, Jr., 298
Bartram, John, The, Arboretum Association, Philadelphia, PA, 298
Bartram, William, 298
Bartram's Garden, Philadelphia, PA, 286, 288, *297*, **297–98**
Beasley, Bruce, 247
Beck, Walter and Marion, 128, 129
Belcher, Daniel, 59
Bellamy, Reverend Joseph, 26, 27
Bellamy-Ferriday House & Garden, Bethlehem, CT, 16, *26*, **26–27**, *27*
Bensel, John A., 232
Bethlehem Land Trust, Bethlehem, CT, 27
Biddle, James, 293
Biddle, Jane, 293
Biddle, Letitia, 293
Biddle, Nicholas, 292, 293
Bill, Max, *136*
Black, Caroline, Garden, Connecticut College, New London, CT, 16, 40, **41**
Blackburn, Dr. Benjamin C., 285
Blanchard, Jr., Peter P. and Sofia, 243
Blanchard, Peter P. and Adelaide, 242
Blithewood Garden, Bard College, Red Hook, NY, 98, 104, *106*, **106–7**
Boboli Gardens, Florence, Italy, 137
Bogart, John and Nathan F. Barrett, 223
Bogusch, Rick, 189
Bonazza, Antonio, 111
Bon Séjour, Bergen Point, NJ, 346
Boothe, David, 28
Boothe, Stephen, 28
Boothe Memorial Park & the Boothe Park Rose & Wedding Garden, Stratford, CT, 16, 20, *28*, **28–29**, *29*
Boscobel House & Gardens, Garrison, NY, 98, 102, *108*, **108–9**, *109*
Bosworth, William Welles, 136, 174
Bowen, Henry C., 80, 81
Branch Brook Park, Newark, NJ, 208, 210, *223*, **223–24**, *224*
Branch Brook Park Alliance, Newark, NJ, 224
Brandywine River Museum, Chadds Ford, PA, 314
Breed, Vera Poggi, 89
Breuer, Marcel, 327
Brewster, Frederick F., 43
Bridge Garden Advisory Committee, Bridgehampton, NY, 189
Bridge Gardens, Bridgehampton, NY, 184, 187, *188*, **188–89**, *189*
Brinckle, John Rodney, 344
Brooklyn Botanical Garden, Brooklyn, NY, 229

Browning, Louisa P., 310
Bryant, William Cullen, 200, 201
Bryce, Lloyd, 200
Buck, Helen, 226
Buck, Leonard J., 225
Buck, Leonard J., Garden, Far Hills, NJ, 208, 212, *225*, **225–27**, *226*, *227*
Buckenham, Horatio, 238
Bucks County Community College, Newtown, PA. *see* Tyler Formal Gardens
Burgess, Caroline, 168
Burlingham, Cora Weir, 89
Burns, Sister Mary Grace, Arboretum of Georgian Court University, Lakewood, NJ, 208, *228*, **228–29**, *229*
Bush, David, 30
Bush-Holley Historic Site, Cos Cob, CT, 16,18, *30*, **30–31**, *31*
Bushnell, Reverend Horace, 32
Bushnell Park, Hartford, CT, 16, 22, 23, *32*, **32–33**, *33*, 34, 36
Bushnell Park Foundation, Hartford, CT, 33
Bussey Institute, Harvard, MA, 358
Butler-McCook House & Garden, Hartford, CT, 22, 23, *34*, **34–35**, *35*
Buttrick, White & Burtis, 33
Byrne, James, 204

Cabot, Frank and Anne, 167, 168
Calder, Alexander, 133, 137, 170
Camden Children's Garden, Camden, NJ, 303
Cannon, Arnout, 182
Caramoor Center for Music & the Arts, Katonah, NY, 16, 18, 98, 101, *110*, **110–11**, *111*
Carey, Brian, 245, 246, 247
Carnegie Institute, 156
Carnegie Steel, 202
Carrère, Robert, 128
Carrère & Hastings, 350
Carvill, William, 304
Cassatt, Mary, 63
Catherine the Great, 351
Cedar Grove, Thomas Cole National Historic Site, Catskill, NY, 98, 104, *112*, **112–13**, *113*
Cedar Hill Cemetery, Hartford, CT, 16, 22, 23, 34, *36*, **36–37**, *37*
Cedar Hill Cemetery Foundation, 37
Centennial Exhibition, 1876, Philadelphia, PA, 302
Central Park, New York, NY, 86, 118, 223
Cézanne, Paul, 296
Chanticleer, Wayne, PA, 286, *299*, **299–300**, *300*
Chateau de Sceaux, France, 351
Chihuly, Dale, *196*, 197
Chinni, Peter, 78
Church, Frederic Edwin, 154, 155
Church, Louis, 155
Citibank, 180
Citizens Committee, Montclair, NJ, 264
City Park, Hartford, CT. *see* Bushnell Park
Clayton Estate, Roslyn Harbor, NY, 200